Journeys of the
Muslim Nation
and the
Christian Church

Herald Press Titles by David W. Shenk

Creating Communities of the Kingdom
(with Ervin R. Stutzman)

Global Gods

God's Call to Mission

A Muslim and a Christian in Dialogue
(with Badru D. Kateregga)

Practicing Truth
(with Linford Stutzman)

Surprises of the Christian Way

Journeys of the
Muslim Nation
and the
Christian Church

exploring the mission of two communities

David W. Shenk

**Herald
Press**

Waterloo, Ontario
Scottdale, Pennsylvania

Library of Congress Cataloging-in-Publication Data
Shenk, David W., 1937-
  Journeys of the Muslim nation and the Christian church : exploring the mission of two communities / David W. Shenk.
      p. cm.
Includes bibliographical references and index.
  ISBN 0-8361-9252-4 (pbk. : alk. paper)
  1. Islam—Relations—Christianity. 2. Christianity and other religions—Islam. 3. Religions—Comparative studies. I. Title.
  BP172.S514 2003
  261.2'7—dc21   2003013527

JOURNEYS OF THE MUSLIM NATION AND THE CHRISTIAN CHURCH
Copyright © 2003 by Herald Press, Scottdale, Pa. 15683
      Published simultaneously in Canada by Herald Press,
      Waterloo, Ont. N2L 6H7. All rights reserved
Library of Congress Catalog Card Number: 2003013527
International Standard Book Number: 0-8361-9252-4
Printed in the United States of America

Cover design by Diana Baldwin
Front cover photo by Jeff Greenberg / PHOTO AGORA

12 11 10 09 08 07 06   10 9 8 7 6 5 4 3 2

To order or request information, please call
1-800-759-4447 (individuals); 1-800-245-7894 (trade).
Web site: www.heraldpress.com

Dedicated to my friend,

Adam Jimaleh Farah,

*who created Somali songs about the journey
as a disciple of the Messiah*

Contents

Foreword

For the first part of my life I was closely acquainted with the Muslim journey as I grew up in a devout Muslim home. I participated in the prayers and submitted my body and soul to Allah as I bowed daily in submission to his will as reveled in Islam and the way exemplified in the life and teaching of the prophet Muhammad. I have indeed experienced the attraction and power of Islam.

Then Jesus the Messiah surprised me for he met me and called me to walk in his way. I said "yes" to his call, and now journey in the way of the Messiah whom I confess to be Savior and Lord. That choice has been costly; family and friends could not comprehend why I would choose the way of the Messiah. Yet I have experienced grace day by day in my journey with Jesus the Messiah. For the past thirty-eight years I have experienced the attraction of the power of the Gospel.

As a person who is acquainted with both the Muslim journey and the way of the Messiah, I appreciate this book for its insightful exploration of both the journey of the Muslim nation and that of the Christian church. David W. Shenk is a careful listener who has felt the "tug" of the Muslim way, as well as the "tug" of the Christian way. I am confident that this book will build understanding between Christians and Muslims—it represents a commitment to the biblical mandate: seek peace and pursue it. (1 Peter 3:11)

The author is an Anabaptist-Mennonite who for many years has offered himself for open discussion with Muslim friends at his home and within the mosques. He understands the Qur'an and Muslim theology because he has extensively read their book and listened to their confessions of faith. He loves Muslims. He is also a man who loves the Christian scriptures and loves the Messiah and the church. Consequently this book reveals depth of understanding and empathetic insight.

Journeys of the Muslim Nation and the Christian Church is not for the sake of arguing with the Muslims; rather it seeks to commend the Messiah of the biblical scriptures to all readers, both Muslim and Christian. This book demonstrates both a concern for Christian distortions of, as well as Muslim misunderstandings or objections to, the Gospel. It is also concerned about Christian distortions of Islam and the Muslim community.

I believe that David is right in insightfully perceiving that at the theological core of the Muslim mission and the Christian mission are two different truth centers: the Qur'an for Muslims and the Messiah for Christians. In this book he probes the implications of those two different revelation centers with clarity and insight. How does mission proceed if the Qur'an is the revealed truth center of a community, or if on the other hand Jesus the Messiah is the center?

I highly recommend this book for my Muslim friends; it will help to clarify the nature of the Muslim way, as well as the Christian way. This book will also be invaluable for Christians, who want to become genuine and respectful neighbors to Muslims.

I recommend this book to all casual readers who are looking for an accessible and lively book that compares Islam and the Gospel, a book enlivened with narratives. Students and study groups will discover that this book is structured with discussion questions at the end of each chapter that are in many cases based upon qur'anic and biblical passages. I hope that study groups in churches and even mosques will use this book in comparative studies of the Muslim and Christian communities. Teachers and students of college courses on Islam and the Christian faith will discover that this book is a valuable resource.

I compliment my beloved brother, David W. Shenk, on this work of love and I pray that it will be a blessing to many thousands.

—*Bedru Hussein, Vice President of Mennonite World Conference*

Preface

Somalia was my first immersion within a Muslim society. In 1963 our family began a ten-year sojourn in this Muslim nation where most citizens were camel-herding nomads. We were commissioned by Eastern Mennonite Missions. Prior to Somalia, I had grown up in Tanganyika (Tanzania) and then lived in the United States for about a decade.

As my wife, Grace, and our two daughters, Karen (two years) and Doris (two months) and I struggled through the clamor of Mogadiscio Airport on our arrival in Somalia, I knew that I had never before heard God's name used so freely. Voices expressed God's name mostly in piety and a few in irreverent profanity.

Although my assignment was to work within the Somalia Mennonite Mission educational program, God was really the foremost concern throughout our decade of involvement in that country. God-talk and God-awareness permeated every aspect of Somali life. Islam had rooted solidly within Somali society and culture. We invested many hours in conversation concerning faith with Somali friends in tea shops or at home, as we sipped tea spiced with *garful* and *heil* (cinnamon and cardamom).

When a Marxist revolution forced us to leave, we moved to Somalia's southern neighbor, Kenya, in 1973. Our family settled into the Eastleigh section of Nairobi so as to be within the Muslim community. A Qadiriyya *sufi* mosque was across the street from us. Our home provided a setting for dialogues with Muslims, including key leaders. We would remove all the chairs from our living room, sit on mats in a circle, and drink tea as we conversed earnestly about God and faith and truth and the Qur'an and Muhammad and Jesus and salvation.

While living in Kenya, my interest in the theological realities that Muslims and Christians experience in meeting one another

grew, as did a commitment to a presence among Muslims of loving service and faithful witness that neither avoided differences
nor exacerbated mistrust. The Project for Christian Muslim
Relations in Africa (PROCMURA) provided a network for me to
work with other Christians committed to presence and faithful
witness among Muslims. I served with the PROCMURA team in
leadership training seminars and institutes that helped to equip
Christians for conversation with Muslims and faithful witness.

A team worked with me to develop a Bible study series that
engaged the Islamic worldview and addressed misunderstandings and objections Muslims have concerning the Christian faith.
These courses, entitled *The People of God*, have been or are being
translated into some forty languages; thousands enroll in this
series of biblical studies every year.

A significant development in the conversation with Muslims
has been a long-term dialogue with a Muslim friend, Badru D.
Kateregga. We were teachers of world religions in the Kenyatta
College of the University of Nairobi. We debated and discussed
faith issues together in the presence of our students as we taught
religion classes as a team. Students were delighted and challenged.

These engaging classroom dialogues forged trust between
Badru and me, and so we decided to share our conversation with
one another in the form of a book. Writing the book, *A Muslim and
a Christian in Dialogue*, was a stretch for both of us. We were good
friends. God was the center of our faith. Nevertheless, our understandings of God were formed by our respective journeys within
our respective faiths.

Since my family and I returned to the United States in 1979, I
have continued my conversations with Muslims. Several times a
year, I and other Christians invest an evening sitting on mats in a
mosque listening to our Muslim hosts. When appropriate, we
share also from the faith that we embrace who are disciples of
Jesus the Messiah.[1]

In the last few years several events with Muslims have espe-
cially impacted me. One was a series of six dialogues in the
United Kingdom with Shabir Ally, director of the Muslim
Information Center in Toronto. These events in the fall of 2000
were sponsored by the Muslim Students Association of the
United Kingdom. The venues were five universities and the

Central London Mosque. These three-hour events focused on key dimensions of the conversation between Muslims and Christians: revelation, God, salvation, Jesus, the cross and resurrection, Abraham, and attitudes of Muslims toward Christians and Christians toward Muslims. The Muslim theological ethos of these events was largely Sunni.

Then, two years later in the fall of 2002, I had the surprise of being the dialogue companion of Ms. Hamideh Mohagheghi, hosted by the *Theologische Studientage Der AMG* in Heiligenstadt, Germany. The Muslim participant was a modernist Shi'ite (formerly Iranian). This four-day Anabaptist-Mennonite event was characterized by a theological depth and respectful interchange that is unusual in the encounters between Muslims and Christians.

Complementing the German event was a Shi'i-Muslim and Mennonite-Christian dialogue sponsored by the Imam Khomeini Education and Research Institute in Qom, Iran, and the Toronto Mennonite Theological Center in Toronto, Canada, in collaboration with Mennonite Central Committee. This dialogue grew out of a Qom-Toronto exchange program that was nurtured by the three sponsoring agencies for several years. The theme was modernity. Iranian Muslims, as well as North American Mennonites, experience the challenges of modernity. The Iranians struggle with a commitment to maintain an Islamic social and political order within the ideological crosscurrents of modernity. Those issues have been at the very core of the persistent political discussions in Iran between democratic student movements and theologians; the theological issues addressed in the Toronto conference were not trivial.

This book is a reflection on dimensions of my walk in conversation with Muslims for nearly four decades. It has been a journey with friends whom I respect. Sometimes the journey together has been quite casual, and at other times truly and intensely theological. Occasionally the pilgrimage together has been confrontational.

Bishop Kenneth Cragg, a noteworthy Islamist and theologian, observed in a Middle East conference where I was a participant, that "Within every theological convergence that Muslims and Christians discover in meeting one another, there is also divergence."

Some Christians and Muslims are so committed to highlighting the convergences that they ignore the divergence between Islam and Gospel; others focus only on the differences, condemning the beliefs of the alternative community as utterly false. This book celebrates areas wherein we agree; preeminently Muslims and Christians are both committed to worshiping the God of Abraham. I also explore the divergent paths that Islam and the Gospel invite us to follow in the journey of life and the nature of the mission of the Muslim nation and the Christian church.

The concluding paragraphs of the dialogue that Badru Kateregga and I shared comment on our experience of witness in each other's presence. We participated both in the joy of convergence and the pain of divergence. We wrote:

> While giving thanks for and affirming the faith which unites us, we also confess that our respective witnesses differ in important ways.
>
> In Islam, God's mercy is supremely expressed through the revelation of a perfect law. In Christian faith, God's love is supremely expressed in the suffering, redemptive love revealed in the life, crucifixion, and resurrection of Jesus the Messiah. These are not superficial differences. They deal with the most fundamental questions of the meaning of human existence. There is no way a Muslim and a Christian can honestly proclaim that these differences are irrelevant or insignificant.[2]

This dialogue is polite, forthright, and respectful. The book has been well received by both Muslims and Christians. However, after writing that dialogue with Badru, I have wanted to write a sequel, a confession at a deeper level of the nature of the encounter between Islam and the Christian faith, especially as I have experienced it. Every time I meet with Muslims in a mosque and hear their perplexity, intrigue, or objections to the Gospel, I experience fresh clarity concerning the nature of the Gospel. Islam is a forthright alternative to the biblical Gospel. When the church meets the Islamic alternative, that encounter helps to clarify not only Islam, but the nature of the Gospel as well.

In this book, also written in a dialogical spirit, I seek to commend the Messiah within the context of an Islamic worldview. I hope that looking at Jesus in the context of the Muslim alternative and critique will reveal dimensions of the Gospel that both Christians and Muslims have often missed.

So, I have written first for Christians. Muslims are dismayed by the hypocrisy of Christians who profess faith in the Messiah but deny the Jesus of the Bible in their daily lives. I hope that Christians will hear the Muslim concern that all of life must come under submission to the will of God.

Muslim critique of the Gospel requires that Christians become careful theologians. Careless theology is not possible when Christians meet Muslims in witness and dialogue. Therefore, I hope that this book will commend the Messiah in ways that will challenge those Christians to repentance, for whom their Messiah has become a distorted creation of their own culture. I also hope that the Islamic critique and alternative to the Gospel will encourage Christians to a reengagement with New Testament theology and the Messiah of the Bible.

I have also written for Muslims. I hope that Muslims will thoughtfully consider the fullness of *'Isa* (Jesus), whom the Qur'an and all Muslims confess to be the Messiah. In regards to the Messiah, Muslims are closer to the Christian faith than is Judaism.

The Qur'an exclaims, "And thou wilt find the nearest of them in affection to those who believe (to be) those who say: Lo! We are Christians. That is because there are among them priests and monks, and because they are not proud" (Maida [The Table Spread] 5:82).

Muslims confess that Jesus is *the* Messiah born of the virgin and a fulfillment of the former scriptures. Judaism does not believe this to be true of Jesus. However, although Muslims believe Jesus is the Messiah, within Islam Jesus is really a mystery figure. The Muslim understanding of his messianic ministry is fundamentally divergent from that of the biblical Jesus and the witness of the church. I hope that Muslims will experience this book as an invitation to consider the claims of the Messiah of the biblical scriptures.

I attempt to describe the Muslim community and beliefs truthfully. In my many conversations with Muslims I have experienced the "tug" of Islam, the inner pull that has attracted so many to embrace the Muslim way. I attempt to convey that tug. However, I am not a Muslim; I believe that Jesus is God's Anointed One, the Savior of the world. This means that some Muslims will disagree with some of what I have written. That cannot be avoided. However, I do hope that I have not misrepresented Islam. It is for this reason that I have sought and taken very seriously Muslim critiques of the manuscript before it was published.

Some Christians might feel that I write with too much empathy for the Muslim commitment. When I write about Muslims, I attempt to tell of their beliefs and mission from a Muslim understanding. I attempt to walk in Muslim shoes, as it were, as I describe Islam. I do that deliberately, for I believe it is important for Christians to understand the Muslim faith as Muslims understand their faith.

Other Christians who have experienced the militant and even violent edge of the Muslim nation will conclude that the Islam I am describing is not the Islam they experience. That is true. I have had some experience with violent Muslim militancy, but those encounters have been marginal to my experience. I do comment on themes within the Qur'an that the militant fringe relies upon for their inspiration. But my walk has been mostly with the broad mainstream of conservative Islam, not Islamic militancy.

Some Muslims will conclude that the Jesus and the church I describe is not the Jesus and church they have experienced. Many Muslims view the Christian faith through the prism of violent Christian crusades against Muslim peoples. In our very recent history there is the pathos of Bosnia and Chechnya and Kosovo and Iraq. Often Muslims view these conflicts as wars against Islam and the Muslims, wars that are instigated by nations that Muslims consider Christian.

I comment on Christian crusades, including some of the Old Testament bases for Christian militancy. My focus, however, within the discussion of both Islam and the Gospel, is to explore the core themes that are foundational to the Muslim nation and the Christian church. It is for this reason that I give special attention to the Qur'an and the Messiah. The Muslim nation is established on the conviction that the Qur'an is the criterion of all truth; the Christian church confesses that Jesus is the Messiah, the Son of the living God.

The Muslim nation and the Christian church are diverse, and this short theological exploration cannot be a journey through all the different and varied paths taken by the Muslim or Christian movements. For this reason the exploration of the Muslim journey will especially focus on the mainstream of Sunni conservative communities.

The Christian journey is even more diverse than the Muslim journey. However, I will rely considerably on an Anabaptist theological orientation informed by the *Confession of Faith in a Mennonite Perspective.*[3] The Mennonite Church is one of the denominations that arose in Europe out of the sixteenth-century Anabaptist movement. The Anabaptists believe that every area of life needs to come under the authority of the Messiah and his kingdom. That commitment is understood by Muslims, who are also committed to bring all aspects of life into submission to the will of God. Of course, the understanding of the nature of the kingdom of God within biblical and qur'anic faith is different. Nevertheless, both Anabaptists and Muslims resist dividing life into the secular and the religious, but rather seek to submit every area of life to the rule of God. All Christians who are committed to this vision find a remarkable basis for dialogue with Muslims.

The Anabaptists were a free-church movement that emerged during the early years of the Protestant Reformation. Anabaptists longed to be a New Testament church of faithful disciples of Jesus. Although there were some extremist and violent aberrations within the movement, the mainstream of the Anabaptists were committed to following Jesus of the New Testament in his fullness. They believed that baptism should be a public testimony to that commitment, and therefore practiced adult baptism on confession of faith. They insisted on the separation of church and state. They refused to take the sword or participate in military adventures anywhere, including the wars against the Muslim Turks that were embroiling Europe. They sought to become a community of faithful followers of Jesus the Messiah. They were passionate evangelists. Many were martyred by the authorities because they profoundly challenged the assumptions of the state-church system.

My journey with Muslims has been as an Anabaptist Christian, and this book reflects that reality. I am a follower of Jesus the Messiah. I believe that in the Messiah, God has acted to redeem humankind, and in Jesus I have received forgiveness and reconciliation with God. I believe that the church is called of God to be a sign of the presence of the kingdom of God on earth, a kingdom inaugurated by the Messiah that will be fulfilled eternally at his second coming. That is the reason I seek to commend the Messiah within the pages of this book.

This book reflects on a journey of conversations with Muslim friends. It is not a comprehensive theology. It is a reflection. This is a narrative theology and some of the material is anecdotal. All anecdotes and conversations are as accurate as I can recall. However, in some cases I have used names other than those of the actual participants.

My life motto is 1 Peter 3:15: "But in your hearts set apart Christ as Lord. Always be prepared to give an answer to everyone who asks you to give the reason for the hope that you have. But do this with gentleness and respect."

I arrived in London, in October 2000, for the six days of dialogue with Shabir Ally. One of my first questions to my Muslim Students Association hosts was, "Why have you invited me?"

They responded, "Because your books reveal a person who is committed to the Gospel and who respects us Muslims."

I have written this book in the hope that this will be a further contribution to that legacy. Whether that is so, you as a reader will ultimately decide.

Using This Book

This book is a comparative exploration of Islam and the Gospel as well as the Muslim and Christian communities. It is written for the casual reader as well as for the more intentional focus of a discussion group or an academic classroom. It will be a helpful supplement to courses on world religions or Islam.

The first chapter, "Different Journeys," consists of two sections: descriptions of the nature of the Muslim nation and the Christian church, and a historical overview. What are the historical journeys of the Muslim nation and the Christian church? This provides for a contextual understanding of the different theological journeys of the Muslim and Christian communities.

The theological and missional portion of the book is written in thirteen chapters. This will provide a resource for a three-month weekly study comparing beliefs and mission of the Muslim and Christian communities. The text relies heavily on qur'anic and biblical sources, with ample scriptural references for further reading and study. The questions at the end of each chapter provide opportunity for lively discussion.

Students and study groups will want to have a copy of the Qur'an as well as the Bible on hand, because many of the questions are derived from the Muslim or Christian scriptures.

Biblical references are from the *New International Version*. References from the Qur'an are from Mohammed Marmaduke Pickthall's rendition, *The Meaning of the Glorious Koran*. For purposes of readability in non-Arabic script, vowel signs for transliterated Arabic words are omitted; however, the ' ('ayn) and the ' (hamza) are included.

A topical and annotated bibliography is included as a supplementary resource at the end of this book. This bibliography was developed by Dr. Jon Hoover, assistant supervisor of the Islamics Studies Program at Dar Comboni for Arabic Studies in Cairo. I am most grateful for this significant contribution to this book.

Acknowledgments

A team of friends have walked with me in this effort. Many have read the manuscript and critiqued it. I am especially grateful for two Muslim friends who have contributed thoughtful counsel. First I mention a Philadelphia surgeon and longtime friend, Dr. A. R. Safi, who reviewed a number of the most pertinent chapters and provided forthright critique. I also explored in some depth concepts within the manuscript with Imam Shabir Ally, who directs the Islamic Information Center in Toronto. These associates have given insight into Muslim perceptions of the approaches I have developed.

Several scholars of Islam have carefully critiqued the effort. Samuel Schlorff addressed issues of accuracy and theological integrity. So did two Dutch Islamists, Roelf Kuitse and Anton Wessels. Jon Hoover gave pertinent suggestions in regards to scholarship, as did Gordon Nickel, Calvin Shenk, and Roy Hange. Others gave helpful counsel in regard to clarity, relevance, theological content, and sensitivity: Ray Reitz, David Witmer, Leon Miller, Harold Reed, Darren Schaupp, Barbara Witmer, Urbane Peachey, and Jewel Showalter. Tilahun Beyene gave pertinent counsel with an internationalist insight. Janet Kreider and her sister, Elizabeth, reviewed the effort with special attention to editorial matters. Of course, ultimately, I take personal responsibility for what I have written.

This effort was incubating within me for many years. During

my four years at Lithuania Christian College, the college provided opportunity for me to interact with expressions of Islam within the European context. Eastern Mennonite Missions encouraged this effort and invested seed funds. Mountville Mennonite Church, where I am a member, has encouraged and prayed for me throughout this writing enterprise.

I am especially indebted to those many Muslims who have become my friends and from whom I have learned so much, especially in regards to submission to the providence of God. A special word of thanks to Badru D. Kateregga, with whom I wrote *A Muslim and a Christian in Dialogue* many years ago. That effort has been the source of the vision to write this book. Also of special significance to this exploration have been the insights of friends who have once walked in the way of Islam and now walk in the way of the Messiah.

Grace, my wife, has applauded this effort. She has brought many cups of tea into my writer's den as one way to encourage this journey. Without her support, this book would be only a thought in my mind. I thank her!

— 1 —

Different Journeys

"THE twin towers!" we heard our hostess gasp into her cell phone.

My wife, Grace, and I were in Tashkent, Uzbekistan. The evening of September 11, 2001, we had just joined friends for a quiet dinner in a downtown restaurant when the news of the catastrophe in New York, Washington, D.C., and Pennsylvania invaded our tranquillity.

Grief overwhelmed us. "This is about Jerusalem," we surmised. It seemed to us that the faiths, histories, traditions, and ethnicities that meet and collide in Jerusalem were intertwined in this disaster.

Paradoxically, Jerusalem, the City of Peace, as is true of no other city, is the place of meeting for the *shalom* of Israel, the *salaam* of Islam, and the peace of the Gospel. Each of these three peace movements, Jewish, Christian, and Muslim, trace their origins to Abraham, who was called by God to bless "all peoples on earth" (Gen. 12:3). The Zionist hope, the Christian church, and the Muslim nation all are inspired by a vision: peace to the nations. There are gracious touches of peace among Muslims, Christians, and Jews living as neighbors in Jerusalem. Yet there are also persistent, dangerous, and powerful theological, ethnic, and cultural undercurrents that are incipiently destructive. What has gone wrong?

Peacemaking

The way of peace is what we talked about in a seminar in Tashkent the day after the September 11 calamity. Friends took us to a basement room in a ramshackle tin and concrete labyrinth that was the first stages of a construction that would someday be a church facility. Seventy Uzbek or Russian pastors and church leaders were present in that basement. Probably all of them were only recently Christian; their backgrounds had been secular atheist or Muslim. It became a holy morning as we considered the different understandings and commitments to mission revealed in the peace of the Messiah and the peace of Islam within our world of conflict. We invested much of our day exploring what it means to be ambassadors of the Prince of Peace, whose peace is created through the cross. We remembered that two thousand years ago, the Messiah had sat on a colt overlooking Jerusalem and wept because that which brings peace "is hidden from your eyes" (Luke 19:42).

In that Tashkent seminar we discerned that our approaches to peacemaking were grounded in our theologies. For example, twenty-three years earlier (1978), United States president Jimmy Carter (a Christian) had hosted Egyptian president Anwar Sadat (a Muslim) and Israeli prime minister Menachem Begin (of the Jewish faith). They met at Camp David in Maryland for thirteen days to focus on peacemaking. Their first act of business was to call on the faith communities they represented to pray for peace. Carter had his Bible nearby during the negotiations, and he and Begin looked into portions of scriptures that they mutually accepted. Sadat persisted with the hope that someday Jews, Muslims, and Christians would meet at Mount Sinai as a commitment to an enduring peace. All three leaders recognized that the respective faith journeys of the peoples they represented profoundly informed the peace process.[1]

The journey and mission for peace is treacherous. Anwar Sadat was assassinated just three years later, and another advocate for peace, Israeli prime minister Yitzhak Rabin, was slain in 1995. Is such suffering a necessary dimension of peacemaking? This book explores a Muslim and Christian response to that question and the core theological foundations of the Muslim and Christian journeys and mission.

The Legacy of Abraham

Muslims, Christians, and Jews gather weekly in their mosques, churches, and synagogues to worship the God of Abraham. Each of these communities believes itself to be an expression of the faith and people of Abraham. The personal Creator God is the focus of worship and loyalty within each of these communities, but God is understood and revealed differently. All three faiths believe that God reveals truth. The believers in each community seek to live in faithfulness to the truth that is at the center of their understanding of God and his will: Torah for the Jews, the Gospel for the Christians, Qur'an for the Muslims. Each of these respective centers creates and nurtures different communities of faith: Israel, church, and *ummah*. We will comment on *ummah* and church.

The Muslim Nation (Ummah)

Ummah means a people or nation. Islam means submission; the Arabic root s-l-m, is also the root of salaam, peace. The Muslim nation is the worldwide community (*ummah*) of believers who submit to Islam. "Submission-peace": this is the Muslim understanding of the meaning of the word Islam. Commitment to the nation of Islam transcends all other national loyalties. A core function of the community is to preserve Islam and protect the Muslim believer from ever going astray. Islam forms the community, and the community preserves Islam.

Humanity is divided. All people who have submitted to the rule of Islam are within the Muslim nation; those who have not submitted to Islam are outside. The *ummah* gives witness: *La Ilaha Illa'llah Muhammadan Rasulu'llah* (There is no God except Allah, and Muhammad is the apostle of Allah). Humanity is divided into two groups: those who make this confession and are, therefore, within the *ummah*, and those who have not yet made this confession and are, therefore, not within the *ummah*.

In Medina the Muslims under Muhammad's leadership developed a constitution. The constitution clarifies that the Muslims "are a single community distinct from other people."[2]

The Muslim *ummah* is not complete until it possesses all dimensions of power and authority. That authority is extended over territory. Many Muslims who live in areas that are not under

Muslim authority yearn for the completion of their community that is only possible when the Muslim nation has established political control over the territory where they reside. That yearning is the reason for the Muslim insurgencies in regions such as Kashmir, Mindanao, Macedonia, and Chechnya. Nevertheless, there are, of course, some Muslims who are not committed to this kind of political agenda, and are quite content to be an island of faith within a non-Muslim society.

Muslims believe that the *ummah* is the "middle nation." It is the nation that emerged from Arabia, a region in the middle of other nations. It is perfectly balanced, not given to the extremes of asceticism or the debauchery of hedonism. Muslims perceive that Judaism focuses on this world, and the church on the hereafter. The Muslim middle nation combines both this world and the next. The *ummah* is "assembly" of the "party of God."[3] It is the best nation and has a mission to be a witness over the nations.

The Qur'an proclaims,

> Thus We have appointed you a middle nation,
> That ye may be witnesses against mankind
> (Baqara [The Cow] 2:143).

The Christian Church

Church means "gathering." The New Testament Greek term for church is *ecclesia*, the group who gather for a purpose and then scatter. The Christian church is the gathering of those who confess, as Peter, one of the first disciples of Jesus, did two thousand years ago, "You are the Christ, the Son of the living God" (Matt. 16:16). That confession is the foundation of the church. The church around the world gives witness: Jesus Christ is Lord and Savior.

The apostolic writings refer to the church as a "holy nation" (1 Pet. 2:9). Within the New Testament this concept does not entail the political and territorial authority that is significant in the Muslim understanding of the Muslim nation, however. The church as a holy nation is a redeemed people called out from among the peoples. The boundary of the church is all believers in Jesus as Savior and Lord, the sign of inclusion is repentance from sin and baptism, and the evidence of membership is the fruit of the Holy Spirit. This is to say that territoriality and political control were contrary to the nature of the New Testament church.

Jesus commissioned the church to be a witness among the nations. In his last command before his departure from earth, he said:

> Therefore, go and make disciples of all nations, baptizing them in the name of the Father and of the Son and of the Holy Spirit, teaching them to obey everything I have commanded you (Matt. 28:19-20).

Christians refer to this command as the "great commission." It has inspired the church in its global mission for two thousand years.

Witnesses do not possess political or territorial control. A witness does not control the outcome—the outcome depends upon the response of those who hear the witness. The New Testament church was a fellowship of people who heard the Christian witness and believed that witness and therefore chose to believe in the Messiah.

The Nation State

Nation states are not universal communities. They might or might not recognize the authority of God.

That is not true of the church or the *ummah.* Both these communities are committed to the ultimate authority of God. Both are universal communities. During Independence Day celebrations in the United States I heard two teachings about the relationship of the community of faith and the secular nation state. The first was in a Sunni Muslim mosque. The second was in a Mennonite Christian church.

The Muslim imam said, "Patriotism is good, but within boundaries. Our first loyalty is to the Muslim nation, which is a universal community that supersedes all nation states."

The Christian pastor said, "Patriotism has its place, but be cautious. Our first loyalty is to Christ and his church. The church is a universal community called out from within communities and nations around the world."

More comment is necessary about the journeys in history of the church and the *ummah.* This framework is essential for an understanding of the theologies and mission of the Christian and Muslim communities, as well as the present-day meeting of the two communities as neighbors in the global community of humankind.

The Church Among the Nations

First, a brief perusal of the story of the church. The apostolic church flowed within the spirit of the command of Jesus to go and become witnesses of the Gospel to all nations. Within the lifetime of the apostles of Jesus, the church had taken root in communities from Spain to India, from North Africa into Central Europe. That rapid growth happened within the context of suffering.

Occasionally the wrath of the authorities turned with fury against the church, and a number of the apostles were martyred. Why the opposition? The church confessed that Jesus is the ultimate authority. Empires and nations are inclined to claim ultimate authority; the Roman authorities perceived the followers of Jesus the Messiah to be dangerous atheists who would not worship the traditional gods nor bow their knees in veneration of the emperor. Within the Roman Empire, one of the most horrendous persecutions lasted for nine years (303-312).

Constantinization of the Western Church

Then it all ended. The Roman emperor Constantine made peace with the church. In the year 313 the Roman Empire proclaimed the Edict of Toleration. There would be no more persecution of Christians. Constantine went even further: The authority of the empire soon favored the Christians, and he became quite involved in the affairs of the church. In fact, Constantine convened a council of bishops at Nicea in 325 to develop a creed that would clarify who Jesus was.

Persecution on the Margins

That was disturbing to a lot of Christians, especially in the Asian East. That unease is related to the later successes of the Muslim community. So, it is helpful to have some awareness of what all this meant, especially for the churches on the margins of the Roman Empire. After the Council of Nicea, the Roman emperors and the Western bishops developed an unseemly union of empire and church. Before long some bishops were depending on the power of the empire to enforce church doctrine, even violently.

The churches in Egypt, North Africa, and the Asian East were especially vulnerable. For example, in North Africa, Donatism was a popular independent church movement among the

Berbers. That indigenous North African church was persecuted and marginalized by the Roman church-empire alliance. The issues were complex. Heretical beliefs were part of the issue. Nevertheless, at the heart of the conflict was the reality that neither the Roman Empire nor the church authorities would tolerate an independent church within the regions under imperial control.[4] Consequently when Muslim armies marched west across North Africa in the seventh century, they met a weakened church because two centuries earlier, "Christian" Roman imperial power had undermined the widespread indigenous and independent Berber church.

Terrific Persecution in Persia

The union of caesar and pope in the European West also had devastating consequences for the churches of the Asian East. For the first three centuries of the Christian era, it was mostly the churches within the Roman Empire that were persecuted. However, with the conversion of Constantine and the emergence of caesaropapacy in the West, it was the churches in the Asian East that began to experience the wrath of the persecutors. Under Constantine, Christianity in the West had become the religion of empire. Peace had come to the Western church; as Bishop Mar Jacob of Edessa wrote, "Constantine, the chief of victors, reigns and now the cross the emperor's diadem surmounts."[5]

In Persia there was no such rejoicing, for the Persian church was caught in the conflict between empires. For three centuries Persian shahs and Roman emperors had made intermittent war with one another. With yet another war threatening, Constantine wrote to the Shah of Persia, Shapur II, "I rejoice to hear that the fairest provinces of Persia are adorned with . . . Christians. . . . Since you are so powerful and pious, I commend them to your care, and leave them in your protection."[6] For the shah, this meant only one thing: The Christians were a Roman fifth column sabotaging Zoroastrian Persia from within.

Twenty years later Constantine massed his troops for war against Persia with bishops accompanying his armies. According to the contemporary church historian, Eusebius, the bishops accompanied Constantine "to battle with him and for him by the prayers to God from whom all victory proceeds."[7]

Consequently the rage of the Persians against the Christians knew no boundaries. For more than twenty years, the Christians were systematically hunted from one end of the Persian Empire to the other, tortured and killed. The Persian church was nearly eradicated by this, "the Great Persecution." It has never recovered from that blow.

Churches of the Asian East

This development made it clear that the church in the Asian East had to forthrightly distance itself from the church in the West. Constantine and the subsequent emergence of Christendom and later the Holy Roman Empire forced the churches of the East to define themselves as alternatives to Western Christianity, even though those alternative definitions (for example, Nestorianism) might be considered "heretical" by the Western church.[8]

However, Dutch historian of religion Arend Theodoor van Leeuwen, observes that this separation provided an open door for Islam. He writes, "Islamic power . . . offered to anti-Byzantine sentiment a far more effective ideology than anything that heretical Christianity was able to provide."[9]

Yet not all Christians converted to Islam as a protest statement against the Western church and empire. The church in the Asian East sometimes manifested its alternative expressions of the Gospel in mission. For a thousand years Eastern missionary outreach extended far into the heartland of Asia. These minority churches of the East were a non-imperial expression of the mission of the church. This was in dramatic contrast to much of the Western expansion of the church subsequent to Constantine, where empire and church did "mission" in concert.

The Eastern churches were always minority churches, often persecuted, sometimes to the point of near decimation. Yet some of these same churches engaged in a thousand years of persistent mission even into far-away China. It is a remarkable story. The international outreach of the Persian church persisted for half a millennium after these churches came under Muslim political authority.

Division in the Western Church

Now a brief excursion into later developments. In 1054 the Western church experienced a separation largely along the lines that developed within the Roman Empire when its administration was divided between Rome in the west and Byzantium in the east. A result of the Western church division was the development of Orthodox and Catholic Christian communions.

However, these different church communions continued to embrace a commitment to the unity of church and state. So the Western church, often referred to as Christendom, means the ethos of political and church unity within the Western church after Constantine, whether the region later became Orthodox or Catholic or Protestant.

Three modern examples: Russian Orthodox bishops praying for Russian victory over the Chechnya rebels; Christian Serbs fighting to cleanse the Balkans of Muslims; and American evangelical leaders asserting that a war against Iraq is a just war that Christians should support.

Thus even in modern times, the Eastern churches often need to define themselves as other than the Western church. Currently, the U.S.–led "war on terrorism" and some of the Christian rhetoric that has accompanied the campaign has rekindled the need for Eastern churches to clearly define themselves as different from the Western churches. Rage against Washington, D.C., is sometimes vented against the small minority Christian communities in the East. The legacy of Constantine or eleventh-century crusaders marching to the East under the sign of the cross persists. Modern Western Constantines and crusaders create new vulnerabilities for the Eastern churches.[10] Millions of Asians disillusioned with the West see Islam as an attractive alternative.

Alternative Commitments

There are communities of Christian faith within the Western church that do not embrace the alliance between church and state that Constantine developed. In fact, these alternative commitments expressed through groups such as the Baptists in North America were a significant voice in providing for the separation of church and state in the United States Constitution.

Other church communities such as the Anabaptists, who emerged during the sixteenth-century Protestant Reformation, have quite consistently committed to being New Testament churches. These fellowships embrace a vision of living as disciples of the Messiah in all areas of life. They seek to unite faith and the ethics of Jesus, including his call to peacemaking. That means, of course, that church and state must be separate.

The *Ummah* and the Nations

Now we will consider a brief historical overview of the Muslim journey. For twelve years, beginning in 610, Muhammad preached in Mecca. He encountered severe opposition. Then in 622, he and his followers secretly migrated to Medina, about 250 miles north. This is the *hijrah* (migration) that marks the beginning of the Muslim era.

Why is the *hijrah* so significant? It is because in Medina, Muhammad could continue his prophetic proclamations while also forming the Muslim believers into an effective community. He developed the *ummah* into an organization with the political, economic, and military institutions necessary to establish, defend, and extend the Muslim nation. The Medina base was very effective; within ten years most of Arabia, including Mecca, had come under the authority of the Muslims.

Before Muhammad's death in 632, he had sent envoys to neighboring nations such as Abyssinia, Persia, and Byzantium. The plans were developing for an expansion of the Muslim nation beyond the confines of Arabia. Within the next several years, the Muslim armies overpowered nations on the Arabian periphery. Modern Muslim apologists make the case that all these conquests were in self-defense,[11] just as the Qur'an commands:

> Fight in the way of Allah against those who fight against you, but begin not hostilities. Lo! Allah loveth not aggressors. And slay them wherever ye find them, and drive them out of the places whence they drove you out, for persecution is worse than slaughter. . . . And fight them until persecution is no more, and religion is for Allah. But if they desist, then let there be no hostility except against wrongdoers (Baqara 2:190-191, 193).

However, the military victories could not camouflage the internal tensions as the Muslims struggled to clarify and solidify leadership after Muhammad's death. The beginnings tested the resolve of the Muslims to be a community. For twenty-nine years after Muhammad's death, a series of four "rightly guided caliphs" ruled the emerging Muslim nation. The movement was severely tested. The last two of the rightly guided leaders,

Uthman and Ali, were murdered.

A bitter division, including a civil war, developed between the Shi'ites and Sunnis that has never been fully healed. The Shi'ites have persisted in the conviction that the legitimate head of the movement had to be a descendant of Muhammad; the Sunnis opted for a leader chosen by the community. Nevertheless, even though there was strife within the leadership, by the time of Ali's death in 661 the Muslims occupied the whole of the Middle East from Egypt to Persia.

Only six years after Muhammad's death (638), Muslim armies captured Jerusalem. The Muslims believed that their *ummah* should be a "witness over the nations," and thus extending Muslim authority over this city of great significance to both Jews and Christians was in full harmony with that mission.

The Dome of the Rock

It was in the spirit of self-confident assurance in their mission that in 691 Caliph Abd al-Malik built the Dome of the Rock mosque in Jerusalem on the site of the first and second Jewish temples. The mosque was built as a place for pilgrimage. The architectural style is that of the Syrian churches. It was and remains a remarkable structure. It towered above the churches and all other buildings in Jerusalem. It was well-built; today it is the oldest Muslim structure on earth.

This mosque was undoubtedly built to make a statement: Islam supersedes both Judaism and Christianity. It is built at Al-Aqsa (the farthest place), where Muslims believe Muhammad went in a miraculous nighttime journey from Mecca. They believe that from the spot on which the mosque is built, he ascended into heaven, where God encouraged him to continue his prophetic vocation. Inscriptions inside the mosque are a witness to the conviction that Islam clarifies and supersedes Judaism and Christianity.[12]

There are several statements extolling Islam and Muhammad at different locations. This inscription is beneath the dome, a quote from the qur'anic *sura* Nisaa (Women) 4:171.

> O People of the Scripture! Do not exaggerate in your religion nor utter aught concerning Allah save the truth. The Messiah, Jesus son of Mary, was only a messenger of Allah, and His word which He conveyed unto Mary, and a spirit from Him. So

believe in Allah and His messengers, and say not "Three."
Cease! (it is) better for you! Allah is only One Allah. Far is it
removed from His Transcendent Majesty that He should have a
son. His is all that is in the heavens and all that is in the earth.
And Allah is sufficient as Defender.

Christians Under Muslim Rule

The imposition of Muslim authority over Jerusalem was only
one of many astonishing successes of the Muslim armies. Within
one century of the *hijrah*, half the Christian population on earth had
come under Muslim rule. Christians and Jewish people were given
the status of protected communities, or *dhimmi*. (The next chapter
comments on that status.) Muslim armies pressed forward in conquest, both east and west. Within four generations Muslim authority was established from the Indus River, throughout the Middle
East, across North Africa, through Spain, and into southern France.

Decline in the Number of Christians

In regions where Muslims ruled for an extended period of
time, the church has declined in membership because of the
Muslim commitment to assure a movement from church to the
ummah. In Yemen, North Africa, Libya, and northern Sudan, the
ancient churches have, in fact, vanished. The death of these
churches never happened instantly. For many centuries the
churches persisted, but eventually Islam smothered these ancient
churches, including the martyr churches of North Africa.

Interestingly, none of these churches that died out had the
Bible in their native languages before Islamic rule was extended
over them. Wherever churches had the Bible, they have endured:
Egypt, Syria, and Ethiopia are noteworthy. In contrast the church
in North Africa always relied on a Latin translation of the scriptures. Latin was the language of the European colonizers. This
made it much more difficult for the church to become indigenous
and for the Gospel to become incarnated within the soul of North
African worldview and culture.

Interaction with Civilizations

In the early phases, the Muslim advance into regions far
beyond Arabia was on the whole quite orderly. This was not a
destructive rampage. Furthermore, the Umayyad and Abbasid
dynasties that carried forward the expansionist mission of Islam

had a remarkable ability to bring diversities within the system of Muslim authority.[13] The Abbasid caliphate presided over the Golden Age of Islam (eighth to eleventh centuries). The great centers of learning and culture—Christian, Hebrew, Hellenistic, Aramaean, Egyptian, and Assyro-Babylonian—were included within the expanding Muslim nation.[14]

During these four hundred years of grandeur, these diverse civilizations contributed synergy to the Muslim movement. As Europe entered the "Dark Ages," the Golden Age of Islam flourished as the Muslims interacted with exceedingly diverse civilizations in the realms ruled by the Muslims.

Nevertheless, as Islam took root, that synergy and creativity waned. There was much within these other systems that could never be absorbed by the Muslims. This was especially the case with Greek political practice and speculative and rational philosophy. Although over time these Greek streams have enormously formed Western civilization, the Muslim nation resisted these influences.[15] This was true of other streams as well.

Van Leeuwen comments:

> It has been part of the mysterious power of Islam to impose upon the civilization that flourished under its patronage its own outwardly sovereign forms, without itself being materially affected by or fundamentally transforming the content.[16]

The scholar of Islam, H. A. R. Gibb, writes:

> The struggle to subordinate all intellectual life to the authority of religion went on for many centuries in successive regions of the Muslim world. Where no fresh stimulus arose to prolong and revive flagging energies, the religious culture caught all other intellectual activities on the rebound, and by minor concessions held them and converted them into its own instruments. Those which it could not use, such as medicine and mathematics, stagnated or ultimately died away.[17]

Gibb adds:

> The study which in some sense took the place of the discarded sciences was not, however, theology. The master science of the Muslim world was law.[18]

This is to say that as islamization progressed, civilizational diversity waned. Some scholars dispute this observation.

Nevertheless, in education all areas of knowledge were subservient to the sent-down will of God, and that guidance from God was explicitly defined in systems of law.

Islam and the West

The Muslim nation and the West have experienced difficulty in developing a trusting relationship. A common meeting place has been elusive. These different communities have frequently fought wars with one another. Early in the Muslim era there were the Muslim expansionist wars into Byzantium, across North Africa, and into Spain. European counter-attacks culminated in the Battle of Tours in southern France in 732, one century after Muhammad's death. Three centuries later the crusades to retake the "Holy Land" for the Christians commenced in the late eleventh century. The pogrom that the First Crusade inflicted on the Muslim and Christian inhabitants of Jerusalem was horrendous. That genocide has never been forgotten.

A Lebanese journalist, Amin Maalouf, writes, "[T]here can be no doubt that the schism between these two worlds [of Islam and Christianity] dates from the crusades, deeply felt by the Arabs, even today, as an act of rape."[19]

These crusades were only one expression of the conflict. Over the course of fourteen centuries, periodic wars have erupted between the West and the Muslims; after the crusades the Muslims rebounded with vengeance and the wars extended into the eastern regions of Europe. By the sixteenth century Vienna was under siege. Much of Europe mobilized for war. It is in that context that the Protestant Reformation began. Some reformers joined hands with the Catholics in supporting the military defense of Europe. However, Martin Luther was ambivalent. He admonished that you cannot fight as a Christian, but you must fight as a citizen.[20]

An Anabaptist Response

Luther's stance was rooted in his theology of the two kingdoms that the Christian lives in. However, not all Protestants agreed with Luther. The Anabaptists agreed that there are two kingdoms, but that the first commitment of followers of Jesus is the kingdom of God. Jesus demonstrated love, not violence, toward his enemies. Christians must do likewise.[21]

Therefore, at this time of distress and fear in Europe, the Anabaptist Christians refused to join the wars against the Turks, for whom Christ had died. Anabaptist leader Michael Sattler expressed this conviction well at the trial in Zurich that preceded his martyrdom.[22] They would love and proclaim the gospel to the Turks, but never take the sword against them. These Anabaptists were considered traitors, and many were martyred for their commitments to peacemaking. These Christians rejected a Christendom where empire and church joined together. The Anabaptists insisted that Christendom was not the kingdom of God.

Western Intrusion

The political-military balance teetered between the Muslim and Western powers for some time. Then in a final fight for Vienna in 1683, Muslim armies were forced into retreat. A century later, in 1798, Napoleon landed his forces in Egypt. That was a major turning point in regard to modern realities. The wars in Eastern Europe were far from the center of Islam, but Egypt was near the center. This Western engagement in the center of the Muslim world has persisted ever since Napoleon's imperial adventure two centuries ago.

The power and attraction of Western economics and culture is an enigma for the Muslim nation. The mission of the Muslim *ummah* is to be a witness "over the nations." For the last several centuries it has not been that way.[23] Just one example: Muslim graduate students in any field are grateful when they can study in Western universities, but students from non-Muslim societies are not pursuing opportunities to study in Muslim universities. What has gone wrong?

The cultural questions are nagging. The political and military developments are even more troubling. From the time of Napoleon onward, the Muslim nation has been under sustained pressure and threat from the West. Here are other dates that mark the journey into misunderstanding and alienation, especially within the heartland of the Muslim world today.[24]

The Balfour Declaration (1917) instituted by the British government supported Jewish Zionist commitments to a homeland for Jews in Palestine. Palestinians were not consulted on that decision.

The Ottoman Empire was dismembered in the Treaty of Versailles (1919) following World War I; subsequently European powers occupied the Middle East.

Turkey became a secular republic under the military rule of Kemal Ataturk (1924). The Sunni Muslim caliphate was abolished.

The state of Israel was formed in 1948, resulting in 750,000 Palestinian refugees, according to the United Nations Conciliation Commission. Then in the 1967 war, Israel occupied Jerusalem, the West Bank, Gaza, and the Golan Heights of Syria. For several years Israel also occupied the Sinai Peninsula. Later Israel occupied southern Lebanon. Israel began to plant settlements in the Palestinian territories. By 2002, 140 settlements in the occupied territories were home to two hundred thousand Israeli settlers.

In 1991 a United States–led coalition fought Iraq for the liberation of Kuwait. Thereafter, for over a decade, U.S. forces have remained in Saudi Arabia, the heartland of the Muslim nation. All of these developments have contributed to deeply held feelings of grievance.

The Temple Mount/Al-Aqsa Mosque

However, there is nothing more tendentious than the Temple Mount in Jerusalem, which Muslims refer to as Al-Aqsa. This introduction has commented on the construction of the Dome of the Rock mosque in the seventh century over the site of the first and second Jewish temples. That mosque has stood on the mount for more than thirteen hundred years. However, since 1967 Israel has extended its authority over the mount.

Peace cannot come between Israel and the Palestinians until the issues of control over the Temple Mount are resolved. In July 2000, Unites States president Bill Clinton convened a meeting with Palestinian Authority president Yasir Arafat and Israeli prime minister Ehud Barak. During the two weeks they met at Camp David, they focused on Jerusalem and especially on the Temple Mount. The participants believed that if that issue could be resolved, the other matters related to the Israel-Palestinian conflict could be negotiated.

Representatives of the churches in Jerusalem were not invited, although they asked to be involved. The noninvolvement of the churches was in recognition that the mount does not have the same status as a "holy place" that it does in Judaism and Islam. Jerusalem is significant for Christians, but not in the way that the Temple Mount is for Jews and Muslims. Although all three of the participants were people of faith, none of them seemed capable of "hearing" the spirituality of the other as it relates to the Temple Mount.[25] The negotiators stumbled over that intractable mount.

Then about two months later, on September 28, Ariel Sharon visited the Temple Mount with about one thousand heavily armed Israeli soldiers, and he said, "We want to clearly exert our sovereignty over the Temple Mount." "This is our holy place."[26] That event and those statements were the match that ignited a renewed Palestinian *intifada* (rising).

About a year later, on September 11, 2001, Muslim militants hijacked planes and flew them into the Pentagon in Washington, D.C., and the World Trade Center in New York. The United States administration responded to this attack by declaring a war on terrorism. The Taliban regime in Afghanistan and the al-Qaida group based there seemed to be the epicenter of the terror network. Muslims worldwide felt on the defensive. Some felt that the United States was leading a modern crusade.

Then beginning on March 19, 2003, the United States led a coalition "of the willing" into a war against Iraq. The Middle East exploded in rage. Middle Eastern Arab governments who in any way appeared to support the U.S.–led invasion were on the defensive. Many Muslims identified with the notion that this invasion was another expression of a Western war against Islam and the Muslim nation.

Middle Eastern Christians

Thus even in modern times, the Eastern churches often need to define themselves as other than the Western church. Currently the U.S.–led war on terrorism and some of the Christian rhetoric that has accompanied the campaign has rekindled this need. Rage against Washington is sometimes vented against the small Christian communities in the East. The legacy of Constantine or eleventh-century crusaders marching to the East under the sign of the cross persists. Modern Western Constantines and crusaders create new vulnerabilities for the Eastern churches.[27]

Turmoil within the Middle East during much of the twentieth century has contributed to a phenomenal attrition in the number of Christians. In 1914 the official statistics of the Ottoman Empire reported that 24 percent of its citizens were Christians. This included present-day Turkey, Syria, Iraq, Lebanon, Palestine/ Israel, Jordan, and Egypt. At the dawn of the twenty-first century, the number of Christians in these countries was but 4 percent.[28]

A major blow to the Christians was the disintegration of the Ottoman Empire early in the twentieth century. That turmoil unleashed devastating intercommunal violence. A pogrom against the Armenian Christians eradicated most of that large community. They were either killed or fled as refugees into Greece or other parts of Armenia. It is noteworthy that this genocide against Middle East Christians happened at a time when Muslim political power was collapsing; it did not happen under the watch of a stable Ottoman Muslim political order.

Another reason for the decline of the Christian population is the choice of Christians to become Muslims. However, except for the Turkish pogrom, the most significant factor has been Christian immigration out of the Middle East during the last half of the twentieth century.

Immigration has dramatically reduced the percentage of Christians in the Middle East, and especially in Israel/Palestine. In 1947 the Arab Christian population in Israel/Palestine was between 20 percent (the churches' estimate) and 13 percent (British Mandate estimate). Fifty years later, at the end of the century, less than 2 percent were Christian.[29] Today there are more Christian Arabs from Jerusalem in Sydney, Australia, than there are Arab Christians in Israel/Palestine.[30]

In a conversation with a Christian journalist, Prince Hassan of Jordan said, "I am not only concerned but saddened that this migration has taken place. How can you have plurality without the participation of the Christians in this part of the world? It is a very real question for us."[31]

The decline of the Christian voice in the region means that the region has become less pluralist, with an increasing number of villages having exposure to only one perspective, that of Islam, and in some communities in Israel, only Judaism. The decline in the number of Christians also means that there is far less possibility for anyone to hear any witness to forgiveness and reconciliation, that gift of grace that is at the center of the ministries of Jesus.

Although they are a minority, the influence of Christians in the Middle East has been significant. Indigenous Middle Eastern Christians have cultivated a ministry of prayer and presence within the Muslim milieus where they live. Some are involved in reconciliation efforts in the Palestinian-Israeli impasse. Occasionally local Christians and Western mission agencies have joined hands in developing ministries of service that are received with much appreciation. Nazareth Hospital in Israel is just one example of many fine signs of Christian presence, some of which have served the peoples of the region for many generations. Excellent educational institutions are also a legacy of the church.

Recently in a mosque dialogue where I was present, there were accusations that Christians are blasphemers. The atmosphere quickly became less than congenial.

Then an engineer from Pakistan softened the rhetoric with this comment: "When I was growing up in Pakistan, the Christian schools were the very best. I would not be an engineer if it were not for those Christian teachers. I will never speak critically of the church or the beliefs of the Christians."

Christians would do well to imitate the spirit of that Pakistani Muslim. The Bible counsels: "Keep [your] tongue from evil. . . . Turn from evil and do good. . . . Seek peace and pursue it" (1 Pet. 3:10-11).

— 2 —

Out of Arabia

THE Muslim mission emerged at a time when Christians were debating theology. Here are examples of the kinds of discussions that were happening among the Christians:

"The virgin Mary is the mother of God."

"Oh, no, that is impossible! How could a woman give birth to God? The holy virgin is the mother of Christ!"

"God's Son was crucified and died on the cross."

"But it is impossible to kill God! Only the human Jesus was crucified, but the divine Son was not crucified; he was rescued from the cross and death."

"Jesus became the Son of God."

"No, Jesus Christ is the eternal Son of God; he didn't become the Son!"

"Christ is God!"

"That cannot be! God is Christ!"

Muhammad was born nearly six centuries after Jesus the Messiah in an era of sometimes divisive theological debate among Christians. Muslims believe that God commissioned Muhammad with a mission to clarify faith for confused Christians. The Qur'an exclaims:

> And with those who say: "Lo! We are Christians," We made a covenant, but they forgot a part of that whereof they were admonished. Therefore We have stirred up enmity and hatred among them till the Day of Resurrection, when Allah will inform them of their handiwork. . . .
> O People of the Scripture! Now hath Our messenger come unto you to make things plain! (Maida [The Table Spread] 5:14, 19).

The Muslim community developed six centuries after the church. What was the Arabian context? And what was the relationship of the early Muslim *ummah* to the Jewish and Christian communities? Why did the Muslims believe that they had a responsibility to clarify theology for the Christians? This chapter explores those questions.

What were the religious, theological, or cultural influences in the formation of the Muslim movement and the Qur'an? That is a Christian quest, for in biblical revelation there is a dialogical interaction between God and humankind within their historical context. However, questions of influence are not a Muslim vocation, because the Muslim community believes that the Qur'an is a sent-down revelation that transcends history. The Qur'an is noncontingent revelation, with "no relationship in its form to the passage of historical time."[1] (Chapters 5 and 6 explore those themes.) In the next paragraphs we briefly review questions of context and influences, while being aware of the concerns of the Muslim community about such questions.

Muhammad's Arabia

Muhammad was born in Mecca in the Year of the Elephant (570 A.D.). That was the year an Ethiopian Christian military commander attacked Mecca with an army that used elephants as war tanks. The battle symbolized the power of the Christian communities that encircled sixth-century Arabia. It also suggested that Arabia was a cultural backwater. Some Arabian leaders, who knew the world beyond their nomadic tribal societies, probably hoped for the time when the Arabian peoples would stand on equal footing with the civilized nations and empires. The Arabian prophet born in the Year of the Elephant would fulfill that hope. What is the Arabian context in which this hope was fulfilled?

There are four streams that we explore: 1) the polytheistic environment; 2) the Christian presence; 3) the Jewish presence; 4) the Arabian monotheists.

The Jahiliyya

The first reality is the *jahiliyya*. The Qur'an refers to the *jahiliyya* as the time of ignorance before Muhammad, who was to "warn a folk unto whom no warner came before" (Qasas [The

Narration] 28:46). Arabian polytheism thrived in the *jahiliyya* era. The Ka'bah in Mecca was the center of polytheistic worship during the *jahiliyya*. A sacred black stone was enshrined within the Ka'bah temple. The Ka'bah and the region around it was *haram*. For the Arabians, *haram* is that which is forbidden. Within the *haram* of the Ka'bah, that which was forbidden was acts that were against peace.

Arabian clans at war, whenever they made peace, brought their gods to the Ka'bah. In that way they established peace, because their gods were living in peace together within the Ka'bah. Both the sacred shrine and the surrounding region were, therefore, *haram*; it was a region of sacred peace. Arabian clans made annual pilgrimages to the Ka'bah to renew the peace with other clans. Some traditions assert that 360 divinities resided in the Ka'bah, each representing different clans.[2]

Muhammad and his Muslim followers developed their locations of worship as the alternative places of peace, because the Ka'bah was desecrated by idols and divinities. However, when Mecca finally came under the authority of the Prophet, the Muslims cleansed the Ka'bah in Mecca from the many divinities who resided there, and they dedicated the Ka'bah to the worship of Allah. Thus the sacred peace of the Ka'bah was transformed from the peace of the polytheistic gods to become the peace of the one God, Allah. This meant that the peace of the mosque and the traditional quest for the peace of Arabia were merged.[3]

A Christian Presence

A second influence was the Christian presence. Muhammad, like many of his fellow Arabians, was aware of the Christian communities and kingdoms that encircled Arabia, the island of the Arabs. Elements of Christian and Jewish thought had unobtrusively permeated Arabian consciousness. Muhammad had exchanges with Christians, who were at least acquainted with the oral traditions of the Christian faith. The Qur'an hints at a lively interchange between Christians and the Muslims. There is considerable respect, although sometimes the exchanges between the Muslims and Christian individuals seem to have been rather polemical.

The Muslims were aware of some aspects of the Christian debates about the nature of the Messiah, and, as mentioned above, Muslims believed that one dimension of the Muslim mission was to clarify these theological disputes. In the modern African Christian experience there are several thousand independent churches. Some of their theologies seem to move beyond biblical norms; all of them are a critique of the churches planted by missionaries. Is it going too far to suggest that the early Muslim community was in some ways an Arabian independent church movement with a critique of the "mainline" Christian movement? The Muslims were surprised and disappointed when the Christians did not receive Muhammad as one of their prophets.

A Jewish Presence

The Jews are a third stream influencing the development of the Muslim *ummah*. There are remarkable similarities between Judaism and Islam: God as transcendent Creator, revealed scriptures, prophets, and a profound commitment to obeying the whole law of God. Nevertheless, Muhammad was dismayed that many of the Jews, especially in Medina, did not accept him as a prophet of God. In Medina the confrontation became polemical—and eventually violent—as the Muslims dealt with the people they believed were sabotaging the Muslim movement.

The Jewish influence on the early Muslim community seems to be very significant, even though relations between Muslims and Jews were, on the whole, confrontational. Qur'anic civil instructions and rabbinic Judaism converge in remarkable ways.

Fuller Theological Seminary islamist scholar Dudley Woodberry calls the Muslim movement "an after-Christ form of Judaism."

It was in this confrontational setting that Muhammad gave up on efforts to conciliate with the Jews. A decisive sign of this transformation was the change in the direction in which Muslims bowed in prayer: Mecca replaced Jerusalem. Furthermore, Friday became the day for Muslims to gather in worship, not the seventh day of Jewish rest, nor the Sunday of the Christians. At first, Muslims fasted on the Jewish Day of Atonement, but as the conflict with Jews deepened, the Muslims abandoned the Jewish fast for a newly established one whole month of fasting. The Muslims were commencing a new movement that was neither Christian nor Jewish.

The Religion of Abraham

The *hanifs* are a fourth stream that is present within the Arabian context. The *hanif* were Arabian monotheists. Some of them were aware of Abraham, and some believed that they worshiped the God of Abraham.

Muhammad's spiritual journey was apparently in harmony with the *hanif*. Their possible spiritual connection to Abraham became significant to the Muslims. As the Muslim *ummah* began to define itself more clearly as different from Jews or Christians, the Muslims developed an emphasis on Islam as *the* religion of Abraham. Religious ritual centered in the Ka'bah was interpreted as commemorating an Abraham/Ishmael pilgrimage to the Arabian "House of God." Ishmael was the forefather of the Arab people, and the blood of Abraham and Ishmael flowed in the veins of Muhammad, Islam was the restoration of the religion of Abraham, and the Muslim is the person who surrenders to God as Abraham surrendered when he obeyed God's command to sacrifice his son.

With Abraham and Ishmael as the spiritual forefathers of the Muslim movement, the choice had been made: Judaism and Islam would develop as faith movements that were different from one another. In fact, the Muslim *ummah* supplants Israel as the "light to the nations."[4]

The Abraham-Ishmael legacy was probably already present in Arabia before Muhammad. The legacy may have been nurtured by those *hanifs* who traced their faith origins to Abraham. In the midst of Arabian polytheism, these monotheists worshiped Allah, the one and only Creator. Muhammad stood within that spiritual tradition. When he discovered that the Jewish people, especially in Medina, did not accept his claims to being a prophet of God, the *hanif* linkage to Abraham became even more significant.[5]

These four steams influenced the formation of the Muslim *ummah*: *jahiliyya*, Christian, Jewish, and *hanif*. For an in-depth study of the Arabian background to the Muslim movement, Philip Hitti's classic, *History of the Arabs*, is thorough and excellent.[6]

This exploration is especially concerned with the theological foundations of the *ummah* and the church. Therefore, further comment on the Christian environment at the time of Muhammad is helpful.

The Christian Environment

In the seventh century, Christian communities thrived on the Arabian periphery. South Yemen was probably Christian. So were Ethiopia and Egypt, with the Bible translated into the national languages. Egypt had three dialect translations. Palestine was largely Christian, as were Syria and Mesopotamia, where the kingdom of Edessa was involved in sustained missionary outreach into Persia and even into China. Chapter 1 mentioned the church in Persia and the horrendous persecution in the fourth century, but that church was slowly recovering. Like Edessa, the Persian church was also a missionary-sending community. Their outreach touched Central Asia and China.

Furthermore, there were Christian communities and individuals living in Arabia. However, the Arabs had no translation of the Bible. They had no book from God, as did the surrounding Christian communities.[7] In this context Muhammad and his followers received the advent of the Arabic Qur'an (Rad [Thunder] 13:30-31, 36-39) in the heartland of Arabia as an astonishing miracle, good news for those who had been despised and sidelined by the civilizations on Arabia's periphery.

Some Christian communities were struggling theologically, especially in regards to Christology. The churches were also in the throes of enormous transformations in the way that they related to the political order. These two issues—Christology and church-state relations—were very significant. The turmoil surrounding these issues influenced relationships between the Muslim nation and the Christian church in the first decades of the Muslim movement. For this reason we explore these developments particularly pertinent to the emergence of the Muslim community and its relationship to the seventh-century churches.

Who Is Jesus?

For the first three centuries of the Christian era, church growth was steady but not phenomenal. Occasional sharp bursts of brutal persecution kept church growth in check. However, persecution within the Roman Empire ended when the Edict of Toleration was proclaimed in 313. Soon the imperial authorities actually encouraged people to become Christians. Millions of former polytheists entered the church. How should the church explain Trinitarian theology for the millions of new believers? The early apostolic church was quite diverse and did not feel a need to develop precise creeds. However, with entire societies being baptized in the early fourth century, it was tempting to view the Trinity as another form of polytheism. And Christology was at the center of the discussion. Who is Jesus?

Then at a church consultation in Egypt, Arius shocked the pastors by insisting there is one God and that Jesus Christ is not truly the *eternal* Son of God. That statement unleashed a hurricane of christological debate. All of Egypt got into the fray as street vendors, farmers, and camel caravan merchants debated the nature of Jesus Christ. In the fourth century, Arianism spread like a prairie fire far beyond Egypt. For Christians from a polytheistic background, Arianism was an attractive way to explain trinitarian theology.

Even the Emperor Constantine weighed in on the debate. Imagine the astonishment of Christians everywhere when the Western Roman emperor convened a meeting at Nicea of bishops from throughout the church. Just a few years before (303-312), Christians had undergone the Great Persecution under Roman imperial authority. Now thirteen years later, in 325, Constantine officially convened the Council of Nicea. Three hundred bishops attended. They met for about three months. This council developed the Nicene Creed, which declares that the Lord Jesus Christ is "God of God, Light of Light, true God of true God; Begotten not made: of one substance with the Father."[8]

Islam and Arianism

Eventually the Arian movement died out. The church as a whole never accepted the doctrines of Arius, as was evident at the Council of Nicea. Sadly, after the Council of Nicea, church and imperial authorities sometimes used force to crush Arian communities. However, the ideas of Arius were not in harmony with the New Testament witness about Jesus Christ nor with the faith experience of ordinary Christians. That is the main reason Arianism died out within the church. Although it was attractive for a while, the movement did not communicate the power of the Gospel. It withered away.

However, three hundred years later, when the Muslim nation emerged, the qur'anic teachings about Jesus the Messiah raised concerns about the nature of Christ that are in some ways similar to the teachings of Arius. The *'Isa* of Islam is honored as the Messiah, but not as the One in whom God is fully revealed. He is the Christ, but not the eternal Son of the Living God. So, although Arianism withered away within the church, Islamic beliefs about Jesus have some similarities to the concerns of Arianism.

Jesus and the Philosophers

Within a century of the Arian controversy, another theological issue ensnared the church. Arianism was a response to polytheism, but the new issue related to Greek Neo-Platonism, which taught that spirit is good and material is not good. That is not a biblical teaching, but it was a widespread philosophical belief.

Philosophers asked, "How could God, who is both good and Spirit, be one with the human Jesus of Nazareth? And how could God, who is eternal Spirit, be crucified and die?"

The Council of Chalcedon (451) and other councils addressed such issues. It was a tumultuous time.

In the midst of it all the churches of the Asian East felt that they had to distance themselves from the Western church, where imperial power helped to define and enforce doctrine. This is one reason that Nestorianism took root in some of the Eastern churches of Asia as an alternative to the orthodoxy of the Western church. Bishop Nestorius suggested that it might be best to refer to the virgin Mary as mother of Christ rather than mother of God. That unleashed a tremendous firestorm of controversy. The credibility of the Asian Eastern churches within their societies demanded that they define themselves as different from the union of empire and pope in the Western church. They expressed this difference in a variety of ways, including doctrines. Some of these churches became Nestorian.[9]

In the seventh century, when the Muslims imposed their authority over the churches in vast regions, both East and West, they ruled with the conviction that they had a mission to simplify and clarify Christian theology: there is no Trinity; Jesus was only a man; he was not crucified. Jesus could not be both God and man and he could not be crucified. That is final, the Muslims insisted. Debate finished.

In time, many Christians concluded that the Muslims were right. The majority of the ancestors of all Muslims throughout

North Africa and the Middle East were at one time Christians. Of course, the doctrinal attractiveness of Islam must not be overstated; Christians often turned to Islam because they became weary of the disadvantages that Christians usually experienced when they lived under Muslim rule.

A Faith from the Edges

The Christian movement emerged from the margins: the virgin from Nazareth, the baby in a manger, shepherds on a hill, wise men from the East, a refugee family in Egypt, a cross on a hill outside Jerusalem, the resurrected Lord meeting his fishermen disciples on a lakeshore. Likewise, throughout history the church has experienced renewed vitality as it touches those on the margins of power. The Constantinian revolution was that the bishops of the Western church were now at the centers of power. The church had migrated from the powerless edges of society to become the possessor and protector of power.

It is in that context that the early Muslim mission emerged from the edges. It was a mission from the underside, from the less powerful, from those who had been sidelined by the progress of the neighboring nations. The Muslims believed that in the providence of God, the Muslim nation was destined to be a witness over the nations.

The Muslims were convinced that their *ummah,* emerging from the marginalized tribes of Arabia, was destined to be the nation that would bring peace to the factional Christians and Jews. The mission included a commitment to clarifying the christological controversies of the church. The Muslims had a grand vision: They believed that they were commissioned by God with the final and universal mission over the nations, a mission that was inaugurated by an unlettered Arabian orphan—Muhammad, the Seal of the Prophets. Muslims observed that the Arabic language, the language of the peoples that the nations considered to be of no account, was the language of the final revelation. The people who were ignored by other peoples had become the carriers of the final message from God to the ends of the earth.

A Faith for All Regions

This is the context and self-understanding of the Muslims. They not only invited people to believe, but they also extended the rule of God over territory. Mission and authority over territory went together. They believed that extending Islamic authority over peoples and territory was the same as extending God's rule, for Islam was the revelation of God's perfect will. Their mission was to extend perfection: Islam, the perfect religion; the Qur'an, the perfect revelation; Muhammad, the perfect man; Muslim law, the perfect guidance; and the Muslim *ummah*, the justly balanced and best nation.

As the harbingers of perfection, there was no need for critique. What the Muslim nation did was right. Submission to the perfection of Islam created assured self-confidence.

Muhammad had set the stage for Muslim relations to Christians in the regions ruled by the Muslims. The Muslims were to protect the Christians. Christians became *dhimmi* (protected) communities. The arrangements for protection were further developed early on in the Islamic expansion. We will not detail this extensively. Christian communities often experienced protection to be proscription. The Christians were to be free to worship, but with clearly defined restrictions about converting others. Wherever Muslims ruled, Islam was expected to grow, not other religions. All the regulations were honed by that commitment. Marriage regulations, church building laws, regulations on conversions, and tax laws were developed in ways that encouraged movement into Islam. Sometimes Christians fared quite well under Muslim rule, but at other times the restraints were stifling, and on occasion there was repression and persecution. For example, in 807, Caliph Haron al-Rashid commanded the destruction of all newer churches.[10]

In all of this, the Muslim *ummah* that had emerged from the edges very quickly moved to the centers of power. And the churches throughout the Muslim nation were marginalized. How should Christians respond?

A Witness from the Margins

But is that not exactly where the church should be—at the margins—just like Jesus often was? There is something about the powerlessness of the church within Muslim regions under Muslim authority that authenticates the witness of the church, just as was true for the Western church prior to Constantine. After all, Christians do believe that the God of all creation entered human history from the margins, in a baby whose first home was a cattle shed and whose first bed was a manger.

Readings from the Bible:
    John 1:1-18, 29-34
Readings from the Qur'an:
    Baqara 2:135-147

Questions for Reflection and Discussion:
    1. What have you learned about Islam that surprised you? What has surprised you about the church in the seventh century?
    2. How does it make you feel to learn that Muslims believe that one of their responsibilities is to clarify for Christians who Jesus is? How should Christians respond to that Muslim commitment?
    3. Both the Christian and Muslim movements began as movements from the powerless edges of society. Do these movements continue to identify with the powerless? Give reasons for your response.
    4. Account for the emergence of the Muslim *ummah* in seventh century Arabia.
    5. Comment on the four streams that the emerging Muslim *ummah* related to as it was developing in seventh century Arabia. Which of these four streams was the most significant?
    6. Why was an Arabic Qur'an so important for the Arabian people?
    7. Give reasons for the need for the churches of the Asian East to define themselves as other than the churches of the European West.
    8. How would you express your faith and witness if you were part of a protected Christian community (*dhimmi*) in a majority Muslim society? What can Christians in more free societies learn from churches that experience restrictions?

— 3 —

In the Garden

"LOOK at the signs of God!" Abdulahi exclaimed. "The breeze, the trees, the donkeys, your own body. It is all so miraculous. The *ayaat* (signs) of God are everywhere. These signs reveal God's power!"

Abdulahi and I were sitting on the steps of a government office in Johar, Somalia, waiting for an appointment. As is true so often in a Muslim society, our conversation that morning turned to God, and the signs of God in creation.

Creation

Both Muslims and Christians believe that God created the heavens and the earth, and that Adam and Eve *(Hawa)* were the first human residents in the garden God had prepared for them. Both faiths teach that the creation is good, and that God is other than creation (transcendent). Both believe that God reveals himself through his creation.

The Bible declares, in Romans 1:20:

> For since the creation of the world God's invisible qualities—his eternal power and divine nature—have been clearly seen, being understood from what has been made, so that men are without excuse.

The Qur'an, in Gashiya (The Overwhelming Event) 88:17-21 also invites people to reverently consider the signs of God in creation:

> Will they not regard the camels, how they are created?
> And the heaven, how it is raised?
> And the hills, how they are set up?
> And the earth, how it is spread?
> Remind them, for thou are but a remembrancer.

Both the Bible and the Qur'an proclaim that the earth and the whole universe are God's good creation, the majestic handiwork of God. God speaks and the creation is formed! (See Gen. 1:3-31; Baqara [The Cow] 2:117; and Nahl [The Bee] 16:40.) The creation is a sign revealing the majesty of God. We are commanded to respect those signs and give honor to God. Furthermore, the creation has purpose.

The Qur'an exclaims, "We created not the heaven and the earth and all that is between them in play" (Anbiyaa [The Prophets] 21:16). Then there is forthright warning against those who equate creation with God or who in any way deify creation: "We hurl the true against the false, and it doth break its head and lo! it vanisheth. And that will be woe for that which ye ascribe (unto him)" (Anbiyaa 21:18).

What then is an Islamic understanding of the purpose of creation? Most certainly the earth is God's gift to humankind to use, care for, and enjoy. The Qur'an explains:

> And the cattle hath He created, whence you have warm cloth-ing and uses, and whereof ye eat; and wherein is beauty for you, when ye bring them home, and when ye take them out to pasture. And they bear your loads for you onto a land ye could not reach save with great trouble to yourselves. Lo your Lord is Full of Pity, Merciful. And horses and mules and asses (hath He created) that ye may ride them, and for ornament. And He cre-ateth that which ye know not (Nahl 16:5-8).

Islam commands people to honor the signs (*ayat*) of God in creation with reverent awe. Trees should not be cut, unless there is need for the wood. When I was teaching Muslim students in East Africa, a North American colleague shot a sickly stray dog.

Students protested, "You have no right to kill a dog for no purpose!"

My colleague explained, "I killed the dog as an act of mercy, for it was ill and dying."

The students were satisfied.

Water should not be wasted; when bathing, water must be used in restraint. No food may be wasted, for there are those who do not have enough to eat.[1] Care for God's creation; do not consider any aspect of his good creation as of no consequence.

Creation inspires all creatures to worship God. Again from the Qur'an:

> Have they not observed all things that Allah hath created, how their shadows incline to the right and to the left, making prostration unto Allah, and they are lowly? And unto Allah maketh prostration whatsoever is in the heavens and whatsoever is in the earth of living creatures, and the angels (also) and they are not proud. They fear their Lord above them, and do what they are bidden (Nahl 16:48-50).

In a public dialogue in a university setting my Muslim companion commented, "The creation is the sign of God, just as the verses of the Qur'an are the signs of God. Even without the revelation of scripture, we can discern the truth of God through creation."

In the Bible creation is also celebrated as God's good handiwork, and we are invited to enjoy God's good earth. However, the Bible is more skeptical than is Islam about the likelihood that people will discern the truth of God in creation. The human inclination, the biblical scriptures warn, is to honor the creation more than the Creator (Rom. 1:25). In fact, within many religions people actually worship expressions of creation, rather than the Creator. Furthermore, in modern times, people who embrace an atheistic approach give science and nature an authority that ignores God.

Both qur'anic and biblical faith forthrightly critique all such inclinations to honor creation more than God. The Creator is transcendent; he is other than creation. God sustains creation, but he is not one with creation. All who worship creation in any form are worshiping a false God. Only the Creator is worthy of worship.

Adam and Eve

These understandings of creation proceed from the biblical and qur'anic descriptions of newly created Adam and Eve (*Hawa*) in the garden. In all cultures and religions stories about the origins of the earth and humankind form the understandings of the human condition. These stories are immensely significant for they communicate belief about who we are and where we are going.

In the following paragraphs we will reflect on the biblical account and then the qur'anic. For the purposes of comparison, I describe the two accounts, even though the material might be familiar to the reader. The conclusion of the chapter compares the implications of the Christian and Muslim descriptions.

The Biblical Account

The first three chapters of the Bible provide several portraits of Adam and Eve, the parents of all humanity. God created Adam and Eve on the sixth day, when the other mammals were created. God created them in his own image. They were covenant beings whose fullest humanity was expressed in a right and joyous relationship with God. God's first covenant with them was rooted in a series of quite "secular" commands: have children, have dominion over the earth, till and care for the earth and the trees and the animals, name the animals.

God placed them in the garden of Eden. There were two trees of special significance in the garden: the tree of the knowledge of good and evil and the tree of life. God commanded them not to eat of the tree of knowledge of good and evil.

In a parallel portrait, God formed Adam from the dust of the earth. He then took a rib from his side and formed Eve, because none within the animal world was fit to be his companion.

Adam was jubilant and exclaimed, "This is now bone of my bones and flesh of my flesh; she shall be called 'woman' for she was taken out of man" (Gen. 2:23).

Then we read this biblical declaration (Gen. 2:24-25), "For this reason a man will leave his father and mother and be united to his wife, and they will become one flesh. The man and his wife were both naked, and felt no shame."

Here we encounter the first description of marriage in the Bible, a statement that provides a foundation for subsequent reflection on marriage throughout the Bible. This covenant understanding of marriage is further elaborated in a New Testament admonition that the husband should love his wife like the Messiah loves the church (Eph. 5:25). The wife should respect her husband and his leadership role in the home (Eph. 5:22-24,

33). This passage begins (in Eph. 5:21) with the command to "submit to one another out of reverence for Christ."

Marriage was only one of God's good gifts. All his purposes for humankind were marvelous.

Then tragic disaster struck. The serpent beguiled Eve to eat from the tree of the knowledge of good and evil. Adam also ate the fruit. This forbidden tree has a variety of meanings. It is a tree that grew in the garden, and in that sense it is a sign of the temptation to look to nature rather than to God for our ultimate authority. In their choice to disobey God, Adam and Eve placed themselves and nature at the center of their lives, not God.

In their choice to turn away from God, they lost their innocence. They were ashamed of their nakedness and made aprons of fig leaves. They hid behind the bushes when they heard God coming near.

"Adam and Eve, where are you?" God called out to them.

God found them hiding in the bushes. God was devastated. He revealed to them the consequence of their decision to turn away from their life-giving Creator: pain in childbearing, alienation between the man and the woman, with the man dominating the woman and she acquiescing, alienation from work, alienation from creation; instead of caring for the earth, humankind exploits it and the earth experiences our exploitation. We curse the earth rather than make the good earth better. God sent Adam and Eve out of the garden of Eden lest they eat the tree of life and live forever. In turning away from God, Adam and Eve and all of us experience sinfulness and death. Shortly murder entered the first family, with Cain killing his brother Abel.

Yet after these sad events at the beginning of the human story, God did not abandon Adam and Eve or the human race. Just as God personally entered the garden of Eden looking for Adam and Eve, so he seeks each of us wherever we are and whatever our sin might be. And God made a promise to the serpent, who is the representative of evil and the temptation to turn away from God. God declared, "I will put enmity between you and the woman, and between your offspring and hers; he will crush your head, and you will strike his heel" (Gen. 3:15).

What does that promise mean? Many Christians believe this is the first promise in the Bible about the Messiah.[2] His mission was to redeem us from death, save us from our sinfulness, and

reconcile us to God. He suffered in that mission, for he was crucified by the forces of sin and rebellion against God. His "heel" was
wounded. Yet he rose from the dead; in his crucifixion and resurrection he has crushed the head of evil, sinfulness, and death.

This stream of Christian biblical interpretation believes that
Genesis 3:15 is fulfilled in John 3:16: "For God so loved the world
that he gave his one and only Son, that whoever believes in him
shall not perish but have everlasting life."

The Bible also states that God made clothing of animal skin
and covered Adam and Eve with these clothes, more dignified
than the leaf aprons they had made. Those skins required the sacrifice of an animal. Is this a sign of the sacrifice of animals in the
quest for forgiveness that permeates traditional religions everywhere?[3] A question to ponder: Is it possible that this first sacrifice
made by God himself in order to clothe Adam and Eve is a sign
right at the beginning of human history of the future sacrifice of
the Messiah for the sins of the world? One of the Messiah's names
(in John 1:29) is "the Lamb of God, who takes away the sin of the
world."

The Qur'anic Account

The Qur'an describes God creating Adam in paradise (*janna*).
He formed Adam from clay; the *jinns* (spirits), from fire. God
breathed his Spirit into Adam. Thus God gave Adam intellectual
capacities that are superior to *jinns*, angels, or animals. The superiority of Adam over angels is dramatically expressed in the
qur'anic declaration: "So when I have made him and have
breathed into him of My Spirit, do ye fall down, prostrating yourselves unto him" (Al-Hijr [The Rocky Tract] 15:29).

Perhaps that is the reason the angels were not keen about
God's plan to create Adam. The Qur'an describes the protest of
the angels:

> And when thy Lord said unto the angels: Lo! I am about to
> place a viceroy in the earth, they said: Wilt Thou place therein
> one who will do harm therein and will shed blood, while we,
> hymn thy praise and sanctify Thee? He said: Surely I know that
> which ye know not (Baqara [The Cow] 2:30).

Adam's intellectual capacities were superior to all other creatures, including the angels. Adam readily learned all the names of

the animals and all other aspects of creation as God taught them to him, a feat the angels could not accomplish. Satan was jealous of Adam's capability, and when God commanded the angels to bow in honor of Adam, Satan (*Iblis*) refused to do so. He protested to God that Adam was made only of clay, and he, Iblis, was created of fire. He would not bow down. So God sent Satan down from paradise.

But Satan was not finished with his mischief. After God created a wife for Adam, Hawa by name, Satan enticed Adam and Hawa to eat fruit from the tree in the garden of paradise that God had forbidden. God, therefore, sent this first couple, Adam and Hawa, from paradise to earth where they and their descendants would need to reside for a period of time for testing. What was the test? The test was whether they would submit to God's guidance, and that guidance was Islam. And they were given a special responsibility: Be caretakers of the good earth (*khalifa*).

The Qur'an comments that Adam and Hawa pled with God for forgiveness, "They said: Our Lord! We have wronged ourselves. If Thou forgive us not and have not mercy on us, surely we are of the lost" (Araf [The Heights] 7:23).

God was merciful to Adam and Hawa. The Qur'an elaborates:

> And We said: Fall down, one of you a foe unto the other! There shall be for you on earth a habitation and provision for a time. Then Adam received from his Lord words (of revelation), and He relented toward him. Lo! He is the Relenting, the Merciful" (Baqara 2:36-7).

The mercy that God gave to Adam and Hawa was supremely expressed in the gift of guidance, which is Islam. This guidance is described as righteous clothing to cover the shame of humanity. The Qur'an proclaims this surprising act of mercy in this way:

> O Children of Adam! We have revealed unto you raiment to conceal your shame, and splendid vesture, but the raiment of restraint from evil, that is best. This is of the revelations of Allah, that they may remember (Al-Hijr 7:26).

Adam was the first prophet to whom God revealed Islam. Muslims believe that their home on earth was on the plains of Arafat, where Mecca and its environs are today. Adam was the first prophet, and Adam and Hawa were the first Muslims. They worshiped God as Muslims at the site of the Ka'bah in Mecca, just as all Muslims today also face the Ka'bah as they bow in worship. (A black stone is at the center of the cubic building in Mecca known as the Ka'bah. Muslims believe that Adam built the first house of God at this site and that Abraham and Ishmael reconstructed the house of God, the Ka'bah, at the site of the black stone where Adam and Eve had bowed in worship.)

The time of testing on earth for Adam and Eve and their descendants was not a punishment for sin, for Adam and Eve and all humanity are born good. The first parents were created with a good *fitrah* (pattern), just as is true of all humanity. In fact, Muslims believe that every one is born a good Muslim, whether they know it or not, for all are created in accordance with the good pattern determined by God. The Qur'an explains:

> So set thy purpose . . . for religion as a man by nature [*fitrah* or pattern] upright—the nature (framed) of Allah, in which he hath created man. There is no altering (the laws of) Allah's creation. That is the right religion, but most men know not (Rum [The Roman Empire] 30:30).

The Islamic conviction is that since all babies are born as good Muslims, they can only depart from their innate goodness through ignorance or wrong information. So all these innately good Muslims around the earth need guidance on how to live, and Islam is that guidance. This guidance enabled Adam and Hawa, as well as all humanity, to live responsibly as caretakers of the earth.

Caretaker is actually not adequate to capture the awesome responsibility that God has bestowed on Adam and upon all humanity. Adam was created to be God's *khalifa* (vicegerent or deputy). That is why God taught Adam the names of creation—to know the name is to have authority.

That authority is given to Adam when God teaches him the names of all created beings; the authority was also bestowed on Adam at the time of his creation. God bestowed his Spirit on Adam. Muslim theologians debate what it means for humankind to have received the Spirit of God at creation. Some believe that this special gift has something to do with authority. The idea of *kahlifa* is helpful in explaining the meaning of the Spirit of God in humanity. Kateregga states that this special gift is:

(a) the intelligence (or knowledge) to discern between right and wrong, good and evil, reality and illusion
(b) the will to choose freely between good and bad, true and false, right and evil
(c) the authority to acquire and make use of things around him
(d) the power of speech—to be able to express his worship of his Creator.[4]

The accounts that we have explored above help to set the sail, as it were, for the different journeys of the Muslims and Christians. There are similarities, yet at a very foundational level, the biblical and qur'anic scriptures we have explored take the believers in different directions.

Different Journeys

A Muslim missionary to Nairobi who came from Pakistan insisted to me that he was taking a different journey than the Christians. He often preached Islam on the street corner a few yards from our home. He came to our home on occasion to dialogue. So, I gave him reflections I had written on the biblical narrative concerning Adam and Eve. About a week later I returned to his home to hear his response.

In his British Oxford English, my friend exclaimed, "This narrative is most obnoxious. It has made me exceedingly chagrined, exceedingly chagrined!"

The issue that chagrined this Pakistani Muslim missionary revolved around this question: What does it mean to be human? He was perturbed by the biblical proclamation that we are created in God's image; he was utterly appalled that in our turning away from God we have become sinful and in need of a redeemer. This imam[5] insisted that humanity is good; we need guidance, not a redeemer.

Some years later in an evening dialogue at the Central London Mosque in the United Kingdom, I said, "The Bible is realistic about human nature. It does not gloss over our sinfulness. Even biblical prophets had their flaws. For example, Abraham, the father of faith, sinned for he told a lie about his wife."

"Oh! No!" It seemed that all five hundred voices in the audience were objecting in irresistible spontaneity.

My Muslim colleague in his rejoinder said, "Abraham was a

prophet and, therefore, did not sin. His lie was a justifiable lie, and it was not sin. All prophets are righteous; they are not sinners."

These conversations provide insights into divergences between a biblical and qur'anic understanding of the human condition. Here are several further statements that summarize themes that the accounts of creation portray.

1. Muslims and Christians recognize that the earth and all things, seen and unseen, are God's good creation, and that God sustains the creation. The creation is a sign revealing God's power.

2. Both agree that Adam and Eve (or Hawa) are the first human parents, and, therefore, all people are one humanity.

3. Christians and Muslims believe that people partake of the animal and material world, created from dust or clay.

4. The Bible describes both Adam and Eve as created in God's image. This is a concept filled with many dimensions of meaning; a core reality is that people are created for fellowship with God. God intends for us to be his covenant partners. The Qur'an describes Adam as receiving the Spirit of God. Muslim theologians debate the meaning of this gift; it probably means that people have authority to serve as God's *khalifa* on earth.

5. A core description of marriage is included in the biblical narrative of the garden. Subsequently the Bible describes tragic departures from this commitment; nevertheless, the seed of biblical understanding of marriage is planted within the first human marriage: One flesh union. One man and one wife. An indissoluble covenant united by God. Children are a gift, but not essential. The husband is to love and cherish his wife as he does his own flesh. Open communion and trust. Singleness fully acceptable, for our completion is in fellowship with God, not marriage.

The Qur'an includes an allusion to the meaning of marriage in a comment on the first couple (Nisaa [Women] 4:1). However, the Qur'an as a whole does include considerable specific teaching about marriage and womanhood. It is unlikely that a non-Muslim can comment in a way that adequately represents a Muslim viewpoint. Here are several statements from Muslim sources, given without comment.

Muhammad exclaimed on one occasion, "The best among you is the one who is best toward his wife!"[6]

The next two statements are qur'anic admonitions:

Men are in charge of women, because Allah hath made the one of them to excel the other, and because they spend of their property (for the support of women). So good women are the obedient, guarding in secret that which Allah hath guarded. As for those from whom ye fear rebellion, admonish them and banish them to beds apart, and scourge them. Then if they obey you, seek not a way against them. Lo! Allah is ever High Exalted, Great (Nisaa [Women] 4:34).

Your women are a tilth [field] for you (to cultivate) so go to your tilth as ye will, and send (good deeds) before you for your souls, and fear Allah, and know that ye will (one day) meet Him (Baqara 2:223).

In Muhammad's farewell pilgrimage to Mecca he proclaimed:

And I command you to treat women well, because they are like captives in your houses, possessing nothing for themselves, and you on your part take them as a deposit from God, and permit yourselves the enjoyment of their persons by means of a word of God. Have therefore the fear of God with regard to women, and I order you to treat them well. Attention! Have I communicated? O God, be witness![7]

One evening a decade ago, a cluster of Christians and Muslims gathered for conversation in a mosque in Baltimore. The imam shared in length about the Muslim understandings of womanhood and marriage. Then I shared briefly from the biblical ideal.

The imam exclaimed, "Islam is practical. The Christian commitment that you have described is an impossible ideal."

One of us commented, "That might be true. Yet the Spirit of God brings about a new creation that empowers disciples of the Messiah to participate in the biblical vision of marriage or singleness that we have described."

6. The Bible describes the garden of Eden as located on earth, in a real earthly geographical setting. However, the biblical drama does not stop in a garden. The final pages of the Bible describe a marvelous city, as God's grand plan for the culmination of history. From a garden, all people are invited to journey toward the culmination of all things in that grand city.

In the Qur'an Adam and Hawa's first home is in paradise in the heavens. They are sent down to earth for a period of testing.

The human sojourn on earth is within a parenthesis, between a paradise lost and a paradise that the faithful will regain at the final judgment.

7. In the Bible God entrusts Adam with the authority to name the animals. In the Qur'an God teaches Adam the names of the animals and all creation.

In biblical revelation, God entrusts people with astonishing freedom and responsibility. God stands to the side, as it were, and listens in as we take the responsibility to name his creation. That is risky! Humanity has done some horrible things with God's creation; they have also accomplished astounding achievements. Humans have used nitrogen both for fertilizer and for chemical warfare.

In the qur'anic worldview, God stays fully in charge; we are recipients of God's instructions in regards to naming his creation. We are God's vicegerents, responsible for carrying out his instructions as we serve as his deputies or caretakers for the good earth.

How do these understandings influence a society's approach to economic and community development or scientific inquiry? I have often pondered that question. Here are two examples of that pondering.

Abdi Muhammad stopped by our home in Somalia for an evening cup of tea. He was a high school student. He mused, "I want to be a secular man, but I do not want to be an atheist. Could the Christian faith be the faith for a secular man?"

I asked him, "Why do you ask?"

"Because I observe that the Christian missions in my country are pioneers in secular development," he said. "Look at the fruit of the church: secular schools, medical programs, vernacular literacy, agricultural and economic development, business enterprise, girls' education."

I often thought of Abdi's question when I lived across the street from a mosque in Nairobi. Every evening at about nine o'clock, I heard neighbors going to the mosque for the evening prayers, and seven hours later, at about four o'clock, I would hear them going for the first morning prayers. I was still sleeping. Our little Christian center was developing a reading room so high school students could study for their exams in subjects such as math and science. We provided school fees for poor students to attend high school; even the daughters of the imam received

money from our center for that purpose. The mosque was invest-
ing funds from Arabia to expand Arabic and qur'anic studies.
The Muslims were far more engaged in religious practices than
was the Christian team working in the secular involvements of
our center.

Early on in my journey as a global Christian, I had read two
books that explored the revolutionary influence of biblical faith in
energizing the secularization process: *Honest Religion for Secular
Man*, by Lesslie Newbigin, and *Christianity in World History*, by
Arend Theodoor Van Leewen.[8] These authors asserted that the
presence of biblical faith in a culture brings about a worldview
transformation that stimulates and energizes a significant commitment to secular development. Are they right? Abdi's question
is profound. To what extent does our understanding of human
responsibility, freedom, and the purpose of history influence our
commitments to secular development?

8. The Bible describes Adam and Eve turning away from God
and the consequences of the outworking of sinfulness in human
relations with God, one another, work, and creation. Adam and
Eve pushed God out of the center of their lives, an inclination that
all humanity experience. Consequently the image of God within
each of us, as well as humanity as a whole, is tragically distorted.

The Qur'an views the disobedience of the first parents as a
mistake that God forgives. There is no effect on the perfect pattern
of humanity that Adam and Hawa demonstrate; we are all born
good.

9. In the biblical account, God entered the garden and found
Adam and Eve hiding. He sent them from the garden, but clothed
them with skins. He promised that someday a Son born to the
woman would be wounded by the serpent, but he would triumph
over evil by crushing the head of the evil one.

In the qur'anic account God sent guidance down upon
Adam, the first prophet.

After a public dialogue with a Muslim theologian, he advised
me, "We Muslims are offended at the thought of God entering the
garden to find Adam and Eve."

I replied, "I know that is true. Yet that is the Gospel. God does
not just send his will down to us. Rather he enters our history personally and searches for us. He meets us within our various gar-
dens, even though we might be hiding from him. Supremely, he

finds us and redeems us through the Messiah in whom we experience God seeking us with wounded and outstretched hands.[9]

Hope and promise permeate the biblical narrative.

Questions for Reflection and Discussion:

1. The Qur'an teaches that we are vicegerents, deputies, or representatives of God on earth and the Bible teaches that we are created in God's image (Baqara 2:30; Gen. 1:27). Reflect on the significance of these understandings.

2. Comment on the qur'anic and biblical approaches to "naming" the animals (Baqara 2:30-2; Gen. 2:19-20). What is the significance of these different understandings?

3. How would you respond to Abdi's question: Is biblical faith the right faith for a secular man?

4. Compare the qur'anic and biblical understandings of sin and its consequences (Baqara 2:36-37; Al-Araf 7:14-23; Gen. 3:1-4:9).

5. Would people today find the Muslim doctrine of the shortcomings of people more attractive than the biblical doctrine of sinfulness? Give reasons for your response. Which understanding is most realistic when compared with our real experiences in life?

6. What is the difference between God sending guidance to us and God redeeming us (Qur'an 2:37-38; Genesis 3:15)?

7. Comment on or critique this statement: The faithful *ummah* idealizes Adam of the past and the faithful church faces a Jesus of the now and the future (Rum 30:30; Gen. 3:15; John 3:16; Rev. 1:7; 22:20).

8. Respond to this statement: The Qur'an (Nisaa 4:34; Baqara 2:223) portrays a natural and realistic view of womanhood and marriage, while the biblical view (Gen. 1:27; 2:20-25) is unnatural and idealistic.

— 4 —

Sons of Abraham: Ishmael—Isaac

"REMEMBER, the faith of Islam is the religion of the natural man. Objective logic and philosophy will lead a person to agree with Islam," the imam urged his audience.

About seventy-five Christians and Muslims were together at a mosque in Devon, Pennsylvania, for an evening dialogue.

I responded, "In that case, the Gospel is different from Islam. No human philosophy or religion has ever imagined the Gospel. The Gospel is the amazing news that God loves us so much that he has entered our history in the Messiah. In Jesus the Messiah God suffers for us and because of us. In the Messiah we discover that God loves sinners, and seeks to redeem all sinners. We cannot find this truth through philosophy. We can only discover the revelation of God's costly grace by receiving his grace."

The imam responded quite emphatically, "But God cannot love that much!"

The Journey of Faith

Probably the iman overstated his case for Islam as only natural; Muslims consider the Qur'an to be a miracle. Nevertheless, the religion of the natural man, or a faith touched with astonishing surprises of grace; that was what our dialogue was about in the mosque that night in Devon. That was also the perplexity in Abraham's home four thousand years ago. The modern-day *ummah* and the church live in the shadow of that abiding perplexity within Abraham's soul and home. Just as was true in Abraham's soul, so we also struggle between living in a natural way, or in the surprising way that God's unmerited promises and grace provide.

Abraham's struggle revolved around this question: How can God's promises be fulfilled? God had promised Abraham descendants. Yet his wife, Sarah, was barren. Should he sleep with Sarah's maid, Hagar, or continue a hopeless wait for Sarah to conceive? Should he act naturally, or live expecting that God would fulfill his surprising promises? Abraham and Sarah doubted that Sarah could conceive, especially when she was past her menses. So Abraham and Sarah agreed that they should act in a natural way. He slept with Sarah's maid, Hagar, and Ishmael was born (Gen. 16).

After Ishmael was born, God (in Gen. 17) came to Abraham and renewed the promise: "As for your wife, . . . I will bless her and will surely give you a son by her. I will bless her so that she will be the mother of nations; kings of peoples will come from her."

Abraham tried to reason with God. He thought the promise was impossible. Abraham pled, "If only Ishmael might live under your blessing!"

God responded, "Yes, but your wife Sarah will bear you a son, and you will call him Isaac. I will establish my covenant with him as an everlasting covenant for his descendants after him. As for Ishmael, I have heard you: I will surely bless him . . . and I will make him into a great nation."

Abraham and Sarah thought the messengers of God must be joking when they persisted in insisting that ninety-year-old Sarah and one-hundred-year-old Abraham would indeed give birth to a son. On one occasion the messengers overheard Sarah laughing behind her tent flaps at the ridiculousness of it all. As for Abraham, he collapsed on the ground in laughter.

The conception of Abraham's second-born son, Isaac, was indeed an astounding surprise; the birth of his first son, Ishmael, surprised no one.

In fact, the name Isaac means "laughter"; his birth brought chuckles of surprise and joy. Sarah rightfully predicted that throughout the centuries people would chuckle when they hear that she conceived Isaac when she was ninety years old. Her son, Isaac, was indeed the son of promise, the astounding gift of God.

However, Ishmael was also a son born of faith. His name means, "God hears." God had promised that Abraham would have descendants. Abraham and Sarah decided to help God fulfill his promise. That is why Abraham slept with Hagar. This act was faith expressed in a logical and rational way.

The Journey Toward Righteousness

The realism of the biblical accounts is surprising. Abraham was the father of the people of faith. Yet his actions sometimes reveal a struggle to really believe. Twice he told a lie about his wife, saying she was his sister lest the locals kill him so that they could sleep with his beautiful Sarah. Was that kind of action based on faith in God's ability to care for them?

Abraham's family system was quite dysfunctional. After Ishmael was born, Sarah harassed her maid Hagar until she ran away for a while to escape from it all. After Isaac was born Sarah insisted that both Ishmael and Hagar leave for good. This was because the two boys did not get along with each other (Gen. 16, 21:8-14).

Abraham's nephew, Lot, and Lot's two daughters were involved in incest when Lot was too drunk to know what was going on. In later years Isaac lied about his wife, Rebecca, denying that she was his wife. Then Rebecca deceived her husband and fanned the flames of a dangerous conflict between their sons, Jacob and Esau.

Righteousness Based on Faith

Nevertheless, God's grace and faithfulness prevailed among these very human people whose lives were not immune to sinfulness. Even though both Abraham and Sarah struggled to fully believe God's astounding promise that Sarah would conceive in her old age, God did indeed bless them with Isaac when she was ninety years old.

God honored Abraham's faith, whether expressed in the natural way or in his trusting in God's astonishing surprise. God recognized Abraham's faith even though his life and his family system were flawed.

The Bible declares, "Abraham believed the Lord, and he credited it to him as righteousness" (Gen. 15:6).

It was hard for Abraham to believe God! He struggled. Sometimes he wavered. Yet he persisted in following God's call and wanted to believe his promises. In response to Abraham's faith, God accepted Abraham as a righteous man. None of us, not even Abraham, are worthy of God's grace. Yet as we respond to God in faith, he clothes us with the garments of his righteousness and salvation (Isa. 61:10).

Two thousand years later, the meaning of righteousness by faith broke into human experience with blazing clarity. This was the mission of Jesus the Messiah, for in the ministry of the Messiah we discover in new and surprising ways that God does indeed love sinners.

We read, "For all have sinned and fall short of the glory of God" (Rom. 3:23).

"But God demonstrates his own love for us in this: While we were still sinners, Christ died for us," says Romans 5:8.

The apostle Paul describes this gift of grace in this way:

> For in the gospel a righteousness from God is revealed, a righteousness that is by faith from first to last, just as it is written: "The righteous shall live by faith" (Rom. 1:17).

> For it is by grace you have been saved, through faith—and this not from yourselves, it is the gift of God—not by works, so that no one can boast (Eph. 2: 8-9).

That is the soul of the Gospel, salvation by grace through faith. The seed of that Gospel was planted in human history in the experience of Abraham, who was counted righteous because of faith, not because he did everything right. That seed was fulfilled and greatly clarified in the mission and ministry of the Messiah.

Islam speaks of the compassion and mercy of God extended to righteous people. The Qur'an proclaims:

> Lo! those who believe
> And do good works,
> The Beneficent will
> Appoint for them love (Maryam [Mary] 19:96).

After a long evening in public dialogue with a Muslim about Abraham in a university setting, my colleague concluded, "Abraham bowed with his face to the ground in prayer. That is the right way to pray. I invite you to bow in that way so that you might receive the mercy of God."

Why did God extend grace to Abraham? Was it because in sincerity he performed ritual prayer in the right way? Or did he receive God's grace because he really did want to believe God's promises?

The remainder of this chapter explores the nature of mercy and grace more fully. The Ishmael-Isaac narratives are crucial to this exploration.

Abraham and Ishmael

The ultimate test of faith for Abraham was when God commanded him to sacrifice his son. The Qur'an tells of Abraham's preparation for the sacrifice. Both the father and his son submitted to the will of God in agreeing to the sacrifice (Saaffat [Those Ranged in Ranks] 37:99-113). Then surprisingly, God intervened to redeem the son from death by providing a ram as a substitute sacrifice. The Qur'an exclaims, "Then We ransomed him with a tremendous victim" (Saaffat 37:107).

The biblical account describes Abraham preparing to sacrifice Isaac, who was redeemed by a substitute animal sacrifice (Gen. 22). The qur'anic account does not name a son; however, Muslim scholars exegete the accounts to claim that the son is Ishmael.[1]

Every year during the annual pilgrimage to Mecca (*hajj*), Muslims around the world sacrifice and eat an animal in remembrance that God intervened by providing a substitute sacrifice of an animal to save Ishmael from death. The pilgrims make the sacrifices on or near the hill of Mince near Mecca. The rituals surrounding these sacrifices are a memorial for the Abraham-Ishmael saga.

Muhammad and Ishmael

The Abraham-Ishmael narrative significantly influences Muslim self-understanding. Some members of Muhammad's family were *hanifs*. They were a faith movement within Arabia who were monotheistic. Some believed that their monotheistic faith was a legacy of Abraham. They worshiped the Creator God, Allah, the name for God that the Muslims embraced.

Allah is the Arabic version of the name for God used by Abraham, who referred to the Creator as *El* or *Elohim*. Prior to God's revelation to Abraham, *Elohim* was considered to be the Creator God who hovered around the hills. The Allah of the Arabians was an ancient Arabian name for the Creator God. Of course, in polytheistic Arabia many deities were venerated, including Allah. In fact, there was a stream of belief among the polytheists that Allah had progeny—three daughter goddesses: *al-Manat, al-Lat, al-Uzza* (Fate, Moon, Venus). Biblical monotheists critiqued all such notions in polytheistic societies anywhere as damnable idolatry; so did Muhammad in Arabia. Muhammad proclaimed that Allah, the Creator, had no progeny and no associates. Islam broke with polytheism: Only Allah is God.

There are, therefore, some analogies between the Islamic Allah and Abraham's biblical *Elohim*. Muslims are totally confident that the God of Abraham *is* the God of Muhammad; they believe that Allah *is* the God of Abraham. It was the *hanifs* who preserved the worship of Allah in Arabia for many centuries before Muhammad and the establishment of the Muslim *ummah*. The *hanif* were Arabian monotheists who seem to have gone against the stream of the polytheistic religions of Arabian traditional societies.

For Muhammad, a connection to the God of Abraham and Ishmael became especially important in Medina, where he experienced rude rejection by members of the Jewish community.[2]

"The prophets are Jews, descendants of Abraham," the Jews chided. "An Arab cannot be a prophet."

The Muslims developed a strong offense. They argued, "Muhammad is *hanif*. These people of faith originate from Abraham and Ishmael."

Genealogy

In fact, the claims are made that Muhammad's family genealogy goes all the way back to Ishmael himself. Muhammad was not only *hanif*, enjoying Ishmael's spiritual heritage, but his family was also the Quraish, who traced their ancestry to Ishmael. The blood of Abraham and Ishmael flowed in Muhammad's veins.

Some Arabian poet genealogists went even further, tracing Abraham's genealogy to Adam. Of course, everyone on earth is a descendant of Adam and Eve. Nevertheless, through these genealogical linkages, Muhammad could claim not only descent from Abraham, but also from Adam. The lineage of Muhammad linked him to the middle prophet of Islam, Abraham, as well as to the first prophet of Islam, Adam.

Just as genealogy became an important consideration for Muslims in Medina, genealogy has likewise become quite significant for Muslims in later centuries. The Shi'a separation from the Sunni shortly after the death of Muhammad was based on genealogy.

"The imam must be a descendant of the Prophet," insisted the Shi'a.

The Sunni demanded, "The *khalifa* (caliph, political *and* spiritual leader) must be chosen by community consensus, not genealogy."

The Shi'a leadership believed that 'Ali b. Abu Talib, cousin of Muhammad and his son-in-law, was the rightful person to carry forward the spiritual leadership of the Muslim *ummah* as the imam, followed by his son Husayn. Civil war ensued. Husayn was killed. The Shi'a-Sunni division has never been fully healed.

However, even among the Sunni Muslims genealogy is valued. To this day many millions of both Sunni and Shi'a Muslims, or their community leaders, trace their genealogy to Muhammad, at least in their legendary lore. So do many of the spiritual leaders of *sufi* (mystical) orders.

The Somali people are an example of the power of genealogy. All Somalis claim descent from Muhammad. I once asked a Somali son of nomads, "What is your genealogy?"

With a great smile, he commenced, "I am Mohammed, the son of Omar, the son of Ahmed, the son of Fidow, the son of Robleh, the son of Abubakar, the son of Odowa, the son of Gueld, the son of Halane, the son of Samatar, the son of Yusuf, the son of Gu'ug-Addeh, the son of Gurey, the son of Baso-Gab, the son of Hussein, the son of Mohammed, the son of Abdallah, the son of Samo-Talis, the son of Hawadleh, the son of the Mohammed, my clan father." He then continued the genealogy of his clan father concluding with a triumphant, "the son of Fatima, the daughter of the prophet Muhammad, peace be upon him!"[3] This Somali son of illiterate nomads reveled in the belief that the blood of the prophet Muhammad, and, therefore, Islam, flowed in his veins.

However, a word of caution on all of this genealogy fascination. The Qur'an insists that the true descendants of Abraham are the people of faith: "Those of mankind who have the best claim to Abraham are those who followed him, and this Prophet [Muhammad] and those who believe" (Ali 'Imran [The Family of Imran] 3:68).

The First Born

Ishmael was the first-born son of Abraham. Muslim theologians point out that in all Semitic cultures, the first-born was the one primarily responsible for carrying on the family heritage. The Abraham-Isaac saga was, therefore, interesting, but the community of blessing for all nations was the Muslim nation that was derived from Abraham's first-born son, Ishmael.

Muslim theologians explain that for a limited period of time, God had preferred Israel to all others (Baqara [The Cow] 2:122). However, with the coming of Muhammad, God's promise to Abraham that he and his descendants would be "imam to the nations" was now fulfilled through the Muslim *ummah*. In fact, Abraham was neither Jew nor Christian, but rather he bowed in submission to the true revelation of God's will, which is Islam (Ali 'Imran 3:67).

The Muslim scholar, Abdullah Yusuf Ali, writes, "The arguments about the favor to Israel are thus beautifully rounded off, and we now proceed to the argument in favor of the Arabs as succeeding to the spiritual inheritance of Abraham."[4]

The Muslim nation revels in the legacy of Ishmael. Muslims appreciate the logic and rationality of it all. It is not surprising that the first-born son of Abraham carried forward the torch of the true faith of Islam and prepared for the formation of the Muslim nation in Arabia many centuries later. It is to be expected that the final prophet would be a descendant of Abraham's first-born. To the Muslim mind it is logical that as Israel's significance among the nations fades, God would call forth the Muslim nation as a light for all nations, a calling that surpasses the temporary ministry of Israel, who traces their origin to Abraham's second-born son.

"The logical person will appreciate the reasonableness of Islam," a Muslim sheikh explained to me.

Abraham and Isaac

The biblical Isaac narratives invite us into a quite different journey than does the Islamic Ishmael saga. We have explored aspects of the qur'anic Abraham-Ishmael journey; now we reflect on the biblical Abraham-Isaac journey. We do this with caution, recognizing that in Islam Isaac is blessed, and in the Bible Ishmael is blessed. This is significant. Islamic theology revels in the primacy of Ishmael, but respects and blesses Isaac. Biblical theology views Isaac as the one who brings blessing to all nations, but blesses Ishmael. In fact, a great nation and twelve rulers will come from the first-born son of Abraham, the Lord promised in Genesis 17:20.

A Struggle Between Two Sons

The surprise of Isaac is a sign of the surprise of the Gospel. Isaac was a gift, undeserved by Abraham and Sarah. Such also is the nature of the Gospel; it is God's astonishing gift that shatters all human philosophical and religious categories. No system of logic or philosophy or religion has ever imagined the Gospel, that God loves us so greatly that he enters human history in a man who lives among us and suffers with us and because of us. That good news of God's extravagant grace is a gift offered. We cannot earn that gift; we can only receive it in faith and thanksgiving.

Twenty centuries after Abraham, the New Testament scriptures reflect theologically on the struggle in Abraham's home between Sarah and Hagar and between Ishmael and Isaac (Gal. 4:21-31). Paul presented this conflict as an example or metaphor of the tension between faith expressed in an ordinary way, and faith that is open to all the surprises of grace that God lavishes upon us in Jesus the Messiah.

These New Testament scriptures describe Abraham's liaison with Hagar and the birth of Ishmael as a metaphor of religious activity that seeks to please God. On the other hand the birth of Isaac was God's initiative of grace; no religious activity or effort could produce Isaac. The story of these two women and two sons reveals the difference between faith receiving God's grace as an unmerited gift and faith seeking to acquire God's promises and blessing in an ordinary human way that includes religious activity that seeks to solicit God's favor.

Paul wrote that these two varied journeys are about freedom

from the need to acquire God's favor through religious rituals and effort. Does religious activity and human effort attract God's grace? If so, how much religious activity do I need to perform in order to receive his grace? Or is God's grace a gift received by faith alone?

Once after I had been traveling with Muslim friends for a week, one of them commented, "If the Gospel is what you claim it to be, then becoming a Christian would be enormously freeing for me as a Muslim."

What did he mean?

I am not sure. I do know that as we traveled, my devout friends were quite concerned that there would be breaks in the travel plans so that they could perform their ritual prayers.

Different Faith Responses

What do the narratives of Ishmael and Isaac have to do with the *ummah* and the church? Could it be that the core difference between the faithful *ummah* and the faithful church is a continuation of the difference between Ishmael and Isaac? This does not necessarily mean the difference between the two sons as such, but rather the struggle within Abraham's own soul as he responded to the promises of God.

Should Abraham work to establish the will of God (Ishmael), or should he obediently follow God's call and wait upon God to establish his promises in God's own way and time (Isaac)? Should he fulfill God's promise in an ordinary way (Ishmael), or wait upon God to fulfill his promise in his own miraculously surprising way (Isaac)? Do these narratives reveal something about the difference between Islam and Gospel?

However, as mentioned earlier, the struggle is not so much *out there* between the *ummah* and the church, although it is out there to be sure. Rather, the struggle resides within our own souls in regard to our approach to situations that we face each day. Shall we seek to establish God's kingdom in a natural way or wait upon God to establish his kingdom in his own surprising way?

The Ancestors

The ordinary human way is governed by genealogical relations: Who was your mother? I think I knew your grandfather; he was a great person. My great-grandfather was a great preacher. You are my third cousin. One of my ancestors was an Anabaptist martyr in the sixteenth century. Muhammad, likewise, and the Muslim *ummah* are grateful for Muhammad's Quraish genealogy that reaches back to Ishmael.

The biblical narrative concerning Abraham puts those connections into perspective. Genealogies have some importance—yet they are ultimately irrelevant.

Tucked into the biblical Abraham narrative is an obscure priest of the Most High God named Melchizedek. At a time of adversity related to a raid by a robber band, this priest blessed Abraham and gave him and his men bread and wine. Abraham gave Melchizedek a tithe of everything he possessed.

Melchizedek was "without father or mother, without genealogy" declared the New Testament writer of Hebrews 7:3. Nevertheless, Melchizedek was greater than Abraham, for he blessed Abraham and Abraham gave him a tithe of his possessions.

Beware! Ancestors are less important than one might think. That is one of the meanings of the mystery person, Melchizedek.

The biblical Isaac account also turns genealogy on its head. The second born is the son of promise. Ishmael is blessed, but the son of promise through whom God will bless the nations is the second born. That is hard to fathom within most cultures.

The Family of Abraham

Half of the world's people trace their faith to Abraham: Jewish, Christian, and Muslim. Seeds of faith were planted within that home that have flourished and spread around the world for the past four thousand years. Significant dimensions of the similarities and tensions between these faith movements were already present within Abraham's own home. We live within the long shadow of Abraham's faith. His journey gave birth to two sons: Ishmael and Isaac.

Abrahams journey is a most significant root event for Jews, Christians, and Muslims. Not only the Torah, but the New Testament and Qur'an are also significant responses to that faith journey. Surely this reality should provide a basis for dialogue.

Readings from the Bible:
Genesis 21:1-20
Readings from the Qur'an:
Baqara 2:124-29

Questions for Reflection and Discussion:
1. God promised Abraham descendants. His wife, Sarah, was barren. The Ishmael and Isaac accounts reveal the nature of Abraham's struggle to have faith in God and his promise. In what ways do you identify with that struggle?

2. Comment on this statement. The struggle between Ishmael and Isaac reveal dimensions of the struggle between an Islam-centered and a Gospel-centered faith (Gal. 4:21-31).

3. The discussion above mentioned a comment by a Muslim friend that the Gospel would be very freeing for him as a Muslim. What do you think he meant by that comment? Is he right? Give reasons for your answer.

4. Account for the importance of genealogy within the Muslim *ummah*. Consider examples of Christan emphasis on genealogy. How does the Melchizedek account critique an overemphasis on genealogy (Quraish 106:1-4; Gen. 14:18-20; Heb. 7:1-10)?

5. Compare the significance of Abraham as the middle prophet for Muslims and the father of faith for Christians (Ali 'Imran 3:96-97; Rom. 4:12, 16).

6. To what extent can the Abraham legacy contribute to peacemaking efforts between Jews, Muslims, and Christians?

— 5 —

Leaders:
the Seal of the Prophets—
the Messiah

JESUS is the Messiah! On that confession Muslims and Christians have unanimous agreement. All Muslims and all Christians also believe in prophets who proclaim the word of God.

Nevertheless, the meaning of the Messiah and the prophets is different for the Muslim *ummah* and the Christian church.

For example, all Muslims believe that Muhammad is the Seal of the Prophets, the one who proclaims God's final, clarifying, and definitive truth. However, Christians do not agree that Muhammad's message supersedes that of the Messiah. This is because all Christians confess that Jesus the Messiah is Lord and Savior, a confession that is quite different from that of the Muslim *ummah*.

These differences in the understandings of the Muslim Prophet and the Messiah are not trivial. This chapter explores these different understandings. What are the Christian under-standings of the life and ministry of the Messiah? What are the Muslim understandings of the Messiah? What is the Muslim understanding of the role of the Seal of the Prophets? What are the areas of agreement? What difference does this all make?

The Messiah in Christian Faith

The third chapter reflected on Adam and Eve and God's commitment to them after they had disobeyed God in eating the fruit from the tree of the knowledge of good and evil. In the Qur'an, God sent down guidance to Adam, the first Muslim prophet of Islam. In the Bible God promised that a son born to the woman will crush the head of evil (the serpent); however, evil will "strike his heel" (Gen. 3:15). Christians believe that the Messiah is the suffering Savior that God promised.[1] In Islam God promised guidance. In the Bible God promised redemption.

Biblical Hope—The Messiah

From the garden onward, again and again, the biblical scriptures written before the coming of the Messiah convey confident hope that God will send a Redeemer who will triumph over sin and death. In this brief study we will not detail all those signs of hope and promise. Nevertheless, century after century, the prophets communicated the promises of God in regard to this Son of Hope.

Probably the prophet Isaiah summarized these themes of hope as winsomely as any of the prophets when he wrote,

> For to us a child is born,
> to us a son is given,
> and the government will be on his shoulders.
> And he will be called
> Wonderful Counselor, Mighty God,
> Everlasting Father, Prince of Peace.
> Of the increase of his government and peace
> There will be no end (Isa. 9:6-7a).

However, many centuries before Isaiah, early seeds of this hope were planted firmly within human history in God's call to Abraham: leave your people; begin a pilgrimage into a new land; through your seed all nations will be blessed (Gen. 12:1-3). Surely this blessing referred to the covenant people of God who embrace the faith of Abraham. Yet the biblical scripture affirms that this promise also refers to a person, a savior, who is the Messiah (Gal. 3:16).

God formed the descendants of Abraham who walked in his way of faith into a covenant people known as Israel.[2] God formed them into his covenant people with a mission: they were to be a light to the nations (Isa. 49:6). To our way of thinking it is rather amazing that these people, Israel, who were just beginning to understand a little of what it means to be God's covenant people, became slaves to the pharaohs of Egypt.

God Reveals Himself as I AM

About five hundred years after Abraham, God called Moses to lead Israel into freedom from their enslavement to the pharaohs. The event of God meeting and calling Moses is very significant, and it helps to clarify the mission of the Messiah. It was also an event that was very significant in giving Israel an unforgettable identity as the covenant people of God.

Moses was in the desert near Mount Sinai herding sheep. He saw a fire in a bush, but the bush was not consumed. He drew near, and God called to him from the bush, "Moses, Moses!" God then commanded Moses to go to Egypt and lead Israel into freedom.

Moses was astounded. "What is your name?" he asked.

God said, "I AM WHO I AM" (Exod. 3:1-15).

In the course of time, biblical scholars have attempted to capture some of the meaning of I AM in the name, *Yahweh*. Yet in a real sense I AM means that God cannot be captured in any name. He is I AM, I WAS, I WILL BE. He is the one who meets us in personal encounter. He is the personal, righteous, covenant God, who reveals not only his will, but also himself to us. And in his revelation he acts for us and with us in order to free us from bondage. He freed Israel from slavery to pharaoh, and God wants, likewise, to free all who follow him from evil and destructive bondage.

God's meeting Moses at the burning bush is a watershed in biblical theology. Abraham knew God as *Elohim*. (The previous chapter noted that Allah is probably an Arabian expression of *Elohim*.) But to Moses God revealed himself as I AM, the personal covenant God who seeks to meet us in a person-to-person encounter. When we repent and say "yes" to his call and encounter, we learn to know I AM (*Yahweh*) as "my God" and "your God."

The biblical account describes this transformation in knowing God in this way.

God also said to Moses, "I am the Lord (*Yahweh*). I appeared to Abraham, to Isaac, and to Jacob as God Almighty (*Elohim*), but by my name the LORD (*Yahweh*) I did not make myself known to them" (Exod. 6:2-3).

Names of the Messiah

The ministry of the Messiah is in harmony with God's revelation as I AM. If God is primarily concerned with revealing his will to us but refrains from personal encounter with us, then the ministry of the Messiah as revealed in the Gospels makes no sense. However, when an angel announced the birth of the Messiah, he gave two names to the Messiah that are consistent with God's beginning revelation to Abraham and the further revelation to Moses.

The first name is *Jesus*. The angel said that his name will be "Jesus, because he will save his people from their sins" (Matt. 1:21). Jesus is derived from the Hebrew name, *Yahshua*, and means "Yahweh saves." What does he save us from? The angel announced that he will save from sins. How will he save? In the Messiah, God enters our human history and our personal lives with much more than guidance. He enters into our sinful situation, whatever that might be, in order to redeem us from sin and death. We will explore more of this amazing initiative by God in later chapters.

The second name is *Immanuel*, which means "God with us." As Jesus' ministry began, people were often totally astonished because he functioned with the authority of God. His life demonstrated that he really is the One who is "God with us." Jesus declared, "Anyone who has seen me, has seen the Father" (John 14:9).

There is a third name for the Messiah that we mention here: the *Lamb of God*. At the time of his baptism, just before he began his public ministry, John the Baptist, who baptized Jesus in the Jordan River, proclaimed, "Look, the Lamb of God, who takes away the sin of the world!" (John 1:29).

Recall that God provided a ram as a substitute sacrifice in order to redeem a son of Abraham from death. Christians believe that sacrifice was a sign pointing to Jesus, the Lamb of God, who has taken our place so that we might be forgiven and redeemed. Later chapters will explore this further.

All of this is to say that the witness of the biblical scriptures is that in Jesus the Messiah, God is fully present and that he reveals himself as our Redeemer and Savior, as our loving heavenly Father. These are not notions concocted by theologians. It is rather that the life, witness, and ministry of Jesus demonstrate this reality.

Here are some examples.

On one occasion Jesus astounded everyone by exclaiming, "Before Abraham was born, I AM!" (John 8:58). That was the same name for the Creator that God revealed to Moses: I AM.

On another occasion Jesus was on a mount with three of his disciples. Moses and Elijah appeared and conversed with Jesus. These were the great prophets of the Old Testament: Moses, the lawgiver, and Elijah, the miracle worker. Then a cloud covered the mount, Moses and Elijah disappeared, and God spoke from within the cloud: "This is my Son, whom I love; with him I am well pleased. Listen to him!" (Matt. 17:5).

After his crucifixion and resurrection, Jesus encouraged his disciples by declaring, "All authority in heaven and on earth has been given to me" (Matt. 28:18).

Who Is Jesus the Messiah?

What does this all mean? How does one put into theological language the meaning of these astounding developments in relationship to the life and ministry of Jesus the Messiah?

Reflecting on all of this shortly after Jesus' crucifixion, resurrection, and ascension into heaven, writers of New Testament scriptures described Jesus in these ways.

> For God was pleased to have all his fullness dwell in him, and through him to reconcile to himself all things, whether things on earth or things in heaven, by making peace through his blood, shed on the cross (Col. 1:19-20).

> In the past God spoke to our forefathers through the prophets at many times and in various ways, but in these last days he has spoken to us by his Son, whom he appointed heir of all things, and through whom he made the universe. The Son is the radiance of God's glory and the exact representation of his being, sustaining all things by his powerful word (Heb. 1:1-3).

When our family first arrived in Somalia, I met one of the Somali disciples of the Messiah in the sandy courtyard of a

Somalia Mennonite Mission school. We observed ants scurrying beneath our feet hoarding food.

He said, "Suppose you want to become a friend with those ants. If you draw near, they become terrified and vanish in their holes. The only way you can ever become a friend of the ants is to become an ant."

He continued, "That is what God has done in the Messiah. We are like ants in his presence. Yet he wants to become our friend. That is the reason that in the Messiah God has become one of us."

And what about the name, Messiah? Messiah means "the Anointed One." What is his mission? Over half a millennium before Jesus the prophet Isaiah described his mission in this way.

> The Spirit of the Sovereign Lord is on me;
> because the Lord has anointed me
> to preach good news to the poor.
> He has sent me to bind up the brokenhearted,
> to proclaim freedom for the captives
> and release from darkness for the prisoners,
> to proclaim the year of the Lord's favor
> and the day of vengeance of our God,
> to comfort all who mourn,
> and provide for those who grieve in Zion—
> to bestow on them a crown of beauty
> instead of ashes,
> the oil of gladness
> instead of mourning,
> and a garment of praise
> instead of a spirit of despair (Isa. 61:1-3).

When Jesus began his ministry, he read portions of the above scriptures to a congregation of Jewish worshipers in Nazareth. Then he astounded everyone by declaring, "Today this scripture is fulfilled in your hearing" (Luke 4:21).

That is the mission of Jesus the Messiah. What about Muhammad, whom Muslims confess to be the Seal of the Prophets? What was his commitment and mission?

The Seal of the Prophets in Muslim Faith

Muslims believe that Muhammad was an apostle or messenger (*rasul*) of God. He was also a prophet or an informer (*nabbi*) of

God. Islam teaches that every people group has been blessed with *nabbi*. However, *rasul* are those messengers through whom God reveals his books of revelation.

Muhammad is the final *rasul* through whom God has revealed the final book of revelation, the Qur'an. He is also the Seal of the Prophets, a title that means consummation and finality. The Qur'an proclaims:

> Muhammad . . . is the messenger of Allah and the Seal of the Prophets; and Allah is ever Aware of all things (Al-Ahzab [The Clans] 33:40).

> And We have not sent thee (O Muhammad) save as a bringer of good tidings and a warner unto all mankind; but most of mankind know not (Saba [The City of Saba] 34:28).

> He it is Who hath sent His messenger with guidance and the religion of truth, that he may make it conqueror of all religion however much idolaters may be averse (Saff [Battle Array] 61:90.

Muhammad is the final prophet sent to clarify and establish the truth proclaimed by all former prophets. Muslims believe that surely, therefore, former prophets anticipated Muhammad's role as the final prophet. That quest takes some Muslim scholars to the Bible.

The Bible and Muhammad

These Muslim scholars review the sayings of Jesus and the writings of all biblical prophets to discover prophecies anticipating the coming of Muhammad. A number of Old Testament scriptures that Christians have applied to Jesus, Muslims apply to Muhammad.

For example, a prophecy from Moses:

> The Lord said to me: ". . . I will raise up for them a prophet like you from among their brothers; I will put my words in his mouth, and he will tell them everything I command him. If anyone does not listen to my words that the prophet speaks in my name, I myself will call him to account" (Deut. 18:17-19).

Quite occasionally Muslims quote this scripture, confident that Moses is anticipating the coming of Muhammad.

Especially intriguing for Muslims is the search for prophecies about Muhammad that Jesus proclaimed. This is because the Qur'an states, "When Jesus the son of Mary said: O children of Israel! Lo! I am a messenger of Allah to you . . . bringing good tidings of a messenger who cometh after me, whose name is the Praised One [Ahmad or Muhammad]" (Saff 61:6).

Where is this prophecy by Jesus? "Ah!" Muslim scholars declare. "We have found the prophecy of Jesus about Muhammad."

"Praises to God!" the imam in the Harrisburg Muslim Center exclaimed. "Jesus the Messiah prophesied that Muhammad would come to lead people in all truth. However, sadly, Christians have changed the original words of their scriptures and have inserted Holy Spirit, in place of Muhammad."

The imam's assertions are taught in Muslim theological centers around the world and merit comment. A brief journey into the Greek original will clarify. In John 14:16, 26; 16:7, Jesus promised that the Counselor would come. The biblical text states explicitly that by this Jesus meant the Holy Spirit. The Greek original word was *Paracleitos* (Counselor). However, Muslim scholars quite universally assert that this is a corruption, and that the original word was *Periclutos* (the Praised One).[3] Muhammad means "the praised one."

It is noteworthy that there are no ancient manuscripts whatsoever that use *Periclutos*; all use *Paracleitos*.

In my response to the imam, I said, "Muslims and Christians pray that God will lead us into the truth. Both the Muslim and Christian scriptures warn against distorting and corrupting scripture. Let us take note. There are some five thousand ancient manuscripts of the New Testament. Not one uses 'Praised One.' All use 'Counselor.' Let us not distort or corrupt the scriptures.

"In these passages Jesus promised to send the Holy Spirit. To replace the Holy Spirit with a prophet is not wise,[4] for it is through the Holy Spirit that we are able to know the truth and to know God."

Muhammad the Example

In the Qur'an, belief in God and his apostle is inseparably linked—God *and* his apostle. There is no such inseparability in the Bible between God and the prophet or apostle. For example, the core of the confession of faith for Israel was the *Shema*: "Hear O Israel: the Lord our God, the Lord is one" (Deut. 6:4). The *Shema* contains only God; prophets are not mentioned. In the Bible, the prophet always stood under the judgment of God. Even Moses never entered the Promised Land, for he did not glorify God in the eyes of the people (Num. 27:12-7).

The very direct linkage of belief in God with belief in his apostle is, therefore, quite different from the role of prophets and apostles in biblical faith. There are other differences as well. For example, Muhammad is idealized as the perfect example. Biblical prophets are not idealized. We know nothing or very little about the lives of many of them, and those whose lives we do glimpse are often quite human indeed, touched with the sinful inclinations of the rest of humanity.

For example, in the Old Testament Moses lost his temper and therefore could not enter the Promised Land. Jonah disobeyed God and fled from his preaching appointment in Nineveh. In the New Testament, Paul and Barnabas had conflict. Peter and the other disciples fled from Jesus at the time of his arrest. However, in Islam, Muhammad is idealized.

Muhammad is the "first" among the Muslims, the perfect pattern and example for all others to follow. The Qur'an declares:

> Say: Lo! As for me, my Lord hath guided me unto a straight path, a right religion, the community of Abraham, the upright, who was no idolater. Say: Lo! my worship and my sacrifice and my living and my dying are for Allah, Lord of the Worlds. He hath no partner. This I am commanded, and I am first of those who surrender (unto Him) (Anam [Cattle] 6:161-3).

Furthermore the Qur'an proclaims that Muhammad was infallibly inspired by God.

> Your comrade [Muhammad] erreth not, nor is deceived;
> Nor doth he speak of (his own) desire.
> It is naught save an inspiration that is inspired,
> Which one of mighty powers hath taught him.
> Then he drew nigh and came down
> Till he was (distant) two bows' length or even nearer,
> And He revealed unto His slave that which He revealed,
> The heart lied not (in seeing) what it saw (An-Najm [The Star] 53:2-5, 8-11).

Within two centuries of the beginning of the Muslim movement, theologians had determined that Muhammad's inspiration
went much further than being the channel through which the
infallible Qur'an was revealed; he was also inspired in all that he
did. Muhammad was the infallible guide for life.[5] He lived his life
in a state of *'isma* (sinlessness), and his *sunnah* (the way he did
things) is the true example of living according the will of God.[6]

In the course of time, Islamic theology embraced the doctrine
that Muhammad was sinless. If the Qur'an was a perfect miracle,
the messenger through whom it came had to be without sin.[7] (One
will recognize in Catholic theology a somewhat similar development in regard to the immaculate conception of Mary, through
whom Jesus the Christ is born. The theological reasoning is that
since Christ was sinless, the virgin Mary also had to be sinless.)

Although Islamic theology has moved in the direction of
'isma for Muhammad, there are themes in the Qur'an that suggest some caution about this development. In Abasa (He
Frowned) 80:1-10 the Prophet is rebuked because he frowned and
turned away from a blind man who came to him seeking guidance. Elsewhere the Qur'an commands Muhammad to seek forgiveness from God for his sin (Muhammad 47:19; Fat-h [Victory]
48:2). Nevertheless, Islamic theology has moved in directions that
greatly honor Muhammad. The Qur'an declares that God proclaimed, "And lo! thou art of a tremendous nature" (Al-Qalam
[The Pen] 68:4). Elsewhere we read, "Verily in the messenger of
Allah you have a good example for him who looketh unto Allah
and the Last Day, and remembereth Allah much" (Al-Ahzab
33:21). Furthermore, the Qur'an proclaims that fealty to
Muhammad is fealty to God.[8]

> Lo! We have sent thee (O Muhammad) as a witness and a bearer
> of good tidings and a warner, that ye (mankind) may believe in
> Allah and His messenger, and may honor Him, and may revere
> Him, and may glorify Him at early dawn and at the close of day.
> Lo! those who swear allegiance unto thee (Muhammad) swear
> allegiance only unto Allah (Fat-h 48:8-10).

All of this is to say that all Muslims should emulate
Muhammad. The mystical devotion of Muslims further develops
this idealization. Muhammad acquires a status that Christians
would give only to Jesus the Messiah, whom Christians confess to

be Lord. These poetic phrases from Muhammad Iqbal (1876-1938) are a small window into the mystical eulogies for Muhammad that pervade Islamic devotional literature.

> The womb of the world never bore Muhammad's like.
> The song of love for him fills my silent reed,
> A hundred notes throb in my bosom.
> How shall I tell what devotion he inspires?[9]

The Muslim community developed a keen interest in the person of Muhammad out of a desire to faithfully emulate him. What kind of a man was he? What did he look like? In subsequent generations some of the legendary descriptions went into trivial detail. The physical details of the perfect man became a matter of great interest to some of his devotees.

> (Muhammad's hair was) neither lank nor short and wooly. It touched his shoulders. Muhammad used to make four plaits with each ear exposed between two plaits. The number of white hairs did not exceed seventeen. His eyes were very wide and black. His nose was hooked. He had a broad chest.[10]

All faithful Muslims honor Muhammad. However, in some of the mystical (*sufi*) streams of Muslim spirituality, Muhammad is venerated. One of the early *sufi* mystics, Ibn al-'Arabi, describes Muhammad as "The Muhammadan Light, the image of God in its primary entity, the divine consciousness, the pre-creation Light from which everything was created."[11] This hovers very close to an incarnational theology wherein God's word is incarnated within Muhammad. Orthodox Muslims wince when Muhammad is described in this way. Nevertheless, a variety of mystical streams do prevail within some expressions of the Muslim movement.

Sunnah

Sunnah is the way Muhammad acted. We learn of his *sunnah*, not through the Qur'an, but through the Hadith (Traditions). The *sunnah* is the path or example Muhammad left for his fellow Muslims.

The minutia of the *sunnah* is intriguing. For example, one of his consorts, 'A'ishah, reported, "The Messenger of God loved to start from the right-hand side in his every act, putting on shoes, combing the hair and performing ablution."[12] Learning of Muhammad's right-to-left habit, multitudes of faithful Muslims try to do likewise.

This way of the prophet has defined the culture of the Muslim *ummah* most remarkably. One can speak of a Muslim personality or a Muslim culture. This is because all faithful Muslims strive to emulate the way of Muhammad. (Chapter 12 will explore the *sunnah* more adequately.)

Jesus in the Muslim Faith

Jesus is also a beloved prophet for all Muslims.

At a gathering with Christians and Muslims in a mosque, the imam began to weep when the name of Jesus slipped into our conversations. Our discussions ceased. We awaited his next comment.

"At the mention of Jesus, I was overcome with tears of joy and veneration. I love Jesus so very much!" Then he added, "But Jesus was only an apostle of God. He was not the Son of God."

In a recent book, *The Muslim Jesus,* Tarif Khalidi peruses a thousand years (the eighth through the eighteenth centuries) of Muslim pious devotion for Jesus.[13] This Muslim Jesus has his roots in the qur'anic Jesus, a Jesus who is a Muslim prophet.

One stream of Muslim piety celebrates Jesus as an eschatological figure who will appear on earth toward the end of human history to prepare the earth for the final judgment.[14] This stream of piety is inspired by the qur'anic assertion that Jesus will be the sign of the coming hour of judgment (Zukhruf [God Adorns] 43:61).

Another image of Jesus is that of a pious ascetic who joins with other prophets in retreat from the world in a quest for pure worship and righteousness. This Jesus is the "patron saint of Muslim asceticism."[15] He is venerated and adored. As far as the practical experiences of life are concerned—well? Let the monks follow him into the desert caves.

Although Muslims throughout the centuries have adored Jesus, this Muslim Jesus is a Jesus who is in dispute with the Jesus of the Gospels and the church.

Tarif Khalidi comments that for the Muslim Jesus:

There is no Sermon on the Mount, no parables, no teachings on the law and the spirit, and of course no Passion. Instead . . . he is humble and pious toward his mother, and he bears a message of God's unity which confirms earlier prophetic messages. . . . Here, then, is the true Jesus, "cleansed" of the "perversions" of his followers, a prophet totally obedient to his Maker and offered up as the true alternative to the Jesus of the Incarnation, Crucifixion, and Redemption.[16]

The Jesus of the Qur'an is "unique in his ability to inspire so much qur'anic tension, the aim being to establish the truth about him."[17] The tension is epitomized at the time of Jesus' birth, when he miraculously speaks proclaiming "Lo! I am the slave of Allah. He hath given me the Scripture and hath appointed me a Prophet" (Maryam [Mary] 19:30). In a defining comment concerning the birth of Jesus, the Qur'an proclaims the "truth" in regard to the dispute between the Muslim Jesus and the Jesus of the Gospels.

> Such was Jesus, son of Mary: (this is) a statement of the truth concerning which they doubt. It befitteth not (the Majesty of) Allah that He should take unto Himself a son. Glory be to Him! When He decreeth a thing, He saith unto it only: Be! and it is (Maryam 19:34-35).

The Qur'an declares that its message will "cleanse" Jesus of the "blaspheme" of those who have ascribed falsehoods to Jesus. Muslims believe that the Qur'an clarifies the truth about Jesus (Ali 'Imran [The Family of Imran] 3:55).

The qur'anic name for the Messiah provides a further glimpse into the differences between Islam and the Gospel. In the Qur'an the Messiah is named *'Isa*. In the biblical scriptures the name the angel proclaimed when announcing his birth is *Yashu'a*; the Arabic translation is *Yasu'a*, the Greek is *Iesous*. The Hebrew *Yashu'a* means, "Yahweh saves!" That meaning is lost in the name *'Isa*; he is only a prophet.[18]

Some Muslims are intrigued by the Jesus images in the Qur'an, for there are mysterious distinctives about him. Here is an abbreviated profile of some of the characteristics of the qur'anic *'Isa*; some of the references from the Qur'an are included.

Messiah, good news (3:45); brought the Gospel (5:49; 19:30); birth announced to Mary by an angel (19:16-20); a sign from God (19:20); born of a virgin (19:16-35); the Word of God (4:171); the

Spirit of God (4:171); not the Son of God (19:34-5; 9:30); only a prophet and apostle of God (4:171); submissive to God (19:30); miracle worker (3:49); established the former scriptures (5:49); a mission for a period of time to the house of Israel (3:49-50; 13:38); rescued from death on the cross (4:157); taken to heaven without dying (3:55-8); returning at the end of history to get the world ready for the final judgment (43:61; The Traditions); prophesied the coming of Muhammad (61:6); without sin (19:19).

A perusal of the above citations reveals that the Qur'an has high esteem for Jesus. Nevertheless, the Muslim Jesus was sent to Israel for a specific people and time. His ethics were quite idealistic, and most likely intended for a small community who retreated from real involvement in the world. Jesus had no universal mission; that was Muhammad's calling.[19] The Messiah is a prophet, but not "God with Us." He was rescued from the cross; another died in his place. The Muslim scriptures do not embrace the central themes of the Gospel: the incarnation, the atonement, and Jesus' bodily resurrection from the dead. Thus, although Jesus the Messiah is honored by Muslims, the qur'anic Jesus is not the Jesus of the Gospel.

Some of the Muslim objections to these foundations of the Christian faith might be attributable to misunderstandings: The notion that the Trinity is polytheistic tri-theism. The notion that a theology of Trinity dissects God into parts. The notion that the Christians believe that God had relations with a consort, Mary, who bore him a son. The notion that Christians believe that God is the Messiah. Later chapters will address these misunderstandings and distortions of the Christian faith.

We also recognize that the soul of the struggle between the Muslim and Christian faith revolves around questions of the nature of God and the human condition. Islam is tremendously concerned about defending God against anything that would detract from his absolute sovereignty and transcendence. To the Muslim mind, the Christian Gospel seems to dangerously compromise those commitments. God in the Messiah on the cross seeking to invite and embrace and redeem and reconcile a lost humanity!— How can that be true of the sovereign almighty God? That is the abiding Muslim perplexity and objection with the Gospel.

Muhammad and the Christians

Muslims often ask Christians how they view Muhammad. That is not a trivial question. The Qur'an is clear: those who do not believe that Muhammad is the final prophet do not have sincere hearts toward God (Al-Mujadila [The Woman Who Pleads] 58:20-22). Nevertheless, Christians are respected as closest in love to the Muslims (Maida [The Table Spread] 5:81-88).

"Is Muhammad the apostle of God?" A Muslim leader prodded during a rooftop restaurant banquet with Muslim friends in Eastleigh, Nairobi.

I responded, "God promised Adam and Eve that a son born to woman would be wounded by the evil one, but in the end he would triumph over evil and death. That promise was about the Messiah. For some two thousand years as the biblical drama unfolded, that promise persisted.

"The biblical prophets proclaimed various dimensions of that promise consistently. The prophets promised that the Messiah would come to offer salvation to all peoples. The Messiah's mission would be to extend the rule of God throughout the earth; he would rule forever. He would proclaim peace and truth to the nations. He would be the Savior of the world.

"The Messiah in his life and mission confirmed all that these prophets over many centuries had promised about him. The biblical witness is clear: Jesus the Messiah is the One whom God has anointed to be the Savior of the world.

"To what extent does Muhammad agree with the Messiah's life, ministry, and teachings and the total biblical witness about the Messiah? That is the question I struggle with. I rejoice whenever a person encourages us to say 'yes' to Jesus the Messiah in the fullness of the biblical witness concerning him."

Jesus and Muhammad

Christians should avoid comparing Jesus and Muhammad. This is because the Messiah is more than a prophet. Muhammad might be comparable to prophets such as Amos or Hosea, who called on people to live righteously and turn away from false gods, although the messages of these biblical prophets is very different from that of Muhammad.

However, it confuses roles of prophet and Messiah when Christians compare the ministry of Jesus with that of

Muhammad. None other is named the Messiah. That name means that Jesus is the Anointed One, a very different role from that of a prophet. Later chapters will explore more of the ministry of Jesus the Messiah.

Is there a Role for Jesus?

What is the role of the Messiah in a Muslim theology that believes that Muhammad is the Seal of the Prophets?

Adam, Abraham, and Muhammad are the first, middle, and final prophets. The first prophet is Adam, who received guidance from God and practiced the true religion of Islam at the Ka'bah. The middle prophet is Abraham, who with his son Ishmael, reestablished the true religion of Islam at the Ka'bah. The final prophet is Muhammad, who, like Abraham and Adam, also established the true religion of Islam at the Ka'bah. In terms of the grand plan of Muslim theology, the Messiah is on the sidelines.

The Messiah is honored as among the other most perseverant prophets: Noah, Abraham, Moses, and Muhammad (Shura [Consultation] 42:13). Muslims eulogize his compassion. However, in the real world Jesus is quite irrelevant, and Muslims believe that the Christians have tragically misrepresented his mission.

Take note! Christians likewise often turn Jesus into an irrelevant mystery figure. Jesus the Messiah is disturbing, not only for Muslims, but for multitudes of Christians as well. Turning Jesus into an irrelevant mystery is not just a Muslim inclination; many Christians do the same. At a time when the sounds of the drums of war roll around the world, what is the relevancy of Jesus—for Christians? In an age when a billion people sleep hungry every night amidst a world of unprecedented wealth, what does it mean to honor Jesus—as Christians? At a time when hundreds of millions know nothing of the hope of the Gospel, what does it mean to follow Jesus—as Christians?

Within the Muslim theological framework, the Messiah has completed his limited mission. Muhammad now steps into the center stage with the final message of all humankind. The Messiah anticipates the universal mission of the Seal of the Prophets and the Qur'an.

A Persistent Jesus

Nevertheless, Jesus does not step aside. In surprising and often unobtrusive ways, Jesus the Messiah persists in being heard and recognized.

Tarif Khalidi observes:

> Nevertheless, he remains a towering religious figure in his own right—one who easily, almost naturally, rises above two religious environments, the one that nurtured him and the other that adopted him. . . . (Jesus) is endowed with attributes which render him meta-historical and even, so to speak, meta-religious.[20]

Several years after the horrible debacle of inter-ethnic and inter-religious war in Sarajevo, I accompanied some Christian Serbian and Bosnian students on a visit with the Muslim Student Association in the center of that wounded city. These young Muslims invited us for tea. The conversation was intensely dynamic. We continued for nearly four hours, and a number in the group agreed to continue the conversations at a later time.

As we were departing, one of the group observed, "A guest joined us this afternoon, and he would not leave."

The guest was Jesus. He not only joined us, but unobtrusively occupied the center of conversation.

Just as in Sarajevo that afternoon, Jesus invites Christians and Muslims to a lifetime journey of exploration and discovery of the meaning of the Messianic secret.

Readings from the Bible:
   Luke 1:26-38; 4:14-30
Readings from the Qur'an:
   Maryam 19:16-36; Al-Ahzab 33:21, 40; Saba 34:28

Questions for Reflection and Discussion:
   1. Both Muslims and Christians agree that Jesus is the Messiah. Describe the differences in the Muslim and Christian understanding of the Messiah.
   2. One can speak of a Muslim pattern of doing things, but hardly of a Christian pattern of doing things. Explain this differ-

ence (Matthew 5:48; Al-Ahzab 33:21).

3. What is the significance for Muslims of the conviction that Muhammad is the Seal of the Prophets (Al-Ahzab 33:40)?

4. What is the significance for Christians of their conviction that Jesus is the Messiah (Luke 4:14-40)?

5. Jesus the Messiah is the mystery person of the Qur'an, with very little real influence on the faith and practices of the Muslim *ummah*. Throughout the centuries the church has likewise sometimes pushed Jesus into the realms of the irrelevant mysterious, away from real life. Account for inclinations to view Jesus as a mystery rather than as reality.

— 6 —

Scriptures:
the Qur'an—the Bible

"PLEASE, lend me a Bible," Ibrahim Muhammad asked me. I gave Ibrahim a *Good News* version with a soft green cover. He wrapped it in brown paper so that others would not notice the book in his hands. He left our home and slipped into the night reverently holding the precious scriptures.

The next evening Ibrahim returned to our home carrying the same wrapped book. His face revealed somber sadness. He entered, sat down, and took the Bible from its wrappings. He laid the book on the desk.

"I thought the Bible is the Word of God. It is not. People have corrupted the Christian scriptures," he said. "What a catastrophe! The Bible is a history book, not the Word of God."

In grieving silence, Ibrahim returned into the night, carrying only the empty brown bag. The "corrupted" *Good News Bible* lay on my cluttered desk.

History and Revelation

Ibrahim was right. The Bible is a history. Some of it is not very inspiring history at that. I suppose Ibrahim began reading Genesis. Within a few paragraphs he encountered the first murder, Cain slaying his brother Abel. A few chapters later he read of an embarrassment, when Noah's sons discovered their father sleeping drunk and naked in his home. Later there is the account of Jacob cheating his older brother, Esau, out of the blessing from his blind father, Isaac, by pretending to be Esau. Then Joseph's brothers sold him to merchants going to Egypt for thirty pieces of silver. Is this scripture? Ibrahim was appalled. He was confident that these stories could not be scripture.

In radical contrast to the Bible, Muslims point out that the Qur'an transcends history. It is God's Word, free from human or historical corruption. It is a sent-down revelation.

The organization of the Qur'an demonstrates that understanding. The organization has no relationship to the sequence of the revelations. Except for the opening chapter, all other qur'anic portions are arranged in a continuum according to the length of the chapters, longest to shortest. Whether a chapter was recorded in Mecca at the beginning of Muhammad's prophetic work or in Medina during his later years is irrelevant. Muslim's believe that God's revelation is noncontingent upon history.

The Qur'an includes references to historical events, such as Noah and the flood or Moses at the burning bush. However, these references are not presented as historical narratives, but rather as parables from history to illustrate a truth. The parables are sketchy, with fragmentary allusions to the events scattered here or there. Muslims believe that revelation is the guidance God sends down. Historical events might illustrate the truths of revelation, but the events are never revelation—except for the event of the sending down of scripture.

This is not to say that the Muslim *ummah* has no interest in history. However, the stories about Muhammad and the early *ummah* are not included in the Qur'an. Rather the stories and sayings of Muhammad are recorded in separate texts known as the Hadith (Traditions). The Hadith is valuable, but has no place in the Qur'an. From a Muslim perspective the Bible is a confusing mixture of Hadith and scripture.

Why does Islamic theology resist the biblical understanding of God revealing himself through his acts in history? Islam is committed to the sovereign transcendence of God. For revelation to partake of the human seems to Muslims to be a demotion of God. God is most great! How can his sovereign greatness mesh with participation in the human?[1] That cannot be.

However, biblical faith is anchored in God's acts in history.

Christians, as well as Jews, believe that the acts of God are the core of biblical revelation. A Jewish theologian, Emil Fackenheim, refers to such events in the Bible as "root experiences" that create an "abiding astonishment."[2] For example, God delivered Israel from slavery to the Pharaohs. Then God met Israel at Mount Sinai (Exod. 1-14, 19-20). The whole of biblical theology is significantly formed by these two events. Of course, Christians believe that the supreme act of God in history is the life, crucifixion, and resurrection of Jesus the Messiah.

Muslims frequently tell me that Paul created the New Testament accounts and theology about Jesus. Of course, they read some contemporary Christian theologians who support such notions. But can that really be true? The event of Jesus filled believers with "abiding astonishment." That was true of Paul.

As a young man, Paul violently opposed the church. However, after he met the resurrected Jesus in a vision, he could never get over the amazement of it all. He researched the life of Jesus. His friend, Luke, joined Paul in that commitment. In that commitment to an accurate account of the life and teachings of Jesus, the Gospel according to Luke was written. Luke writes about this effort saying,

> Many have undertaken to draw up an account of the things that have been fulfilled among us, just as they were handed down to us by those who from the first were eyewitnesses and servants of the word. Therefore, since I myself have carefully investigated everything from the beginning, it seemed good also to me to write an orderly account for you, most excellent Theophilus, so that you may know the certainty of the things you have been taught (Luke 1:1-4).

So the theology of Paul was a response to the Jesus event.[3] Scriptures penned by Paul are included in the New Testament; his writings are in varied ways a response to his abiding amazement about the Jesus event. That is the nature of the Bible. The Bible is the narrative of God's redemptive acts as well as the narrative of our human responses to what he is doing.

Christians believe that the Holy Spirit inspires the whole process. The scriptures explain,

. . . and how from infancy you have known the holy Scriptures, which are able to make you wise for salvation through faith in Christ Jesus. All Scripture is God-breathed and is useful for teaching, rebuking, correcting and training in righteousness (2 Tim. 3:15-16).

Guidance and Fellowship

In the Bible, God meets us; in the Qur'an, God sends his will down to us. Prayer illustrates this difference.

"Our Father, who is in heaven," Jesus taught his disciples to pray, a prayer that Christians refer to as the Lord's Prayer.

"In the name of God, Most Gracious, Most Merciful," is the opening prayer of the Qur'an, a prayer that Muslims refer to as the perfect prayer.

What is the difference between addressing God as "our Father" or bowing in prayer "in the name of God"?

In biblical faith, God meets us personally. God meets me and reveals himself to me. He is "my Father God," who is engaged in my sorrows and yearnings. God has transcended his transcendence to meet us in our humanity; our Father in heaven rejoices and sorrows with us.[4] He participates in our suffering and joys.

In the Qur'an, God is near. In fact, "We are nearer to him than his jugular vein" (Qaf [*possibly meaning* God Knows Best] 50:16). This nearness is his watchful presence to assure that we are performing our duties. Our duty is to bow before God's will in submission. His presence is not understood to be God's personal engagement with us in our sorrows and yearnings. We submit to the compassionate One, but we cannot know him as "my God."[5] God hears our prayers, and responds to our petitions; yet he is not personally affected by our plight. He never suffers with us.

In the Bible, God meets us in the particular event or personal crisis. God met Adam and Eve in the garden hiding behind a bush. God met Noah. God met Abraham and Sarah. God met Hagar. God met Moses at the burning bush. God met Israel at Mount Sinai. Each particular event of meeting God has personal significance; it is also a blessing to others, for as we meet God we also hear his call to live as a blessing to others.

Qur'anic faith takes the believer in a different direction than that of an encounter with God. For example, God sent the angel Gabriel to Muhammad to reveal the universal truth of Islam, but

God himself did not encounter Muhammad in these events of revelation. However, a hint of personal encounter between God and his prophet is present in a qur'anic reference to Moses at the burning bush. Nevertheless, some Muslim theologians believe that it was the angel Gabriel who met Moses, not God; that view prevails quite widely within the Muslim *ummah.*[6]

In the Qur'an, the merciful Allah sends his perfect will down; in the Bible, the loving Yahweh meets us in personal "I-thou" encounters.

All of these diverse themes are found in the Qur'an and the Bible. Now we take a brief look at the Qur'an itself, and then, the Bible.

The Qur'an

"This night is more excellent than ten thousand others!" exclaimed our Arab-Somali host.

We were at an elegant banquet in the riverine village of Jamama in southern Somalia. This was the *'Id al-Fitr* (the three-day Feast of Breaking the Fast). Our host, with the vast majority of all Somalis, had participated faithfully in the one-month day-time fast that is required as one of the five pillars of Muslim duty. Now the fast was over and the feast was at hand.

Before the meal began, our host explained with an expansive smile. "This night is more wonderful than ten thousand nights! Tonight we remember the advent of the Qur'an, when it began to come down from heaven. The month of fasting is to anticipate the gift of revelation. Now on this night, we celebrate because revelation has descended from heaven. The gift is here, the true guidance from God, the Qur'an."

The Qur'an proclaims:

> The month of Ramadhan in which was revealed the Qur'an, a guidance for mankind, and clear proofs of the guidance, and the Criterion (of right and wrong). And whosoever of you is present, let him fast the month, and whosoever of you is sick or on a journey, (let him fast the same) number of other days (Baqara [The Cow] 2:185).

Elsewhere we read:

> Lo! We revealed it on the Night of Power. Ah, what will convey unto thee what the Night of Power is! The Night of Power is better than a thousand months (Qadr [The Night of Power] 97:1-3).

Power! The Qur'an proclaims that it is the overwhelming power of truth. Even the mountains would split asunder and be humbled by the fear of God, had the Qur'an descended upon them (Hashir [The Exile] 59:21). This is the truth that divides believers from nonbelievers. All true believers fall prostrate in belief and submission when they first hear the Qur'an recited in their presence (Inshiqaq [The Rending Asunder] 84:20-22).

Muslims believe that angels were the messengers through whom God sent guidance down through the ages. They believe that the angel Gabriel was the heavenly messenger who brought God's final guidance, the Qur'an, to Muhammad. Gabriel's first appearance frightened Muhammad. He was alone in a cave on Mount Hira just outside Mecca. The year was A.D. 610.

Gabriel appeared and commanded:

> Read [Recite]: In the name of thy Lord Who createth, createth man from a clot.
> Read: And thy Lord is the Most Bounteous, Who teacheth by the pen, teacheth man that which he knew not (Iqraa [Proclaim] 96:1-5).

The first word of revelation was: *Recite*! That is the meaning of Qur'an: "recite." Muslims believe that the Qur'an is a recitation of the revelations that God sent down from the original heavenly book, *Umm-ul-Kitab* (Mother of the Book) (Rad [Thunder] 13:39). After this first revelation, the angel Gabriel appeared from time to time, teaching Muhammad other portions of the heavenly book. The Qur'an declares that nothing in the Qur'an has come from any influences other than the revelation of the angelic messenger.[7]

Muslims believe that Muhammad faithfully recited to his companions all that the angel revealed to him. His companions memorized or recorded the portions in writing. That was an awesome responsibility, for they believed that each verse was an *ayat* (sign) of truth sent to earth from God their merciful creator. All the content of the Qur'an was transmitted during Muhammad's twenty-two years of public proclamation. It was Muhammad alone who first recited each of the portions that comprise the Qur'an.

The qur'anic *suras* (chapters) were collected and recorded in their final form by the caliph, Uthman, in 653. That was twenty years after Muhammad's death. All alternative manuscripts were destroyed. A comparative study of the original manuscripts is, therefore, an impossibility.

The Qur'an is the criterion of truth for the 1.2 billion Muslims around the world. They honor this scripture. Many millions have memorized the entire Arabic Qur'an. I suppose that all Somali children memorized significant portions before they entered first grade. That is normative in devout Muslim societies everywhere. Each verse (*aya*) is sacred. *Aya* means "a sign." Just as creation is filled with the signs of God, so each verse in the Qur'an is a precious sign of God. Muslims believe that in memorizing each sacred *aya* of the Qur'an, the child is imbibing the mystery and wonder of the *ayat* of God.

The Qur'an must always be the highest object in a room. It should only be handled after appropriate ritual ablutions. No markings are permitted upon its sacred pages. It is untranslatable; it is an Arabic Qur'an. Portions are read or recited in the mosques around the world in the times of daily prayer and worship. It is the foundation of the Muslim nation.

The Bible

The biblical writings span at least fifteen hundred years, from Moses to John. The narratives beginning with Abraham and the early history of Israel until the formation of the church embrace more than two thousand years of history.

Perhaps the Bible is best understood as the narratives and theologies of a journey of a people learning to know God. These narratives unfold in grand epochs.

First are the narratives of the nations (Gen. 1–11). This is universal history. For example, Christians believe that the Adam and Eve narratives communicate our universal human condition. All people are created in God's own image; we all come from one original Parent—we are, therefore, one humanity. We all experience in various ways a turning away from God and the pernicious outworking of sinfulness in our personal lives and in our world.

Second are the narratives of call and promise (Gen. 12–50). These are the accounts of God's call to Abraham to leave his people and become the father of a new people who would bless all nations. These accounts describe the saga of three generations of the family of Abraham commencing the pilgrimage as God's called-out people, the forerunners of Israel.

Third is the journey of Israel as God formed them into his covenant community which was called to be a light to all nations (Exodus through Deuteronomy). These are the narratives of Israel's deliverance from enslavement to the pharaohs of Egypt and God meeting them at Mount Sinai. The Torah is the scriptures that describe the pilgrimage of discovery as God met and called the family of Abraham and then Israel; God formed them into his covenant people.

Fourth is the journey of conquest and nation formation (Joshua until the exile). During this era of about eight hundred years, God revealed himself and worked with Israel, showing them how to live as God's covenant people in the midst of conquest and wars, the formation of nationhood, government, the competing claims of gods other than Yahweh, economics, religious ritual, justice, the poor, and aliens. Israel was not always a faithful learner; the community experienced both God's judgment and his grace.

Fifth is the journey into exile and then return. This was a time of tremendous theological reflection and development. Many of the prophetic scriptures were written during this time. How could it be that God's covenant people were overpowered by other nations, had their temple destroyed, and were forced into exile in strange countries? During this era a theology of suffering emerged which has contributed significantly to Christian understandings of the Gospel.

These five epochs are narrated and theologized in the first portion of the Bible, known as the Old Testament. Then comes the sixth development, and this is described and theologized in the second portion of the Bible, the New Testament.

The sixth era is the birth and ministry of the Messiah and the formation of the church. Both the Messiah and the church believed that what was happening was a continuation and fulfillment of what God had been doing from the time of Abraham's call through all the eras noted above. A common prophetic theme within those previous eras was the promise and expectation of the coming of the Messiah: "He will proclaim peace to the nations. His rule will extend from sea to sea and from the River to the ends of the earth" (Zech. 9:10).

The biblical accounts are richly varied. At least thirty people wrote portions of these scriptures. The Old Testament was written in Hebrew, and the New Testament in Greek. Biblical literature includes history, poetry, proverbs, prophetic writings, apocalyptic literature, and letters of encouragement and admonition.

People often question whether the historical narratives are accurate. The historical accounts of the Old Testament were developed at a time when no other societies anywhere were interested in accurate history. Most cultures paid no attention to history because they believed history was a meaningless cycle. Those few who did record some accounts, such as the Chinese emperors, did so to prove something; accuracy did not matter. For example, the Chinese wrote their history to prove that everything goes excellently under good emperors and horribly under bad emperors.

The biblical accounts of history are different. The history unfolds generation by generation. Realism characterizes these accounts. The unseemly is recorded as well as the good. For example, the beloved King David was involved in adultery and arranged for the death of the husband of the woman. During the last century archaeologists have examined the accuracy of biblical historical accounts. The late William Albright, a highly respected twentieth-century archaeologist, observed that biblical history is the only accurate history of ancient times.[8]

Why did the writers of the Bible give such attention to historical accuracy? Surely it is because of their conviction that God is acting and revealing himself within history, and therefore their history had meaning. The covenant people of God took that conviction very seriously. They recorded their history with great care.

Ancient biblical manuscripts provide a basis for confidence that the texts of the modern Bible are an accurate transmission of the original biblical texts. In contrast to the Qur'an, where Caliph Uthman commanded that all alternative manuscripts be destroyed within twenty years of Muhammad's death, there are thousands of ancient biblical manuscripts. This includes manuscripts of the biblical texts as well as texts that were never accepted as trustworthy scripture.

In regard to the Old Testament, the Dead Sea Scrolls are exceedingly helpful. Shepherds discovered these scrolls in caves near the Dead Sea in 1947. These parchments provide scholars with substantial portions of Old Testament manuscripts that are well more than two thousand years old.

Furthermore, scholars are overwhelmed by the abundance of ancient New Testament manuscripts. There are at least five thousand ancient manuscripts. Places that manuscripts are found are often surprising. For example, seventy-five portions of New Testament manuscripts were discovered in the mummy of a crocodile at Oxyrhnchus in Egypt in 1897. One of these manuscripts was a portion of the Gospel of John that is believed to be dated around A.D. 135. Ancient manuscripts such as these enable scholars to provide trustworthy texts of the New Testament. The scholar F. J. A. Hort comments that there is only one possibility in a thousand of deviation from the original texts.[9]

Ancient manuscripts confirm that the texts of our modern Bible are in remarkable harmony with the original biblical texts. However, whenever the early documents suggest that our modern text is different than the most reliable ancient manuscripts, scholars revise our modern texts. The goal of the scholars is to provide texts that are a trustworthy transmission of the original manuscripts.

Christians believe the Bible is the Word of God. Jesus the Messiah is also the Word of God. What does that mean? Redemption is the central theme of the biblical scriptures. And the witness of the New Testament is that God has acted in Jesus the Messiah to redeem us. The Bible as the written Word of God leads us to meet the Messiah who is the living Word of God who redeems us.

Jesus the Messiah said, "You diligently study the Scriptures because you think that by them you possess eternal life. These are the Scriptures that testify about me, yet you refuse to come to me to have life" (John 5:39-40).

Muslims and the Former Scriptures

Muslims are often perplexed about the Bible. Nevertheless, the Qur'an commands Muslims to believe in the previous scriptures. The Qur'an names four such scriptures:

—The *Suhuf* (Pages, now lost) revealed through the prophet Abraham.

—The *Taurat* (Torah) revealed through the prophet Moses.

—The *Zabur* (Psalms) revealed through the prophet David.

—The *Injil* (Gospel) revealed through Jesus the Messiah.

All Muslims believe that these scriptures are revealed by God; furthermore, the Qur'an commands Christians to make these scriptures freely available.[10]

Then there is the final revelation, the Qur'an, revealed through the prophet Muhammad. This scripture is a summary and clarification of the former scriptures. Although Muslims believe that the *Suhuf* of the prophet Abraham have been lost, the Muslim *ummah* recognizes that Christians and Jews are People of the Book (*Ahl al-Kitab*) who possess former scriptures. So, although the Qur'an is the final revelation that clarifies all previous revelations, there is, nevertheless, an abiding respect for the former scriptures. The Qur'an recognizes that these former scriptures nurture the life and faith of the Jewish and Christian people and that they are also "guidance and light" (Maida [The Table Spread] 5:44-47) to all humankind.

In fact, the Qur'an commands Muslims and even Muhammad himself, "If thou (Muhammad) art in doubt concerning that which We reveal unto thee, then question those who read the Scripture from before thee" (Yunus [Jonah] 10:94).

Elsewhere Muslims are reminded that "Allah laid a charge on those who had received the Scripture (He said): Ye are to expound it to mankind and not to hide it" (Ali 'Imran [The Family of Imran] 3:187). However, the Qur'an also warns Muhammad and the Muslims that those who possess the former scriptures (Jews and Christians) might "seduce thee from some part of that which Allah hath revealed unto thee" (Maida 5:49). Nevertheless, the Qur'an portrays a spirit of respect for the People of the Book, and admonishes them to safeguard their scriptures and commands them to make their scriptures available.

"Corruption"

On the other hand, Muslims experience difficulties reconciling the Qur'an with the biblical scriptures. Ibrahim, described at the beginning of this chapter, put his finger on a core problem, but there are other difficulties as well. Here are some of these issues.

First, as mentioned above, a substantial portion of the Bible is historical accounts and narrative.

Second, Christians on the whole do not use the original Hebrew and Greek texts, but other translations of the Bible, and even in a particular language there are different translations. It seems that Christians are not greatly concerned about a commitment to the exact words of the original revelation.

Third, there are numerous and irreconcilable differences between the Qur'an and the Bible. A conversation at the Kenyatta University College campus in Kenya illustrates this last point.

Jama Hussein and I taught world religions together. A student asked Jama, "You say that all Muslims must believe the Bible. However, there is conflict between the Qur'an and the Bible. For example, all four Gospel accounts describe the crucifixion of Jesus, but the Qur'an declares that Jesus was not crucified."

My colleague responded, "That is because the Bible is corrupted. Muslims believe in the original scriptures, not the corrupted scriptures that comprise the modern Christian Bible."

I asked Jama, "On what basis do you dismiss the Bible as a corrupted scripture?"

"On the authority of the Qur'an, for our Muslim scriptures warn that the Christians have corrupted their scriptures."

"Where does the Qur'an make that charge?" I asked.

"I will show you the exact verse after class," my colleague responded.

In Jama's office some minutes later, he showed me this well known qur'anic verse, "And lo! there is a party of them who distort the Scripture with their tongues, that ye may think that what they say is from the Scripture, when it is not from the Scripture" (Ali 'Imran 3:78).

I asked Jama, "Have you or I ever misquoted scripture with our tongues? Is this not a warning against that kind of distortion? However, I see nothing here that hints that the written biblical texts are corrupted."

In fact, both the Qur'an and the Bible declare that God's Word endures. The Qur'an proclaims, "There is none to alter the Words and Decrees of Allah" (Anan [Cattle] 6:34).[11]

The Bible exclaims, "Your word, O Lord, is eternal; it stands firm in the heavens" (Ps. 119:89).

Nevertheless, around the world the assumption of the Muslim *ummah* is that the Bible is not trustworthy scripture. The stance demonstrated by Jama Hussein in the world religions class is heard in mosques everywhere.

Christians and the Qur'an; Muslims and the Bible

Christians are saddened by the mistrust in the Bible that leads many Muslims away from a serious engagement with the Bible. As Christians review the Qur'an, it seems to them that there is little or no qur'anic basis for any judgment that the Bible is not trustworthy. Although Christians need to avoid imposing a Christian understanding upon the Qur'an, nevertheless, it is appropriate to engage a lively discourse on the text of the Qur'an.

It is instructive for both Muslim and Christians to be aware of what the Qur'an says about the biblical scriptures. There are two general themes of qur'anic comments in regard to the former scriptures:

1. God has revealed the former scriptures.

"He hath revealed unto thee (Muhammad) the Scripture with truth, confirming that which was (revealed) before it, even as He revealed the Torah and the Gospel" (Ali 'Imran 3:3).

"And unto thee (the People of the Gospel) have We revealed the Scripture with the truth, confirming whatever Scripture was before it, and (you are) a watcher (protector) over it (God's Book)"(Maida 5:48).

"Say: O People of the Scripture! Ye have naught (of guidance or no ground to stand upon) till ye observe the Torah and the Gospel and that which was revealed unto you unless you stand fast by the Law (*Taurat*) and the Gospel (*Injil*) and all the revelation that has come to you from your Lord" (Maida 5:68).

"The writings of Moses are the *furqan* (criterion) of truth" (Anbiyaa 21:48; Yunus 10:64).

"It is also guidance, light, and mercy to humankind. It is the Book of Allah" (Maida 5:47; Hud 11:17; Anbiyaa 21:48).

"There is no changing the Words of Allah" (Yunus 10:64).

In regard to the Gospel, the Qur'an states: "Wherein is guidance and a light, and confirming that which was (revealed) before it in the Torah—(the Messiah) a guidance and an admonition unto those who ward off (evil)" (Maida 5:49).

The Qur'an also advises the prophet Muhammad: "And if thou (Muhammad) art in doubt concerning that which we have revealed unto thee, then question those who read the Scripture (that was) before you" (Yunus 10:95).

Occasionally the Qur'an insists that God's Word cannot be corrupted. Here is an example of that kind of affirmation: "Messengers indeed have been denied before thee, and they were patient under the denial and the persecution till Our succor reached them. There is none to alter the decisions (or Word) of Allah. Already there hath reached thee (somewhat) of the tidings of the messengers (We sent before)" (Anam 6:34).

2. The People of the Book must respect and protect their scriptures.

There are admonitions for the Christians not to corrupt their scriptures, not to hide their scriptures or sell scripture for a profit, and not to misquote the scripture.

"And (remember) when Allah laid a charge on those who had received the Scripture (He said): Ye are to expound it to mankind and not to hide it" (Ali 'Imran 3:187).

"And lo! there is a party of them who distort the Scripture with their tongues, that you may think that what they say is from the Scriptures, when it is not from the Scripture. And they say: It is from Allah, when it is not from Allah; and they speak a lie concerning Allah knowingly" (Ali 'Imran 3:78).

"O People of the Scripture! Why confound ye truth with falsehood and knowingly conceal the truth?" (Ali 'Imran 3:71).

"Therefore woe be unto those who write the Scripture with their hands and then say, 'This is from Allah,' that they may purchase a small gain therewith. Woe unto them for that their hands have written, and woe unto them for that they earn thereby" (Baqara 2:79).

Of course, the Qur'an is clear about one matter: It is the final revelation and clarifies all former scriptures. Nevertheless, the Qur'an commands Muslims to go to those who have the former scriptures and ask their counsel.

"I invite you to do that," I encouraged a Muslim colleague in a public debate at a university. "Don't accuse Christians of corrupting their scriptures. Rather sit with us and listen to the witness of the Bible, just as the Qur'an commands."

"Yes, but remember, the Qur'an also warns us not to necessarily accept your counsel, because you might deceive us Muslims," my colleague responded.

He was right. Muslims are commanded to go to the Christians and ask them for clarification from their scriptures. Muslims are also commanded to be careful lest Christians lead them from the true faith of Islam. That ambivalence runs deeply within any conversation in regard to the message of the Bible.

"Are there any Muslim theologians who are biblical scholars?" participants asked a Muslim academic who was presenter at a German Anabaptist dialogue with Islam.

"I have never heard of any such Muslim," was the response.

Neither have Muslim universities developed serious biblical or Christian studies departments. This contrasts with a number of Christian universities that have developed noteworthy departments of Islamic and qur'anic studies. There are also Christians who have become highly respected qur'anic scholars; some of them are occasionally invited by Muslims to address them on the meaning of Islam.

Why these differences? The next chapter explores the themes of *tanzil* (sent-down truth) and incarnation, which might be relevant to this question.

Different Understandings of Scripture

"David has clearly stated that the Bible is not the Word of God," my Muslim dialogue colleague proclaimed to the several hundred who had crammed into a mosque in downtown London.

I had said that the personality, idiom, and experience of the writers of biblical scripture are part of the content of biblical revelation.

"The Qur'an has no human cultural or personality influences. It is the pure sent-down word of God," my colleague elaborated.

Our topic for the evening was "Revelation in Scripture." The three hours of dialogue were indeed intense. We agreed that both Muslims and Christians believe in revelation in scripture. Then what? Here are some of the different themes we met that night and meet whenever Muslims and Christians share from their understandings of scripture.

> Biblical: Scripture is revealed incarnationally.
> Qur'anic: Scripture is revealed as sent down (*tanzil*).

> Biblical: God reveals himself in personal encounter.
> Qur'anic: God reveals his will through the prophets.

> Biblical: Scripture is contingent revelation; that is, human action affects God and his response to us.
> Qur'anic: Scripture is noncontingent revelation; that is, human action does not affect God.

> Biblical: The soul of biblical revelation is the acts of God in history.
> Qur'anic: Scriptural revelation transcends history. The allusions to historical events in the Qur'an are parables or illustrations.

> Biblical: The prophets and biblical writers are carried along by the Spirit of God as they interpret the meaning of the acts of God. So revelation is not only the acts of God, but the Spirit-inspired interpretation of those acts. Sometimes the writers "saw" or "heard" the Word of God or the Word was put in their mouths.
> Qur'anic: The prophets through whom scripture is revealed are a mouthpiece through whom revelation comes.

> Biblical: Scripture also includes our story, the human response to the acts of God and the prophetic message. Human rejection of God is part of the content of the biblical accounts.
> Qur'anic: Scripture is only the revealed sent-down Word of God. Any scriptures that include the human story or response are, therefore, corrupted scripture. *Sunnah* (descriptions of the life of a prophet) are not part of revealed scripture.

> Biblical: Scriptures are translatable in the languages and idiom of people everywhere.
> Qur'anic: The Qur'an is an Arabic Qur'an. It can be interpreted into other languages and idiom, but it is only Qur'an in Arabic.

> Biblical: Scripture is dialogical, an "I-thou" encounter and response.
> Qur'anic: Scripture is monologue—God sends down his guidance, and we are commanded to submit to that guidance.

> Gospel: The central event of the Bible is Jesus the Messiah. He is the Word of God incarnate in human form. The Bible finds its fullest meaning and interpretation in the light of Jesus the Messiah.

Islam: The Qur'an is the final revelation of God's guidance for all humankind. It summarizes and clarifies all the former scriptures.

Gospel: The message of the Bible is so astonishing that one can only receive and believe this good news through the revelation of the Holy Spirit.

Islam: The message of the Qur'an is so natural and logical that through rational thinking a person will be Muslim. In fact we are all born Muslim, for Islam is fully in harmony with human nature.

The Messiah: The miracle of God's Word incarnate
The Qur'an: The miracle of God's Word sent down

Muslims and Christians converge in their mutual belief in revelation in scripture. Nevertheless, even within that agreement, we are often surprised at the divergences. However, the differences need not become a wall. It is vital for Christians and Muslims to engage one another in scripture-based dialogue and witness.

Christians will discover that Muslims often have a cautious intrigue in the Bible precisely because the Bible is so different than the Qur'an. Especially captivating are the biblical historical narratives; so is Jesus the Messiah. Although the historical narratives are a perplexity for multitudes of Muslims like Ibrahim, yet these very same characteristics of the Bible are intriguing, winsome, and inviting for many Muslims.

Readings from the Bible:
    Genesis 3:1-20
Readings from the Qur'an:
    Ta-Ha 20:9-24

Questions for Reflection and Discussion:
    1. The qur'anic reference to Moses at the burning bush has significant parallels to the biblical account. How might this event provide a basis for dialogue between Muslims and Christians on the theme of how God relates to people (Gen. 3:1-20; Ta-Ha 20:9-24)?
    2. Ibrahim was perplexed because, unlike the Qur'an, the Bible was mostly a history. How do those differences reveal different understandings of revelation and God's relationship with us (Gen. 3:8-10, 15; Baqara 2:38)?

3. Explain the reason no Muslim would pray, "My God," but rather pray "in the name of God." Reflect on the reason Christians pray, "My God or our Father God" (Al-Fatiha 1:1-7; Matt. 6:9-13).

4. Suggest ways Christians might respond to Muslim concerns that the Bible is corrupted.

5. Note the biblical scriptures that the Qur'an especially mentions (Ali 'Imran 3:3; Maida 5:47-49). How might these scriptures provide a basis for Muslim and Christian conversation concerning faith?

— 7 —

Revelation:
Tanzil—Incarnation

A Middle East Christian told me, "Christians and Muslims in my community have excellent relations. Whenever faith slips into our conversation, we turn our backs to one another and walk away."

Why does that happen? Why is it so difficult to listen to one another? Why are we afraid to share our witness? Is it because the truth claims of the Muslims trouble Christians? Is it because Muslims are disturbed by the truth center embraced by the Christians?

A Muslim professor once illustrated different understandings of truth within the Muslim *ummah* and the Christian church. First, he placed the Qur'an on top of his clenched fist. He explained, "My fist represents Muhammad. For Muslims, the Qur'an transcends Muhammad. The Qur'an is the sent-down truth that transcends all history and all prophets. All truth is clarified in the Qur'an."

Then, he placed his fist on top of the Bible. "My fist now represents Jesus the Messiah. For Christians, the Bible points toward Jesus who is the truth; he is the fulfillment of the biblical scriptures. He is the incarnation of truth, the incarnation of God. Ultimate truth finds its fulfillment in the Messiah and the total biblical witness concerning the Messiah."

Often after an evening of conversation in a mosque, I comment, "Our discussion has revolved around questions of truth centers. Christians confess that Jesus the Messiah is the incarnation of truth. Muslims tonight have given witness to their conviction that the Qur'an is the criterion of all truth that God has sent down upon humanity. These questions are always with us when we meet as Muslims and Christians. What we believe about life and God is wrapped up in our responses to these two questions: Who is the Messiah? What is the Qur'an?"

Revelation as *Tanzil*

The Muslim understanding of revelation is that it is sent down by God; the Qur'an is the final sent-down revelation. That is the meaning of *tanzil*: "sent down." Throughout the eras of human history, that is the way God has always revealed his guidance to humanity, through sending down his instructions through prophets to his vicegerents on earth. The Qur'an is the final and clarifying revelation, and, of course, it is *tanzil* revelation, just as has been true of all other revelations. That is the foundational belief of the Muslim *ummah*.

This understanding is consistent with the Islamic belief that there is the Mother of the Book in the heavens, inscribed on a guarded tablet. That heavenly book is the Qur'an which reveals God's unchangeable and eternal will. Adam was the first prophet upon whom God sent down guidance. That guidance instructed Adam on the ways he should live as God's vicegerent on earth. Later, God sent other portions of that guidance down in books: the Torah, Psalms, Gospel, and finally the Qur'an.

Muslims revel in their claims of proof that the Qur'an is God's sent-down revelation. The proof: it is inimitable (*i'jaz*).[1] That is to say that the miracle of the Qur'an cannot be imitated; this is the declaration of the Qur'an and the Muslims (Baqara [The Cow] 2:23). When detractors challenged the truth of Muhammad's qur'anic recitations, he threw the challenge right back to them: reproduce even a small portion of the miraculous Arabic alliteration and rhythm that comprises the Qur'an. None could replicate it. In modern times Muslims submit the Arabic Qur'an to computer analysis. They describe linguistic and alliteration patterns that are remarkable and that they claim cannot be duplicated; the Qur'an is *i'jaz*.

Other Muslims speak of the scientific insights of the Qur'an.

They perceive that the Qur'an anticipated dimensions of modern scientific discoveries. All of this, Muslims proclaim, is proof that the Qur'an is indeed *tanzil* revelation: It is miraculous, it predicts modern discoveries, it is in harmony with science.

The doctrine of *tanzil* demands that believers preserve revelation from corruption. What is corruption? Is it the human dimension that would consist of corruption? Although Muhammad sought the counsel of others, the doctrine of inimitability means that the Qur'an that he recited had no imprint of external human influence. The Qur'an was uncorrupted; it transcended all human influence (Yunus [Jonah] 10:37-38). The Qur'an is sent down upon humanity; it is not influenced by humanity.

Badru D. Kateregga, a former professor of Islamics in Nairobi writes:

> Revelation which is contained in scriptures or divine books is the true guidance sent down (*tanzil*) directly from God. It is God's Word revealed to chosen prophets. Gifted personalities as the prophets were, their lives and histories did not form part of the divine message or scriptural message.[2]

Revelation as Incarnation

Incarnation is a biblical understanding of revelation; this is in contrast to *tanzil*. Incarnation means "in the flesh"; it refers to revelation that is clothed in the human.

The last chapter observed that when Muslims consider the human dimension of the Bible, the inclination is to conclude that these scriptures are corrupted. If corruption means anything that pertains to the human, then indeed the biblical scriptures are corrupted. All biblical revelation includes the imprint of the human. It is clothed in human idiom, personality, culture, and thought patterns. It is in-history revelation.

In biblical faith it is the advent of Jesus the Messiah who is the fullest expression of God's in-history revelation. God sent his one and only Son into the world (John 3:16). That Son was Jesus of Nazareth, a Jewish carpenter. God in the Messiah is clothed within the "corruption" of humanity.

In the Gospel according to John, the eternal truth of God is called the Word. This refers to God's full self-expression—the

Word through whom he created the universe. Jesus of Nazareth, the Messiah, is the incarnation of this Word.

The Gospel declares:

> In the beginning was the Word, and the Word was with God, and the Word was God. He was with God in the beginning. . . . The Word became flesh [in Jesus of Nazareth] and lived for a while among us. We have seen his glory, the glory of the one and only Son, who came from the Father, full of grace and truth (John 1:1-2, 14).

The Bible proclaims that people are created in God's image. In our sinfulness and rebellion, that image is distorted. God in the Messiah restores the image of God among us that was tragically distorted when the first Adam and Eve turned away from God. Adam and Eve, the parents of us all, turned in directions that have brought death. Nevertheless, God incarnate in the Messiah is the revelation of the full restoration of our true humanity as the image of God creation. He is the new Adam.

We are corrupted by our sinfulness. Nevertheless, in the Messiah, God has entered our corrupted humanity so that he might redeem us from corruption. Through Adam the corruption of sin and death has spread throughout the human race, but in Jesus, God has entered the human race. Through his presence, righteousness and new life spreads within the human race as people respond in faith, repentance, and commitment to Jesus, the new Adam.

The biblical scriptures make the point:

> For just as through the disobedience of the one man the many were made sinners, so also through the obedience of the one man the many will be made righteous (Rom. 5:19).

> For since death came through a man, the resurrection of the dead comes also through a man. For as in Adam all die, so in Christ all will be made alive (1 Cor. 15:21-22).

The Difficulty of Dialogue

Muslims believe that God in his sovereign power sends his merciful will down to us; Christians confess that in the Gospel, God in his sovereignty gives of himself in suffering love for us. This is the soul of the difference between a *tanzil* and an incarnation understanding of revelation.

This difference is evident when Christians and Muslims meet one another in dialogue. For Christians, revelation occurs within history. This means that the historical and cultural context wherein the scriptures were written is essential in understanding the biblical message. Furthermore, incarnational revelation is dialogical. The God who enters into our story both confronts us and also converses with us.

"Come now, let us reason together," says the Lord (Isa. 1:18).

Most Muslims find such notions impossible to apply to the Qur'an because they believe the Qur'an is *tanzil*. It transcends history. God does not invite dialogue; rather, in his compassion and mercy, he sends his perfect will down to us. We must submit. We never dialogue with God.

Here are examples of the difficulties Muslims and Christians meet when sharing their different commitments to God's revelation.

The Crucifixion

A central issue is the crucifixion of Jesus. The biblical witness is that Jesus was crucified. In contrast the Qur'an says, "they slew him not for certain" (Nisaa [Women] 4:157).

I have had scores of conversations with Muslims about the betrayal and crucifixion of Jesus. These conversants come from many societies and levels of education. However, I have never conversed with a Muslim who was open to considering the possibility that Jesus might have been crucified.

In a dialogue with a Muslim theologian, with several hundred university students present, I pressed the point. "About a third of each of the four gospel accounts in the New Testament relate to the crucifixion," I said. "There are multiple trustworthy eyewitness reports. There are both biblical and nonbiblical reports. The soul of the Christian Gospel is the crucifixion—is it wise to discredit all of that because of one sentence uttered by one man six hundred years after the event?"

The response: "The Qur'an has spoken. The Messiah was not crucified; the biblical accounts are corrupted."

The Human Dimension

Another issue is the imprint of the human in all biblical revelation. In a conversation with an academic Muslim colleague I observed, "In the Bible the personality and culture of the writer is included in the scriptural accounts. Paul writes like Paul and Peter like Peter."

My colleague responded, "You have just confessed openly that the biblical scriptures are indeed corrupted, that human personality and culture have contaminated the Word of God. The Qur'an has no such human distortions. Thanks be unto God!"

Transcendence and Power

Muslims are concerned that accepting that scriptures have an incarnational quality will subvert the sovereignty, transcendence, and power of God, as well as the integrity of his revealed will. Muslim theology assumes that a *tanzil* revelation protects the sovereignty and transcendence and power of God.

However, Christians ask Muslims, "Is a sent-down revelation the best way to preserve and express the power and the glory of God?"

"Yes!" is the Muslim reply.

However, is the vulnerability of the incarnation and the cross weakness? The witness of the church is that God incarnated and suffering is the power of God within and among us offering new and abundant life that transforms people and renews and sanctifies all creation.

Bishop Kenneth Cragg has invested much of his life engaged in dialogue with Muslims about this very question. He pleads for a more incarnational understanding of revelation. He has done this by unlocking the human and historical dimensions of the Qur'an and Muhammad's prophetic work. "Look!" he implores. "The Qur'an does include the imprint of the human."[3]

Cragg's hope has been that Muslims might thereby be more ready to hear from biblical incarnational revelation. Cragg has invested patient scholarship and passion in his commitment to commend to Muslims the biblical witness that God meets us within our human context, and supremely so in Jesus. However, his writings reveal some discouragement. Muslims find it difficult to imagine celebrating the touch of the human, cultural, and historical in revelation.[4]

History and Tanzil

Other Christian theologians plead with Muslims to apply the tools of historical, cultural, and critical study to the Qur'an. A respected Swiss Catholic theologian, Hans Kung, observes that it is not possible for Christians to enter into dialogue with Muslims unless there is more openness to a historical-critical approach to the Qur'an. He comments that this is the only way Christians and Muslims can meet one another in mutual dialogue concerning revealed truth.[5]

However, is it possible for a *tanzil* understanding of revelation to ever mesh with a historical-critical commitment? Isn't Kung imposing upon Muslims his understandings as a prerequisite for dialogue? If Christians wait to dialogue until Muslims change their approach to scriptures, will we ever meet in dialogue?

A scholar of Islam, Andrew Rippin, observes, "[U]sing history as a criterion of truth higher than the Qur'an [is] something which no Muslim could accept. . . . [Muslims fear that] watering down the doctrine of the noncontingent nature of the text too far will lead to no defense against claims that the entire basis of the religion may be false."[6]

It is more fruitful to recognize that *tanzil* and incarnation are different understandings of reality and revelation. The Qur'an communicates to the Muslim *ummah* a radically different view of revelation than the Bible communicates to the Christian church. Trying to impose *tanzil* upon biblical understandings or incarnation upon qur'anic understandings is fruitless and a distortion of what Islam and the Gospel are. Each faith gives witness from within these different understandings.

The divergence between *tanzil* and incarnation is quite evident indeed in the respective approaches to mission by the Muslim *ummah* and the Christian church. Both communities are inspired by their conviction that God has called them into a mission to all nations. Their respective scriptures convey the message that they proclaim: Islam or the Gospel. A brief survey of these different journeys in mission follows.

Tanzil and Mission

Muslims believe that God's final sent-down revelation is the Arabic Qur'an. It is, therefore, untranslatable. In any other language, it would cease to be Qur'an. Qur'anic interpretations might be written in other languages, but these are never Qur'an.

How does an Arabic Qur'an affect a Muslim approach to mission? There are significant implications for mission.

One of the most obvious implications is the role of the Arabic language in all Muslim worship. Here is an example, which is repeated in varied nuances hundreds of thousands of times around the world every year as people convert to Islam. Several dozen Christians had joined the Muslim congregation in the Islamic Way Mosque in Baltimore for an evening of conversation. At the conclusion of the evening prayers an old man approached the imam and said, "I want to become a Muslim."

Ripples of, "*Alhumdillah*" (praise be to God) came from the gathered worshipers.

The imam led the new believer through the Muslim confession of faith, in the Arabic language: *La Ilaha Illa'llah Muhammadan Rasulu'llah* (There is no god but Allah, and Muhammad is the apostle of Allah).

The imam proclaimed the man a Muslim and invited the congregation to receive him. He then told the man about the Arabic evening classes in the mosque. He informed the new believer that the Muslim scripture is the Arabic Qur'an, and that all ritual prayers are in Arabic. As a Muslim he would need to enroll in the Arabic school.

An Arabic Qur'an

Lamin Sanneh has written extensively on the relationship between the Arabic language and the mission of Islam. Sanneh grew up in a Muslim home in West Africa. As a young man he became a Christian. His noteworthy academic sojourn has taken him to Yale University Divinity School, where he teaches missiology. His doctoral research focused on Islam in West Africa.

Sanneh has explored the missionary implications of a *tanzil* understanding of qur'anic revelation. This makes it impossible to translate the Arabic Qur'an into local languages. The Qur'an is sometimes put into vernaculars; these are only interpretations of the Qur'an, but not the actual Qur'an. Therefore, wherever the Muslim *ummah* spreads, arabization must follow. Arabic language schools always accompany the mission of the Muslim nation.

Sanneh is quite forthright in his critique. He asserts that the Arabic Qur'an disempowers local culture.[7] The Arab Muslim missionary knows Arabic best, so how can the converts critique the person who is best able to read and understand the Qur'an? There is no local empowerment to critique the cultural imperialism of the Arab Muslim missionary movement.

Yet Islamization can be powerfully attractive. Participation in the powerful cohesion of the universal Arabic language of revelation bonds the new believer with other believers around the world. Whenever she bows in prayer she knows that she bows with hundreds of millions of other Muslims in submission to God's sent-down will. Knowing how to perform the Arabic *salat* is the sign of universal submission to the one will of God.

The Political Order

Respect for the authority of those most conversant with the Arabic of the Qur'an also influences the political order. A Muslim Indian scholar, Rafiq Zakaria, comments on the political dimension of the Muslim movement. Here are three themes extracted from his writing.

First, the role of the political order: "Again, in Islam a ruler, government, or state has to strictly follow Islam's ideology; the Prophet took over the government in order to propagate and nourish the faith."[8]

Second, the authority over the political order: According to a Muslim tradition, Muhammad once said, "An Arab has no superiority over a non-Arab or a non-Arab over an Arab."[9] A twentieth-century Pakistani reformer, Maududi, quoted this saying extensively in his efforts to free Muslim communities from an excessive reliance on arabization. Nevertheless, Zakaria observes that within the Muslim nation as a whole there has always been a strong tug toward giving special honor to those closest to the Arabic language and the Arabian people.[10]

The Muslim nation first emerged among a people, the Arab people, who had been marginalized by the civilizations that surrounded them. The Arabic Qur'an was a tremendous empowerment for these marginalized Arab peoples. In the course of time, however, the Arabic-centric revelation has become an authority that too easily marginalizes those Muslims who are not fully within an Arabic-centric culture. Not only has the movement been Arabic-centric, but the clan family of Muhammad, the Quraish, has always exercised considerable control over the Muslim nation as it spreads.[11] Throughout the centuries,

Muhammad's dictum to avoid an Arab-centric movement has been more easily idealized than practiced.[12]

Third, changing the political order: Zakaria further elaborates:

> Again the classical jurists are all confused about the removal of a ruler; when and how this should be done? Even when rulers were tyrannical, lazy, indolent, impious, and unfaithful to the dictates of religion, the *'ulama* [Muslim theologians/judges] by and large, did not suggest their removal. On the contrary most of them advised obedience, basing their opinion on the oft-quoted saying of the Prophet: "Obey those in authority over you."[13]

These three themes do not nurture democratic values. However, there is a process of *shura* (consultation) among the *'ulama* (experts in Islamic law). *Shura* has nuances of democratic consensus-building within the counsels of the *'ulama*; however, the role of the *'ulama* is to hand down decisions based on their expertise in Islamic law. This is different than democratic government by and for the people. Democratic movements within predominantly Muslim societies have looked elsewhere, not to Islam, for philosophical inspiration.[14]

"Islam is not democracy!" declared some Temple University Muslim students when I suggested that biblical faith encourages a worldview that has been fertile soil for democracy.

A sent-down revelation with a mandate that the Muslim nation must be a "witness against [over, to] mankind" (Baqara 2:143) has sometimes provided a basis for the military-political expansion of the Muslim nation. An African historian, John Alembillah Azumah, describes how this dimension of the Muslim mission has sometimes inspired wars in the African experience. Azumah observes that, especially in West Africa, the militarist approach of *jihad* (war for Islam) has been significant in the growth of the Muslim nation.[15] One might also observe that *jihadist* commitments have fueled the civil war in Sudan for most of the last quarter of the twentieth century. In these tragic circumstances, Christians and Muslims who are people of goodwill heroically struggle to build trusting relations. In times of violence, that calling to reconciliation can be a personally costly one indeed.

Other streams of Muslim missionary commitment emphasize peace-extension themes in the Qur'an as the basis for their missionary efforts. In regions such as East Africa or Indonesia the historic growth of the Muslim nation has been the gradual Islamization of societies through trade, immigration, or the peaceable orders of the Muslim mystics. Yet all Muslim mission, whether *jihadist* or peaceful, give witness: God has sent his will down and all people should submit to that will.

Critical Thinking

How does a *tanzil* understanding of revelation affect attitudes toward seeking truth? Chapter 3 touched that question in the discussion of the authority to "name the animals." A *tanzil* understanding of revelation is completely in harmony with the qur'anic assertion that God taught Adam the names of the animals. One of the dilemmas of commitment to revealed truth is how that relates to an open-minded investigation into truth. Both Christians and Muslims meet that question. However, is there a difference in the way Christians and Muslims approach that question—the difference between a *tanzil* and an incarnation understanding of God and revelation?

A modernist Muslim philosopher, Shabbir Akhtar, comments on his frustration in encouraging open inquiry among Malaysian university students. Akhtar's fellow Muslim intellectual colleagues counseled him: "Believers . . . [have] nothing new to learn. Western free inquiry is aimless. Besides what is the point of free inquiry if God has already revealed to us the whole truth?"[16]

Akhtar challenges his fellow Muslim academics, "How can a modern university thrive within that kind of an intellectual straightjacket?"[17]

He is pushing the borders of Muslim thought, encouraging a much more open spirit of free inquiry. It is a lonely journey sometimes. Can the tensions surrounding a *tanzil* understanding of revealed truth and free inquiry be resolved?

Incarnation and Mission

Now we embark on a brief reflection on the Christian journey in mission that incarnation invites. On the Pentecost birthday of the church, the people throughout Jerusalem were astonished when they heard the disciples of Jesus preaching because "we hear them declaring the wonders of God in our own tongues!" (Acts 2:11). More than a dozen languages are specifically mentioned. This biblical account says that God miraculously assured that every person would receive the Gospel within her own language and culture.

Translating the Bible

Beginning from that Pentecost event, from the very beginning of the Christian movement, the church in mission sought to make the biblical message available within local languages. What is the reason behind this compulsion of the church to translate the Bible into local languages? It is anchored in the incarnation. The message of the Gospel is that Jesus the Messiah is the One who is God with us. In the Messiah, God is incarnated within a person, within a particular culture, language, society, and nation. In fact, as stated above, all biblical revelation is incarnational. God expresses his self-revelation in human idiom. He meets us within our situation, and supremely, fully, and definitively so in Jesus the Messiah.

This means the incarnated Gospel critiques all cultural imperialism. For example, although the New Testament was written first in Greek, by translating the scriptures into Egyptian languages, the same Gospel became incarnated within the Egyptian experience as it did in the Greek people. The Gospel incarnated within Greek culture was not closer to the truth nor superior to the Gospel incarnated within Egyptian culture. Neither did the Greeks have the authority to dominate the Egyptian Christians. (Sadly, sometimes the church in one culture has dominated churches in an alien culture, but this is contrary to the nature of the incarnated Gospel.)

It is noteworthy that for many years the church in Europe departed dramatically from a vulnerable incarnated Gospel. One way the medieval Roman Catholic Church in Europe dominated people was by using only Latin Bibles. These scriptures could not be understood or incarnated among the peasantry.

Then, in the late fifteenth century the invention of printing and the publication of Bibles in vernacular European languages helped to unleash freedom movements across Europe. Bible study groups flourished across Europe, and the Gospel became incarnated within reborn Christian fellowships here and there across the continent. The Protestant Reformation and the Anabaptist movement were results of that sixteenth-century Bible study movement.

Today the phenomenon of Bibles in the languages of people is worldwide. Portions of the Bible have been translated into some three thousand languages, and more than 95 percent of the people on earth have at least a portion of the Bible in their mother tongue.

Empowerment

Translating the Bible into local idiom empowers a people to read and hear the Bible, to welcome the Messiah, and to embrace the Gospel within their own culture. Even the illiterate can hear the word of God read in worship, as well as worship and pray in his or her own language. Those who believe in the Messiah clothe the Gospel within their own idiom. That is profoundly empowering. That is the local church, a community committed to Jesus the Messiah and a community with deep roots in local culture.

Lamin Sanneh observes that this empowerment cuts two ways. First, the newly formed church is empowered to critique the cultural imperialism of the missionaries. Second, the church is empowered to critique evils within their own culture. Either way, translating the Bible into the local language enables the Gospel to become incarnated within the local culture; that incarnation empowers the church to be the salt that transforms from within the culture.[18]

Incarnation and Culture

The translation of the Bible into a local language quite frequently contributes powerfully to the renaissance of local culture and society. For hundreds of societies around the world, the Bible is the first book available in their native language. People want to read that book, so they begin schools. The language and culture are renewed as people gain a new sense of pride in their language and culture.

"After all, God is speaking within our own language," they say. "That is something to celebrate!"

However, it is not just the Bible that the church in mission makes available. For example, in the modern African experience, the church in mission has contributed very significantly to the transformation, preservation, and renaissance of African culture. Secular education, community development, the scientific revolution, medical programs, and public health were all pioneered by the church in mission in the African experience. Furthermore, the biblical insistence that the person is created in God's image, that God loves and respects each person, that God honors the freedom of the person, that tyrannical authorities stand under the judgment of God and should be transformed—these themes have provided the values that are necessary for developing democratic institutions and government.[19]

In India it is a Protestant missionary, William Carey (d. 1834), who is recognized as the father of Indian vernacular languages. Why? He and his team developed schools to teach literacy in the vernacular languages. And they published books in the vernacular languages—on subjects as different as the Hindu scriptures or botany or agriculture or history or biology, and, of course, the Bible.[20]

Prior to the Christian mission movement in modern India, the only languages considered to be significant enough for literacy were the Sanskrit of the Hindu scriptures, the Arabic of the Qur'an, the English of the British East India Company, and a couple Indian languages used in British administration. In contrast, the church in mission believed otherwise. Carey and his team developed the first liberal arts university in Asia, the Serampore Christian College. One of the goals of the college was to train teachers who would develop vernacular schools in language groups across India. Every language is precious! Every person should have the opportunity to read in her mother tongue.[21]

Vulnerability

The incarnated Gospel is always vulnerable. It is never coercive. The Gospel invites, it never forces. The Gospel sows seeds of respect, love, and freedom; the Gospel critiques all that is unjust and dehumanizing. The faithful church is the community of incarnation, in which the life of the Messiah is present for grace and ministry. That ministry of the Messiah is expressed in loving service and witness. This "truth" is vulnerable. That is what the Messiah crucified reveals.

What is truth? Can a person control or enforce truth? How does an incarnated Gospel respond to the open-minded critical thinking that disturbed Professor Shabbir Akhtar's students as described above? This is not a trivial question. Both Muslims and Christians struggle with the tensions between a commitment to revelation and the open-ended search for truth that characterizes the academy. Can truth be vulnerable and yet prevail, or must it be defended against all detractors?

William Carey believed that the Gospel frees and empowers; it needs witnesses but not defensiveness. Therefore, in the liberal arts college at Serampore, students were encouraged to range widely in their studies. Even Sanskrit and Hinduism were lively subjects. The Gospel was also presented. Students were invited to think critically, investigate, and come to their own decisions about the truth claims of the Gospel within the context of a free market of ideas.

Was Carey right in his approach?

The journeys of both Muslims and Christians present the dilemma: how does one reconcile a commitment to revealed truth with a commitment to open inquiry and critical thinking? The two journeys are guided by different understandings of revelation: *tanzil* and incarnation. What difference does that make?

Readings from the Bible:
    John 1:1-5, 14
Readings from the Qur'an:
    Iqraa 96:1-5

Questions for Reflection and Discussion:
    1. Consider examples you are aware of wherein people use their beliefs in "truth" in destructive ways.
    2. Both the *ummah* and the church are committed to revealed truth. Give reasons that the dialogue about revealed truth between Muslims and Christians is so very difficult.
    3. How might a *tanzil* understanding of revelation affect the stance of the Muslim *ummah* toward local culture? How might an incarnational understanding of revelation affect the stance of the Christian church towards local culture (Acts 2:5-12; Yusuf 12:2)?
    4. Account for the fact that the church in mission has translated portions of the Bible into a couple thousand languages while

the *ummah* in mission uses Arabic scriptures (Matt. 1:23; Nahl 16:103; Al-Burooj 85:21-22).

5. Critical thinking and commitment to open investigation are central commitments of the modern Western university. What are the challenges that this kind of university presents to a community committed to the Qur'an? To the Bible?

— 8 —

Power:
the *Hijrah*—the Cross

"**O**UR Muslim friends will reject this book," colleagues warned.

A team of us were developing the *People of God* study course for Muslims. I had just completed a draft of the biblical account of Noah and the flood. I was confident that Muslims would be delighted to learn more about Noah; an event that the Qur'an refers to.

The advisory writing team included about half a dozen disciples of Jesus the Messiah who were from Muslim background. The concern of the team bewildered me.

"What is so offensive about this account?" I asked.

The team quoted this biblical verse, "The Lord was grieved that he had made man on the earth, and his heart was filled with pain" (Gen. 6:6).

"Why is that statement offensive?" I was surprised.

"Don't you understand?" the team was now perplexed by my lack of understanding. "In Islam God is never affected by what we do. He is sovereign and all powerful. God is never sorry because of us!"

We had encountered the great divide between Islam and the Gospel. Both celebrate the power of God. Islam proclaims that the all-powerful God cannot suffer for us. The Gospel proclaims that our all-powerful God has chosen to suffer for us.

This chapter explores this ultimate divergence between the

Gospel and Islam. The exploration follows two journeys that go in opposite directions: the *hijrah* and the cross. The *hijrah* is Muhammad's journey from Mecca to Medina. The cross is the culmination of the journey of Jesus from Galilee to Jerusalem where he was crucified. The difference between the *hijrah* and the cross reveal a watershed understanding of the nature of God, understandings that are at the heart of the meaning of Islam and the center of the Gospel. Does God suffer for us and with us? The different Islamic and gospel answers to that question form the nature of the Muslim nation and the Christian church.

First we reflect on the journey of Jesus to Jerusalem and the cross; then the *hijrah* of Muhammad to Medina. What do these journeys communicate about our beliefs concerning the nature of God and his kingdom?

Jesus Journeyed to Jerusalem

Jesus was in Galilee in northern Israel. He was joyful. Peter had confessed that he and the disciples believed. "You are the Christ, the Son of the living God," Peter said.

With genuine gratefulness, Jesus exclaimed, "Blessed are you, Simon son of Jonah, for this was not revealed to you by man, but my Father in heaven. And I tell you that you are Peter, and on this rock I will build my church, and the gates of Hades will not overcome it" (Matt. 16:17-18).

Not only were Jesus' disciples persuaded that he was the Messiah, he was also very popular among the Galilean people. In fact, he was at the height of his popularity, after feeding five thousand men plus women and children. He fed this multitude through the miraculous multiplication of five loaves of bread and two small fish. The people were amazed. They asked him to become their king.

At that time some Galileans were waging an underground war against their Roman rulers. These were the Zealots. With Jesus as their king, they would have no further problems providing food for their soldiers, for Jesus could miraculously multiply food daily for their whole army. The Galileans were ready to use force to make Jesus become their king (John 6:15).

Jesus refused the offer to become their king; instead he slipped away from the clamor and went into the mountains where he spent the night in prayer. From that time on he "resolutely" set his face toward Jerusalem (Luke 9:51). He knew that in Jerusalem he would be crucified. He told his disciples that in Jerusalem people would take the Son of Man and "mock him, insult him, spit on him, flog him and kill him. On the third day he will rise again" (Luke 18:32-33). Nevertheless, he pressed on in the resolute journey south to that city.

The disciples of Jesus believed that he was the Messiah. They did not and could not believe that he would be crucified. A crucified Messiah was utter nonsense. On one occasion, Peter forthrightly rebuked Jesus for talking about crucifixion.

Jesus was very sharp in his response to Peter, "Out of my sight, Satan! You are a stumbling block to me; you do not have in mind the things of God, but the things of men" (Matt. 16:23).

In Jerusalem, Jesus was indeed arrested and condemned to death on a cross. At that time Jesus declared that he could call for twelve legions of angels (Matt. 26:53). That would be an army of seventy-two thousand angels! However, Jesus would not ask for either human or angelic help to deliver him from the cross.

The arresting officers took him to Pilate's hall for one of his two trials. Pilate was the Roman governor. In that judgment hall, Jesus exclaimed, "My kingdom is not of this world. If it were, my servants would fight to prevent my arrest by the Jews. But now my kingdom is from another place" (John 18:36).

Before his crucifixion Jesus was tortured and mocked. They spit in his face. They placed a crown of thorns on his head. They beat him with a metal-tipped whip. They blindfolded him and mocked him. Then they nailed his hands and feet to the cross, and he was crucified between two thieves. Even as he was dying, the derisive mockery continued.

As he neared death, he cried out, "Father, forgive them, for they do not know what they are doing" (Luke 23:34).

Then his last words: "It is finished" (John 19:30).

> At that moment the curtain in the temple was torn in two from the top to bottom. The earth shook and the rocks split. The tombs broke open and the bodies of many holy people who had died were raised to life (Matt. 27:51-52).

To be absolutely sure that Jesus had died, a soldier thrust a spear into his side. Water and blood poured from the wound.

Friends buried him in a nearby tomb. They placed a large stone over the tomb; the authorities sealed the tomb and placed guards to be sure no one would steal his body. Nevertheless, God sent heavenly messengers who rolled the stone away. This was the third day after his death, on the first day of the week. Several women came to the tomb early on the morning of his resurrection, and they discovered that his tomb was empty. God had raised Jesus the Messiah from the dead!

During the next forty days, the Gospel accounts describe the risen Jesus appearing occasionally to his disciples. There were at least eleven appearances; on one occasion he appeared to at least five hundred people. In a number of those appearances he showed his skeptical disciples his nail-scarred hands and feet.

Here is a description of one of the appearances of the resurrected Jesus:

> On the evening of that first day of the week, when the disciples were together, with the doors locked for fear of the Jews, Jesus came and stood among them and said, "Peace be with you!" After he said this, he showed them his hands and side. The disciples were overjoyed when they saw the Lord.
>
> Again Jesus said, "Peace be with you! As the Father has sent me, I am sending you." And with that he breathed on them and said, "Receive the Holy Spirit" (John 20:19-21).

Muhammad Migrated to Medina

About six centuries later, Muhammad began preaching in Mecca in the heartland of Arabia. He claimed that his messages were revelations from an angelic messenger. For twelve years he proclaimed portions of the Qur'an as they came to him. He preached and he warned the Meccans to leave their polytheistic worship, evil practices, and injustices.

Muhammad's reward was derision. His life was often under threat. On at least one occasion he was stoned; some people threw garbage at him. Very few believed in him or his message. Those who did believe were sometimes tortured, and a few were killed. Others fled to Ethiopia as refugees.[1] The movement was struggling seriously.

If God was sovereign, why did the Muslim believers suffer? If God was all powerful, why was the life of the prophet under threat? If Islam was the will of God, why was it impossible to establish a Muslim *ummah* that submitted to Islam? Such questions touched the Muslims of Mecca with perplexity and even doubt. These questions take us into the soul of the nature of God and his relationship to humanity.

Although the Meccan experience was filled with overwhelming challenges and touched with theological perplexities, there were two migrations that gave the Muslim movement and Muhammad great encouragement: the *mi'raj* and the *hijrah*.

The *mi'raj* is touched with mystery. According to Muslim traditions, this mysterious migration commences with a night flight from Mecca to Jerusalem. The journey has two phases. First is the *isra'* wherein Muhammad is whisked from Mecca to Jerusalem on a winged horse-like animal called *al Buraq*. When they arrive in Jerusalem, the second phase of the migration commences: the *mi'raj*, as Muhammad is carried up into the seventh heaven.[2]

The *mi'raj* has added to the significance of Jerusalem and the Temple Mount within the Muslim nation. As noted in the introduction, for Muslims the Temple Mount is Al-Aqsa, the farthest point that Muhammad went from Mecca in this miraculous travel. Although there is only an allusion to the *mi'raj* in the Qur'an (Bani Israil [The Children of Israel] 17:1), Muslim traditions recorded later elaborate; this miracle gave Muhammad courage.

The other migration, the *hijrah* is of even greater practical significance. In the midst of the Meccan difficulties, good news came to Muhammad from Yathreb (later called Medina). Medina was 250 miles north of Mecca. The Medina town fathers invited Muhammad and his followers to migrate from Mecca to Medina. They offered Muhammad the authority to govern their city; they needed help because of factional strife within Medina.

Muhammad and several hundred Meccan Muslims secretly accepted the invitation from Medina. The year was 622, twelve years after Muhammad began preaching in Mecca. The migration proceeded secretly over several months. When Muhammad arrived in Medina on September 24, many of the town residents celebrated. At that time Medina was experiencing strife; they hoped that Muhammad would establish peace.

In Medina, Muhammad the prophet also became Muhammad the statesman and military general.[3] With these instruments of political power, Muhammad and his fellow Muslims established the Muslim *ummah*. In Medina, the Muslim community became the beginning of the Muslim nation that has spread around the world.

This migration is known as the *hijrah*. This event is the beginning of the Muslim era. It is significant that the Muslim era does not begin with Muhammad's birth in A.D 570. Neither does it commence with the first revelations on Mount Hira in 610. No, the era begins with the migration from suffering and powerlessness in Mecca to the triumph and power of Medina.

Muslims believe that event was further evidence that Muhammad was indeed a prophet of God. With the instruments of political and military power under his control, Muhammad and the Muslim movement could succeed. Muslims believe that this success proved that the Islam he proclaimed and the prophethood that he claimed was indeed of God. The Qur'an elaborates:

> And when those who disbelieve plot against thee (O Muhammad) to wound thee fatally, or to kill thee or to drive thee forth; they plot, but Allah (also) plotteth; and Allah is the best of plotters (Anfal [The Spoils of War] 8:30).

This is to say that Allah will rectify suffering, which is an aberration to be corrected. The Medina experience was a dramatic correction to the aberrations of Mecca; now the Muslims could triumph, and that is the normal way for those who submit to God.

Journeys in Opposite Directions

Jesus the Messiah and Muhammad the prophet of Islam traveled in opposite directions. The Messiah turned his back on the invitation to become a king with an army; instead he resolutely set his face to go to Jerusalem and the cross. Muhammad welcomed the invitation to become governor and left suffering in Mecca for Medina and political power.

These different journeys provide the ethical foundations for the Christian church and the Muslim nation.

The way of the cross is the way of Christian ethics. The biblical scriptures remind Christians of the call of God to walk in the way of the Messiah in his crucifixion.

> To this you were called, because Christ suffered for you, leaving you an example, that you should follow in his steps. "He com-

mitted no sin, and no deceit was found in his mouth." When
they hurled insults at him, he did not retaliate; when he suffered, he made no threats. Instead, he entrusted himself to him
who judges justly (1 Pet. 2:21-23).

The way of the *hijrah* and the subsequent developments in
Medina significantly form Muslim understandings of ethics. The
Qur'an commands violence against the enemy when necessary.

> Fight in the way of Allah against those who fight against you,
> but begin not hostilities. Lo! Allah loveth not aggressors. And
> slay them wherever ye find them, and drive them out of the
> places whence they drove you out, for persecution is worse
> than slaughter. . . . But if they desist, then, lo! Allah is Forgiving,
> Merciful. And fight them on until persecution is no more, and
> religion is for Allah. But if they desist, then let there be no hos-
> tility except against wrong-doers (Baqara [The Cow] 2:190-93).

The issues of the sovereignty and power of God are fundamental in these two journeys that go in opposite directions.

In the Gospel, the Messiah chooses the path of vulnerable suffering. In his very nature he is God. Yet he chose to come to earth.
He became a man. He humbled himself. He became a servant. He
became obedient. He was crucified on the cross.

> Therefore God exalted him to the highest place and gave him
> the name that is above every name, that at the name of Jesus
> every knee should bow, in heaven and on earth and under the
> earth, and every tongue confess that Jesus Christ is Lord, to the
> glory of God the Father (Phil. 2:9-11).

In Islam the success that the *hijrah* provided for Muhammad
is foundational to the Muslim *ummah*'s understanding of the way
God's rule prospers on earth. Political and coercive power are
required in order for God's will to triumph. Vulnerability does
not befit the people who submit to the will God. It is for this reason that Muslims believe that the cross cannot be; the Messiah
could never experience a crucifixion.

A Muslim Defense of the Messiah

In Medina, it is likely that Muhammad encountered Jewish
people who asserted that the Messiah promised in their Jewish

scriptures could never be crucified. That is one of the reasons the Jewish people rejected any notion that Jesus was the Messiah. In line with their convictions about this, the Jewish people in Medina opposed the Muslim claim that Jesus is the Messiah. Jesus cannot be the Messiah, the Jews insisted. He was crucified.

The last chapter commented on the Muslim denial of the crucifixion of Jesus (Nisaa [Women] 4:157). This verse was proclaimed in the context of Muslim conflict with the Jews of Medina. Muhammad differed with the Jews: Jesus was the Messiah—and he was *never* crucified.

God is sovereign and all powerful. Therefore, he would never ever let the Messiah be crucified. Just as God rescued Muhammad from the ignominy of suffering in Mecca, so God also rescued the Messiah from the cross. God sent an illusion; someone else died in his place while God miraculously raised the Messiah to heaven, from which he will return sometime to prepare the earth for the final judgment. God rescued the Messiah from the suffering and ignominy of the cross.

The Muslim *ummah* denies that Jesus was crucified as a way of defending that he is the Messiah. Nevertheless, in that Islamic defense of the Messiah, Islam has turned away from the center and wonder of the Gospel. The denial of the cross runs deep within the soul of the Muslim *ummah*.

The Offense of the Cross

Once I commented to an erudite Muslim theologian-scholar, "As I see it, the qur'anic verses that related to the crucifixion, death, and resurrection of Jesus have some ambivalence about them. Would it be possible for an imaginative exegesis to open the door for a possible Muslim reconsideration of the crucifixion of Jesus?"

He responded, "That is an interesting observation, and that might be possible as far as the qur'anic verse is concerned. However, our Muslim denial of the crucifixion of the Messiah is not just a response to one verse. Rather it is rooted in Muslim theology. Glory cannot suffer."

Christians experience that denial of the cross again and again in their conversations with Muslims. Commenting on this reality, Tarif Khalidi observes in his book, *The Muslim Jesus*, "Unlike the canonical Gospels, the Qur'an tilts backward to his miraculous birth rather than forward to his passion."[4]

Two conversations held on opposite sides of the world will further illustrate this.

In the mid-1980s I joined several Christian theologians for a day of dialogue with Muslim theologians in the "God Box" on Riverside Drive in New York City. The God Box is a nickname for the imposing, box-shaped headquarters of the National Council of Churches. Our guests were Rev. Don McCurry, who directed the Samuel Zwemmer Institute, and Dr. Abdul Rauf, who directed the Islamic Center in Washington, D.C.

Late in the day, Dr. Abdul Rauf asked, "Do you really believe Jesus the Messiah was crucified?"

We responded, "Yes. In the Messiah crucified we meet the fullest revelation of God's suffering, self-giving love for humanity."

With pain etching his face, this gentle Muslim scholar commented, "How can that be? The Messiah crucified suggests that God is vulnerable. That is impossible."

Six months later I was visiting a remote village in Bangladesh. During an evening lantern-lighted gathering with illiterate Muslim peasants, I asked, "Do you have any questions you would like me to comment on as your Christian guest?"

"Yes," they responded quite eagerly. "We have heard it said that Christians believe the Messiah was crucified. What a strange notion that would be. Do you believe that?"

"Yes, I do," I replied.

"That is impossible," my hosts said. "God is sovereign. The Messiah could never suffer in that way."

These were two conversations on opposite sides of the world, one with theologians with doctorates and the other with illiterate peasants. Yet the stumbling block of the cross was at the center of both.

Seeking Peace

Although the Muslim *ummah* denies the crucifixion of Jesus the Messiah, there are some Muslims who are intrigued by the cross. Noteworthy is the book by Muhammad Kamil Husain, *The City of Wrong,* in which he reflects with considerable insight into the spiritual and political powers that unleashed the hatred toward Jesus that led to his arrest and trial. Yet, in the end, amidst the confusing darkness, Jesus escaped![5]

In a four-day dialogue I had in Germany with a Shi'ite Muslim, she commented that she is intrigued by the notion that in the cross the ideals of Jesus were crucified. Yet, she insisted, Jesus himself was most certainly never crucified.

Some Muslim movements do recognize suffering as a consequence of faithfulness to Islam. Nonviolent pacifism is a faith stream in some West African Muslim movements.[6] Some of the *sufi* (mystical) movements in Islam are influenced by themes of suffering and martyrdom. The same is true of some Shi'a streams of Muslim theology. It is important to recognize that a gentle, vulnerable, and respectful spirit prevails within some expressions of the life and faith of the Muslim *ummah*.

Nevertheless, the different Muslim and Christian responses to the New Testament meaning of the cross has enormous significance. As a teacher in Somalia, I sometimes sat with Muslim students in a nearby tea shop. One evening we discussed peacemaking.

"Islam is the practical religion," a student observed. "If you hit me on one cheek, I will hit back so hard you will never hit me again. That is how Islam establishes the peace. However, Jesus the Messiah is not practical. He teaches that you should forgive your enemies, and even turn the other cheek when your enemy strikes you. One cannot establish peace in that way."

I responded, "If I hit you back for the wrong you have done to me, surely sometime you will take revenge. So the cycle of revenge will go on and on. However, when Jesus was crucified he proclaimed forgiveness to those who had wronged him so deeply. That kind of astonishing forgiveness breaks the cycle of violence."

Those drinking tea with me that evening were not impressed with my peacemaking homily. They were far more attuned to the pre-Islamic Arabian wisdom, "He who uses not roughness, him shall men wrong."[7] They saw no contradiction between that traditional wisdom and the Islam they embraced.

I often think of that conversation in the light of the violent debacle that has destroyed the Somali nation. The cycle of inter-clan vengeance and counter-vengeance has gone on and on for too many years.

A theology of the *hijrah* has no space for vulnerability or defeat. Temporary retreat from the ignominy of suffering and

Peace — revenge, forgiveness

apparent defeat are sometimes necessary, just as Muhammad migrated from Mecca to Medina. But in the course of time, the *ummah* must succeed in triumphing over the enemy. Muhammad's triumphant return to Mecca is the normal way for all who are true followers of God. The eventual victory of the Muslim nation over its enemies is assured, just as Muhammad and the Muslim forces eventually triumphed over the powers in Mecca that at first opposed the Muslims.

We have noted above some pacifist streams within some Muslim communities. There is also a persistent qur'anic command to extend mercy to the enemy who repents and abandons his fight against the Muslim community. Nevertheless, within the mainstream of Muslim life, it is difficult for the Muslim *ummah* to discover within Islamic spirituality a way other than retaliation for wrongs experienced.[8] The tragedy is that retaliation nurtures counter-retaliation.

It is, therefore, not surprising that within the Middle East peace process, it has been the Palestinian Liberation Organization (PLO) that engaged in the negotiations with Israel. The PLO is a secular group, not an Islamic organization. Arab Christian presence in the PLO keeps the movement secular. Muslim organizations such as Hamas have not been involved in the negotiations, and are less inclined to negotiate with perceived enemies than would be a secular organization such as the PLO, which includes some of the "salt" of Christian reconciliation themes, would be.

In the fall of 2002, a student group from a Christian college spent a semester in Israel and the West Bank. Three meetings are especially pertinent to this reflection on peacemaking.

First, they met with a Hamas leader. He explained the theology of Islamic *jihad*. He stated that in the present circumstances violent confrontation with Israel was the only possible alternative, that *jihad* was necessary.

Second, they met an Israeli settler group. Their religious leaders explained that Zionism requires that they occupy the land of historic Israel. The violence of the Palestinians against the settlements had to be met with violence. There was no other way.

Third, they met with a Palestinian Christian family on the rubble of their home. This family had lost everything they owned during an Israeli attack. They talked about the way of Jesus, who forgives the enemies. They confessed that they held no malice or bitterness against those who had destroyed their home, and that they were committed to expressing the love of Christ for all who were caught up in the spiral of violence.

The way of the Messiah who went to the cross! Although Muslim theology might deny the cross, an intrigue about the cross persists. One evening during conversations in a mosque in Philadelphia, a woman who was doing her doctoral studies at Temple University asked, "Why does the cycle of violence never stop in Somalia? Although Somalia is Muslim, why are the Christians, such as the Mennonites, so involved in peacemaking among the Somalis?" She was addressing the question to me, for she knew I had lived in Somalia for some time.

I responded, "There are many reasons contributing to the cycle of violence. However, the Christian contribution to peacemaking is the conviction that we should forgive our enemies just as Jesus the Messiah forgave those who had crucified him. One of the tragedies of Somalia is that for many centuries the Somali people have excluded the witness of those who believe that Jesus the Messiah was crucified and forgave those who did him this great wrong. The salt of the way of forgiveness that the Messiah offers is, therefore, largely absent within this wounded nation."

The response in the mosque that evening was almost a chorus: "Oh! Take note! Jesus the Messiah was not crucified."

"We have heard that denial again tonight," I persisted. "The forgiving love revealed in the Messiah crucified is healing for the nations, and for each of us personally. When we deny the possibility of that kind of love, we are rejecting authentic reconciliation and healing."

On one occasion after I described the astonishing reconciliation offered in the cross, a Muslim academic and theologian turned to me and said, "I have never experienced the church as a peacemaking community. This is the first I have ever known that Jesus rejected the way of violence against his enemies. As for the church, we Muslims perceive of the church as a community committed to violence when things do not go your way."

I responded, "May God forgive the church for portraying a violent Messiah who is a distorted masquerade of the Messiah of the Gospel. I hope by God's grace you also can forgive us. Your comments are a call to Christians to repent of the distortions of the Gospel that we so often embrace."

She thanked me, and with deep emotion said, "This is the first time in my life that I have heard a Christian ask forgiveness from Muslims for the sins of the church. In your confession, I have seen an image of the Messiah I have not known."

Authentic Power

The cross is about the nature of power. As the conversation above reveals, however, many who profess to be disciples of the Messiah really embrace an Islamic rather than Gospel understanding of power. A conversation with friends in our home illustrates the different understandings of power.

Three Muslim friends from Somalia spent a couple nights in our home. "What gift does the church offer in peacemaking?" the gray-haired elder of the group asked during Sunday morning breakfast on our patio. "My country is dying. Your Mennonite Church has been helping in the peacemaking efforts. Why?"

"Our peacemaking is an expression of the life and ministry of Jesus the Messiah. Just before his arrest and trial, he washed the feet of Judas, who betrayed him. In that way the Messiah expressed compassion and a servant-like spirit, even toward a man who had turned against him.

"Furthermore, when he was crucified he proclaimed forgiveness to those who had placed him on that cross. That kind of love is not weakness. This suffering love of God seeks to forgive and be reconciled with the enemy."

At that point our friends broke in, "That is impossible, for the Messiah was anointed with the power of God. Power cannot suffer! God cannot love that much!"

"Please," I said. "Let God be God."

We missed the first part of our church worship gathering that morning. So be it. The conversation on our patio was a moment of ultimate significance.

Readings from the Bible:
 John 6:1-15; Matthew 16:21
Readings from the Qur'an:
 Anfal 8:30; Al-Mujadila 58:20-22

Questions for Reflection and Discussion:

1. Comment on this statement: Muhammad and Jesus journeyed in opposite directions.

2. Jesus refused political or military power, but Muhammad welcomed political and military power (John 18:36; Baqara 2:190-93). Explain the difference.

3. How might those different directions influence the attitudes of the Muslim *ummah* towards those who oppose the *ummah*? How might the journey of Jesus to the cross influence Christian attitudes toward those who oppose the church?

4. The *hijrah* is the beginning of the Muslim era. Give reasons for the significance of that event in Muslim self-understanding and theology.

5. Is it possible for God or one anointed by his power to suffer? What does the event of the *hijrah* say to the question? What does Jesus crucified say to the question? What do you say to that question? (Anfal 8:30; Luke 23:34)

6. How do you go about establishing what you believe to be good for you and others? Do you embrace the way of the *hijrah* or the way of the cross?

7. How would a theology of the cross or a theology of the *hijrah* respond to a "just war"?

— 9 —

Holy Cities:
Medina—Jerusalem

MEDINA is the city in Arabia where the Muslim *ummah* was first established. Jerusalem in Israel-Palestine is where the Christian church was born. The *ummah* and the church live within the long shadow of these two formative events. This chapter explores the formation of the *ummah* in Medina and the creation of the church in Jerusalem.

Church—*Ummah*

The Muslim and Christian movements did not emerge out of nothing. Both Christians and Muslims recognized that God had called Israel to be a light to the nations many hundreds of years before either the church or the *ummah* existed. God had formed Israel to be his covenant people, a witness among the nations. Both the early church and the *ummah* believed that their missions were to be a fulfillment and expansion of the mission and calling of Israel. (See chapter 4.)

The New Testament was written as the early church was formed. This community of believers confessed that Jesus is the Messiah and that he is Lord and Savior. As non-Jewish Gentile peoples came into the church, the church was transformed into a genuinely multinational community. The church believed this was the fulfillment of the promises of God that through the seed of Abraham all nations would be blessed.

Jesus proclaimed to his disciples just before his departure

from them, "But you will receive power when the Holy Spirit comes on you; and you will be my witnesses in Jerusalem, and all Judea and Samaria, and to the ends of the earth" (Acts 1:8).

The Qur'an was recorded as the early Muslim *ummah* was formed. The Muslims believed that the *ummah* superseded both Israel and the church as the community of faith for all nations. Israel's mission was for a season, but the *ummah* now carried that mission forward among the nations. Muslims observed that the church was divided over doctrinal questions; the mission of the *ummah* was to provide clarification of the truth for the church.

The Qur'an proclaims, "(This is) a Scripture which we have revealed unto thee (Muhammad) that whereby thou mayst bring forth mankind from darkness unto light" (Ibrahim [Abraham] 14:1).

The church and the *ummah* both claim Abraham as the father of faith. Each community believes that its mission is in harmony with God's promise to Abraham that through his seed all nations would be blessed. The church views its mission as a fulfillment of the promises of God to Israel that the rule of God will extend throughout the whole earth. The *ummah* views its mission as superseding both that of Israel and the church. It is, therefore, not surprising that relations between these communities of faith are often touched with tension.

This chapter explores the formation of both the church in Jerusalem and the *ummah* in Medina. Whereas the church preceded the *ummah*, we will explore the creation of the church first and then the formation of the *ummah*.

The Church Is Created in Jerusalem

After three years of public ministry, Jesus the Messiah was advancing on Jerusalem. The city was in an uproar. He was descending into Jerusalem from the Mount of Olives just east of the city. A huge and exuberant singing army was accompanying him.

Jesus Journeyed into Jerusalem

Jesus was riding on a colt. His army comprised throngs of children singing,

> Hosanna to the son of David!
> Blessed is he who comes in the name of the Lord!
> Hosanna in the highest! (Matt. 21:9)

The authorities were livid. They knew that by riding the colt, Jesus was making a statement, a proclamation that they totally rejected. That statement related to a well-known biblical prophecy concerning the Messiah.

Five hundred years earlier the prophet Zechariah wrote:

> Rejoice greatly, O Daughter of Zion!
> Shout, daughter of Jerusalem!
> See, your king comes to you,
> righteous and having salvation,
> gentle and riding on a donkey
> on a colt, the foal of a donkey.
> I will take away the chariots from Ephraim
> and the war-horses from Jerusalem,
> and the battle bow will be broken.
> He will proclaim peace to the nations.
> His rule will extend from sea to sea
> and from the River to the ends of the earth
> (Zech. 9:9-10).

By riding that colt, Jesus was proclaiming that he was indeed the Messiah, and that he was inaugurating a new kingdom of peace whose rule would extend throughout the world. The Jewish authorities were angry because Jesus was not the kind of king and messiah they wanted.

A real king would ride into Jerusalem on a white stallion with several legions of men armed with swords and spears. He would lead an army that would overthrow the pagan idol-worshiping Roman imperial government and establish the rule of God throughout the city, the region, and the world.

The colt-riding Jesus with throngs of singing children was not competent to be king. They begged Jesus to silence the children, but he would not. In fact, he declared, "If they keep quiet, the stones will cry out" (Luke 19:40).

A British theologian, N. T. Wright, asserts that in that colt-ride Jesus was proclaiming that he is the glory of God entering Jerusalem from the east.[1] This understanding comes from another biblical prophecy, that of Ezekiel. At about the same time that Zechariah was writing prophecy about the colt-riding king, the prophet Ezekiel wrote of a vision of the glory of God coming into the temple of God from the east.

> I saw the glory of the God of Israel coming from the east. His voice was like the roar of rushing waters, and the land was radiant with his glory. . . . The glory of the Lord entered the temple through the gate facing east. . . . I heard someone speaking to me from inside the temple. He said: "Son of man, this is the place of my throne and the place for the soles of my feet. This is where I will live among the Israelites forever" (Ezek. 43:2, 4, 6-7).

When Jesus rode that colt into Jerusalem, he was announcing that he was the fulfillment not only of Zechariah's prophecy, but also of that of Ezekiel. Jesus the Messiah riding into Jerusalem was proclaiming that in his person the radiant glory of God was entering Jerusalem *and* that he was inaugurating God's kingdom of righteousness, justice, and peace that would extend to the ends of the earth.

Jesus Cleansed the Temple

Just as in Ezekiel's prophecy, Jesus, in whom the fullness of the glory of God is revealed, entered the temple. This place of worship was thronging with merchants. They sold animals or food for sacrifice to the worshipers. Jesus overthrew the tables of the money changers and chased the cattle from the temple area. He proclaimed that God's intention was for the temple to be a house of prayer for all nations; not a den of robbers (Matt. 21:13).

The temple authorities challenged Jesus. They wanted him to prove his authority to do all this.

"Destroy this temple, and I will raise it again in three days," Jesus replied (John 2:19).

Of course, Jesus was referring to his death and resurrection after three days in the grave. But there was a double message here, as well. The temple of stone was needed no more. Jesus the Messiah was the new temple in whom God in his fullness and glory dwelt.[2] The temple authorities understood that Jesus was boldly hinting that the old temple built of stone and wood was not necessary.

Not only was the temple unnecessary, but also Jerusalem faced destruction. Jesus wept as he entered Jerusalem on the colt. He wept because Jerusalem would not receive that which made for peace; consequently Jesus mourned as he contemplated the horrible destruction and suffering that would befall the city.

In reality, the kingdom of God that Jesus was inaugurating did not need either Jerusalem or the temple.

Jesus Was Crucified

The anger of the temple authorities concerning all of this could not be quenched. As described in the previous chapter, they arrested Jesus and condemned him to crucifixion. They hurled many accusations against him; one that enraged the court especially was the charge that Jesus spoke against the temple. Another was that he claimed to be the Son of the Blessed.

As described in the previous chapter, Jesus was crucified. His disciples scattered in grief and fear. However, three days after his death, on the first day of the week, some women found his grave empty; he had arisen from the dead. The disciples were astounded. Thereafter, during the next forty days Jesus appeared to his disciples on at least eleven occasions.

Jesus Gave a Command

At one of his first appearances, he showed his disciples his wounded hands and side. Then he gave them a blessing and a promise, "Peace be with you! As the Father has sent me, I am sending you" (John 20:21).

Jesus commanded his disciples to wait in Jerusalem until they received the Holy Spirit. Thereafter, 120 disciples waited for ten days. They met together in an upper room in prayer and fasting. Then on Pentecost Day the Holy Spirit came upon them.

The Church Was Created

Pentecost is the Jewish feast celebrating the first fruit of the harvest. On that day in Jerusalem, the festival took on a new meaning, for the church was created—the first fruit of the Holy Spirit. The Holy Spirit descended like the rushing of a mighty wind. It rested on each disciple like tongues of fire. The disciples proclaimed the wonderful praises of God.

People from nations in the Middle East and North Africa were in Jerusalem. They ran to the place where the disciples were staying to hear and see what was happening. They were "exceedingly amazed" for in a miraculous demonstration of the nature of the Gospel and the church, everyone heard the Gospel in his or her own tongue.

Peter stood and preached the first Christian sermon. This was the soul of his message; it is significant as a clear witness to the Gospel:

> Jesus of Nazareth was a man accredited by God to you by miracles, wonders and signs, which God did among you through him, as you yourselves know. This man was handed over to you by God's set purpose and foreknowledge; and you, with the help of wicked men, put him to death by nailing him to the cross. But God raised him from the dead, freeing him from the agony of death, because it was impossible for death to keep its hold on him.
>
> Therefore . . . be assured of this: God has made this Jesus, whom you crucified, both Lord and Christ (Acts 2:22-24, 36).

"What shall we do?" the people cried.

Peter urged them, "Repent and be baptized, every one of you, in the name of Jesus Christ so that your sins may be forgiven. And you will receive the gift of the Holy Spirit" (Acts 2:37-38).

As these thousands heard the Gospel preached, the Holy Spirit convicted them of sin and truth. Three thousand repented of their sins that day and believed in Jesus the Messiah as Lord and Savior. The apostles baptized all who believed. They were filled with great joy. No one was needy for those that had provisions shared with those who were in poverty.

We read, "They broke bread in their homes and ate together with glad and sincere hearts, praising God and enjoying the favor of all the people. And the Lord added to their number daily those who were being saved" (Acts 2:46-47).

The Church Was Persecuted

Nevertheless, persecution was at hand. Jesus suffered. So did the church. Within weeks of the birthday of the church, Herod arranged for the apostle James to be beheaded. Later, a deacon, Stephen, was stoned to death. The apostles Peter and John were beaten and put in prison. All this happened in Jerusalem as the church was growing. This growing church enjoyed no political power; in fact, it was persecuted by the authorities.

The Jerusalem persecution scattered the church. As the believers moved elsewhere, they carried the good news with them. Wherever the believers went, new fellowships emerged. The church believed this was because of the work of the Holy Spirit.

The Church Is the Temple of God

Any notions that the first Christians had of a Jerusalem-centric church eventually withered away. In fact, within only a generation after the birthday of the church in A.D. 70, the Roman authorities had destroyed the temple. Jerusalem itself came under a horrible siege and much of the city was destroyed. Neither Jerusalem nor the temple was in any sense the center of the Christian movement. The center of the church was wherever people met together in the name of Jesus the Messiah.

"We are the temple of the living God!" Christians exclaimed in wonder and joy (2 Cor. 6:16).

The Church Scattered and Grew

Scattering from Jerusalem did not enable the church to escape suffering. For the first three centuries of the Christian era, the church was usually a powerless and often severely persecuted community. Nevertheless, within two hundred years of the beginning of the church, Origen, living in Egypt, wrote, "By the coming of Christ, the land of Britain accepts belief in the one God. So do the Moors of Africa. So does the whole globe. There are churches now on the frontiers of the world, and all the earth shouts for joy."[3]

Although the church did not possess instruments of political power, the Gospel did penetrate centers of power like yeast in bread dough. For example, Paul wrote from his prisoner's circumstances in Rome that the Gospel was being heard and believed within Caesar's household. How could this happen?

Celsus wrote about this "problem." He was a second-century pagan critic of the church. He was most frustrated because there was no way to prevent the Gospel from entering centers of power. The movement could not be stopped because, Celsus lamented, the Christian servant women doing the laundry for their master whispered the Gospel accounts to the master's children in their care. Alas, the children told their parents, and before long the whole household believed because of the whispering witness of the "uneducated and rustic" laundry women.[4]

Christians sometimes referred to the church community as "the new race."[5] The biblical scriptures proclaim:

> But you are a chosen people, a royal priesthood, a holy nation, a people belonging to God, that you may declare the praises of him who called you out of darkness into his wonderful light. Once you were not a people, but now you are the people of God; once you had not received mercy, but now you have received mercy (1 Pet. 2:9-10).

The early church believed that they were called by God to be a new community within and among the nations, languages, and tribes of humankind. Jesus said it this way in a prayer for his disciples just before he was crucified: "They are not of the world, even as I am not of it. . . . As you [God the Father] sent me into the world, I have sent them into the world" (John 17:16, 18).

The expansion of the church, first in Jerusalem and then in regions far beyond Israel, required solid leadership and good organization. It is hardly surprising, therefore, that the church developed effective leadership patterns very early in its journey. The twelve disciples who had worked closely with Jesus were recognized as apostolic leaders in the early church. (One of the disciples, Judas, had betrayed Jesus, and then killed himself. So the disciples appointed a replacement, Matthias.) Wherever new congregations developed, elders were selected and appointed to provide spiritual leadership for the congregation. Deacons were appointed to serve the financial and material needs of the poor.

So there were three areas of leadership responsibility: deacons, elders, and apostles. Throughout the centuries the church has developed many kinds of leadership, yet variation on this early church model is quite universal: deacons, elders (pastors or priests), and overseers (bishops). Leaders were to be servants of their people, not their bosses (John 13:2-17).

A Changing Church and an Emerging *Ummah*

However, the Roman Emperor Constantine (fourth century) introduced an astonishing revolution into church-state relations. Constantine used the church to help unify and extend the Roman Empire. Thus the role of the church in the West was fundamentally transformed, including leadership patterns. Bishops became increasingly powerful and church authority patterns began to mimic that of the Roman imperial system. This is because from Constantine onward, the Western church has often enjoyed considerable political power. However, in recent decades modern secular culture has significantly eroded the political influence of the church in Western societies.

As noted in the introduction to this book, the changes in church-state relations that began at the time of Constantine were well entrenched within the Western church when the *ummah* was formed in the seventh century. The Western church and some expressions of the church in the Middle East assumed that political power and the church should be united. (An exception would be churches in regions such as Persia or India or Christian communities in Arabia where the churches were always minority movements.)

The arrangements the Muslims developed in Medina for the unity of the *ummah* and the political order were quite similar to the model developed by churches such as the Syrian Orthodox in nearby Syria and the Western church as a whole. Christians, who are inclined to criticize the way the *ummah* developed, should recognize that the Western church had already developed *ummah*-like understandings of its own relationships to the political order several centuries before the *ummah* was formed. We shall now explore the development of the Muslim *ummah* or nation in Medina in the seventh century.

The *Ummah* Is Formed in Medina

There was jubilation in Medina when Muhammad arrived at the conclusion of the nine-day journey from Mecca to Medina. This was the *hijrah*, described in the previous chapter, the beginning of the Muslim era.

Muslims Organized the Ummah

There was also a few hundred other Muslim emigrants from Mecca. They were known as the Muhajirun (exiles). The local Muslims were the Ansar (helpers). Muhammad gave leadership to these two communities so that they would be united into one *ummah*. The local believers shared their possessions so that their exiled brothers and sisters might have adequate provision.

Muhammad then planned the construction of a mosque. This is the first mosque built for the *ummah*. This place of worship and the manner of worship that developed in that mosque has become the model for all Muslim congregations around the world for all time.

The mosque included the *mihrab*, a niche in the wall of the mosque that shows the direction worshipers must face in prayer. At first the Muslims faced Jerusalem in prayer. This was probably a sign of respect and continuity with the Jewish community and their prophets; that continuity was important for the Muslims in the early formation of their community of faith. However, in Medina the Muslims changed the direction of prayer to face the Ka'bah in Mecca. Ever since the development of the first mosque in Medina, all subsequent mosques anywhere in the world include a *mihrab* indicating the direction of the Ka'bah.

The worship of Allah was the bond that united the Muslims in Medina, whether they were Meccan exiles or Medinan helpers. Yet there were political and cultural realities that also had to be addressed. Therefore, after having established the place and pattern of Islamic worship, Muhammad laid the foundations for a Muslim political order. He developed the constitution of Medina.

The Muslims Developed a Constitution

The constitution established the Muslim principles of brotherhood, justice, and consensus. The foundational concern of the constitution was the preservation of the integrity of the Muslim *ummah* or nation. The rights of the person were sublimated to the rights of the *ummah*; this constitution would not pass the test of human rights assumed within modern democracies.[6] However, Muslims are often appalled by the destructive individual liberties that are protected in liberal democracies.

In fact, in recent years the Muslim World League has developed the Islamic Declaration of Human Rights as a Muslim response to the United Nations Declaration of Human Rights. Just as in Medina thirteen centuries ago, the modern Muslim nation functions with the assumption that community rights supersede individual rights.[7]

Muhammad extended Muslim rule over all the inhabitants of Medina, whether or not they were Muslims. Non-Muslims could live within the Muslim governing authority and the Islamic rule of law. In Medina the integrity of these other communities, especially Jews, Christians, and Zoroastrians, were protected to some extent. However, no person or community was allowed to threaten the integrity of the Muslim nation. For example, when Muhammad and the Muslims were convinced that members of the Jewish community were plotting against him, they were killed.

Arabian society was a divided society with clans often hostile toward one another. In Medina, Muhammad welded competing clans and interests together into a new interclan community, the Muslim *ummah*, often referred to as the Muslim nation. This required keen political skill. Within the next several years, the act of uniting disparate clans in Medina into the emerging Muslim nation expanded to become a unifying movement throughout Arabia.

As the Islamic movement extended beyond Medina, Arab Christians were a special challenge for the Muslims. With an Arabic Qur'an as the final revelation, Arab Muslims were convinced that all Arabs would become Muslim. Within two centuries that is exactly what happened within Arabia. However, some of the Arabian Christians' conversion to Islam happened under pressure and even threat. An example of the pressure is expressed in a reprimand from Caliph Walid early in the eighth century. He addressed the Christian leader of an Arabian Christian tribe called the Taghlib: "How can you be an Arab leader and adore the cross? You shame the Arabs."[8]

The Beginning of Dar al-Islam (The Region of Islam/Peace)

In Medina the faith community and the political order were united. Muhammad was both prophet and statesman. The region under Muhammad's rule was considered to be at peace. This region of peace was referred to in Medina as the Dar al-Ahd (The House of the Treaty), or the Dar al-Islam (The House of Islam). It was about three centuries later that the concept of Dar al-Salam (The Region of Peace) as the international rule of the Muslim nation was more fully developed.

Dar al-Islam is the region of peace that is under the rule of the Muslims. The seed of the Dar al-Islam understanding of the world order in regard to Muslims and non-Muslims was planted during the Median experience in the early formation of the

Muslim nation. The Qur'an itself plants those seeds within the community. The Qur'an describes the Dar al-Islam in gracious language.

> And Allah summoneth to the abode of peace, and leadeth whom He will to a straight path. For those who do good is the best (reward) and more (thereto). Neither dust nor ignominy cometh near their faces. Such are the rightful owners of the Garden: they will abide therein (Yunus [Jonah] 10:26-27).

> For them is the abode of peace with their Lord. He will be their Protecting Friend because of what they used to do [practicing righteousness] (Anam [Cattle] 6:127).

The Muslim nation thrived in Medina, where the Muslims had political power. The success of the *ummah* in Medina contrasted sharply with the discouragement the Muslims experienced in Mecca when they did not possess political power and authority.

The contrast between the Mecca and Medina experiences has given Muslims the abiding conviction that political power enables the triumph of truth. The mission and success of the *ummah* is hindered whenever Muslims do not control the political order. Muslim control of political power enables the triumph of truth and secures the well-being of the Muslim *ummah*.

Muslims and Government

Kenneth Cragg comments, "For to study Islam, both in its history and its theology, is to encounter the most resolute and unperturbed of all faiths in placing trust, and finding pride, in political religion."[9]

The Princeton University Islamist, Bernard Lewis, observes:

> The principal function of government is to enable the individual Muslim to lead a good Muslim life. This is, in the last analysis, the purpose of the state, for which alone it is established by God, and for which alone statesmen are given authority over others. The worth of the state, and the good and evil deeds of statesmen are measured by the extent to which this purpose is accomplished.[10]

Can a non-Muslim government provide that kind of support for Muslims? Probably not. However, that issue was cause for intense debate among the *'ulama* (Muslim authorities in Islamic law) during the early nineteenth century. The inclination was to forbid any Muslim from going to live in non-Muslim territory in the West.[11] Yet as modern mobility increased, that became an impossible ideal. In fact, nowadays some Muslims discover that liberal pluralist Western culture can provide space and protection for the Muslim *ummah* as well as the individual Muslim.

This is the position of Hamideh Mohagheghi, an Iranian Shi'ite who has lived in Germany for more than two decades. She is a professor of Islam, and commented to a gathering of German Anabaptists, "The House of Islam is wherever Muslims have peace. That is Dar al-Islam. Germany has become a place of peace for Muslims; it is, therefore, Dar al-Islam."[12]

Medina Is a Model

Nevertheless, Muslims idealize the Medina experience, and for most Muslims that model of establishing the Dar al-Islam is the goal.

In regard to that goal, Mohagheghi commented at the 2002 German Anabaptist consultation, "Even the animals were at peace in Medina after the rule of Islam was established even into the environs of that city. Under the Prophet's rule, there was total peace within and around Medina."[13]

Thus the Medina experience has taught the Muslim *ummah* to seek political power and to use that power to extend the region of peace. The region not yet under the rule of the Dar al-Salam is the region of war, or the Dar al-Harb. The whole world is divided between these two regions—the region of peace and the region of war that has not yet been brought under the rule of the Muslim nation.

Victorious Muslims

Muhammad lived for another decade after the *hijrah*. During those ten years the military and political success of the Dar al-Islam was remarkable. The Dar al-Harb was put to flight and retreat as the successful Muslim nation extended the rule of Islam throughout Arabia.

The conflict between the region of peace and region of war involved military engagement. In battles against the opponents of Islam, the Muslim forces under Muhammad's generalship won several noteworthy victories, even when the enemy forces vastly outnumbered the Muslims. The Muslim victories were celebrated in the Qur'an as vindicating Muhammad's prophethood and the truth of Islam (Anfal [The Spoils of War] 8:5-19). However, there was one exception to these victories. At the battle of Uhud, the Meccan army forced the Muslim military into a temporary retreat; Muhammad was wounded in that battle, losing two teeth, and seventy Muslims were killed.

The Qur'an addresses the theological implications of this defeat (Ali 'Imran [The Family of Imran] 3:134-200). Wars in defense of Islam provide martyrs who enter paradise. God determines the time of each person's death. Whether one is in battle or in the safety of ones home really makes no difference as to the moment of death. The idolaters will never ultimately triumph over the Muslim believers. Victory was at hand, until the Muslims disobeyed the command of the prophet Muhammad— had they obeyed, defeat would have been averted. The battle was a test of faith. Be courageous, and God will give the final victory. God is forgiving and merciful.[14]

Indeed, the Muslims did rally from the defeat at Uhud, and within ten years of the *hijrah*, all of Arabia had come under Muslim rule. Eight years after the *hijrah*, Muhammad led the triumphant Muslim forces into Mecca. By this time, the Meccan resistance had been broken through a series of military defeats.

As Muhammad led ten thousand Muslim soldiers into Mecca, he declared, "Truth hath come, and falsehood hath vanished away" (Bani Israel [The Children of Israel] 17:81).

Truth and the Political Order

Muhammad in Medina united the community of Muslim faith and the political order. In that accomplishment he effectuated a vision that has persisted within the global Muslim nation. The ideal is a Dar al-Islam that integrates the community of faith and the political order.

Muslims observe that Jesus did not seek to control the political arena; in fact, he rejected such possibilities. Consequently his ministry seems, to Muslims, to be impractical and incomplete. Practical faith requires engagement in and control of political power. However, Muslims ask, "How can you govern a nation based on the law of love as Jesus taught?" That is an idealism befitting pious monks, not the cruelties of a tumultuous world. Therefore, it is obvious that the mission of Jesus was limited in scope. Muslims point out that Muhammad, not Jesus, carried forward with a mission to bring all authorities, including political systems, under the rule of God.

Muslims are right in observing that the political commitment of Muhammad was not that of Jesus. In fact, in Jerusalem, Jesus turned his back on a kingdom enforced or sustained by political and military power. However, Jesus did assert that his followers were like "salt" and "light" and "yeast" in the world. This is a vision of righteous people having a powerful and transforming influence for good within all levels of society, including the political. But Jesus did not initiate a plan for his followers to control the political agenda. The political order should hear the witness of the kingdom of God and respond to the demands of righteousness and justice, but Jesus was clear in his life and teachings: No political system is the kingdom of God.

This is not to suggest that cooperation between church and state is wrong, or that the faithful church must always be persecuted, or that the church has no word of witness for the state. No indeed! However, church communities vary greatly in their approaches to church and state relations. In some regions nowadays there is close cooperation; in other regions there are practically no relations between church and state. For example, in Soviet times, governments that embraced a communist ideology were mostly forthrightly hostile toward the church.

The sixteenth-century Anabaptist movement was insistent that church and state are different kingdoms. To this day, Christians with an Anabaptist commitment believe that the very nature of the church is distorted whenever a church co-opts the political and military power of the state to effectuate its mission, or whenever a government co-opts the church to support its nationalist agenda. Jesus prayed and worked for the peace of Jerusalem, but his kingdom was not Jerusalem-centric. Anabaptist Christians believe that the patterns of church-state separation developed in the early church in Jerusalem are helpful models for the church everywhere. These Christians counsel: Let the church be the church and the state be the state.

That is exactly the point where the early church in Jerusalem and the early *ummah* in Medina embarked upon radically different journeys. Within the Muslim *ummah*, the unity of the *ummah* and the political order is a mandate; that is the essence of the Muslim nation. Within Islam, the community of faith is not complete until it possesses and controls the instruments of political and military power. The political power then protects the truth (Islam), and truth thrives when it is supported by political power.

Truth and Power

These issues of faith and the political order introduce another question. Does truth need the assistance of coercive power? What happens in the soul of a person when he "believes" in submission to power that is imposed?

Within Islam this worry is expressed in the qur'anic admonition: "There is no compulsion in religion" (Baqara [The Cow] 2:256).

To what extent have the Muslims been faithful to that counsel? To what extent does the church honor the freedom of people to believe or not to believe?

Jesus revealed truth and proclaimed peace, but he never forced the truth on anyone. He even freed Judas to betray him. This commitment to voluntary decision for or against faith is one of the reasons the Anabaptist Christians in the sixteenth century desisted from infant baptisms, choosing rather to baptize only those who as adults choose to believe in and follow the Messiah. Even parents cannot choose the faith of their children. Of course, even in churches where infant baptism is practiced, there is the later confirmation of faith when the young believer publicly confesses faith in the Messiah. Yet the church has not always lived up to this commitment to an unobtrusive witness to truth that frees the person to say "yes" or "no."

What do the events in Jerusalem when the church was formed, or the events in Medina when the *ummah* was developed, tell us about the understandings of truth and power in the early church and the early *ummah*?

Several years ago I was being interviewed on National Public Radio in Virginia. I was commenting on the difference between Muhammad and Jesus in relationship to power and truth.

The interviewer observed, "It occurs to me that many Christians and their preachers would be more at home with Muhammad in Medina than Jesus in Jerusalem."

I said, "I have often thought that might be true."

This brings us right back to the question we often meet in the conversation between Muslims and Christians: What is truth?

The truth revealed in Jesus the Messiah as he entered Jerusalem on the colt needed no defense. His truth was expressed in his wounded outstretched hands on the cross as he cried out for the forgiveness of those who crucified him, or in the peace he breathed upon his disciples after his resurrection as he promised the gift of the Holy Spirit. In contrast, the truth Muhammad proclaimed as he entered Mecca with the Muslim forces enjoyed the support of military power.

What, then, is the nature of truth? What is the nature of genuine peace?

The Gospel and Islam offer different responses that are engraved on our histories and hearts by two different journeys and two different cities: Jesus of Nazareth saying "yes" to the cross as he traveled into Jerusalem surrounded by singing children; Muhammad of the Quraish migrating to Medina, where he commands political and military power. For the Muslim army entering Mecca, a truth that suffers seemed impotent for establishing the peace of Islam.

Muslims give witness to the peace of Islam. However, the calling of the church is to give witness to the peace of the Messiah. In that calling the church gives witness to the vulnerable truth of the Gospel. This is a gift offered; it is a gift freely received or freely rejected. Such truth needs bold and faithful witnesses. It requires no other defense.

Readings from the Bible:
    Luke 10:28-48
Readings from the Qur'an:
    Anfal 8:5-19

Questions for Reflection and Discussion:
    1. What are the qualities of the kingdom of God that Jesus was announcing when he rode into Jerusalem on the colt (Zech. 9:9-10; Luke 19:28-44)?
    2. What are the qualities of the kingdom Muhammad was establishing in Medina (Anfal 8:37-41)?

3. Describe the birthday of the church (Acts 2:1-47). Reflect on the role of the Holy Spirit in creating the church.

4. Describe the establishment of the *ummah* in Medina. Reflect on the role of Muhammad in establishing the *ummah* (Anfal 8:20-1).

5. How shall the truth prevail? Within the church as formed at Pentecost? Within the *ummah* as formed in Medina?

6. Comment on this statement: Those who embrace the Gospel will turn away from any inclinations to defend truth forcefully or violently.

7. How can the church today journey with Jesus into Jerusalem?

— 10 —

One God:
Tawhid—Trinity

"ARE you a Muslim?" a fellow passenger projected his voice above the high-decibel *gabei* music in a crowded Mercedes bus speeding between Mogadiscio and Johar in Somalia.

"Actually, I am a Christian," I replied.

"Oh!" he exclaimed for everyone to hear. "So you are a polytheist. You believe that Jesus is the Son of God. You believe that God had a consort who gave birth to his Son!"

Muslim-Christian relations cannot avoid this paramount question in the mind of Muslims, "What do you Christians believe about Jesus?" It is always there, either beneath the surface, or explicitly as in that Mercedes bus in Somalia jammed with people.

For example, several years after that bus ride conversation, I participated with other Christians in a day of dialogue with Muslim theologians near the United Nations in New York City. We were exploring global development and peacemaking issues wherein Muslims and Christians might partner. The Muslim participants were highly educated professionals who were in leadership roles in the Muslim World League.

In the midst of the conversation, the director of the league interjected, quite out of the blue, "We must remember that the difference between Christians and Muslims is that Christians believe in three gods, and we Muslims believe in one God."

Objections to the Trinity

All Muslims believe in the *tawhid* (unity) of God. Muslims likewise believe that God as Trinity is a violation of *tawhid*. These concerns are fixated within Muslim doctrine because these concerns recur repeatedly in the Qur'an. Unless the concerns are faced and addressed, it is impossible for Christians and Muslims to develop credible and trusting relations.

Ahmad was a Somali Islamic student who lived near our home in Eastleigh, Nairobi. *Tawhid* was very much on his mind one day when he came directly from the mosque across the street to our home. He called, "*Hodi*!" That is the Kenyan way to ask entrance.

"How dare you teach that there are three gods," he exploded when I opened our door.

"Come in," I invited. "Let's have tea and let me hear what troubles you."

"No!" Ahmad objected as he stepped into our living room. "I shall not sit down with you nor drink tea today. Your deception of the people in this community must stop. God is one, not three."

"I believe in one God," I countered.

"Trinity!" exclaimed Ahmad. "That is polytheism. That is against *tawhid*. God is one! To believe that God has associates is *shirk*. That is the worst sin a person can commit. That sin is unforgivable."

Interpreting the Trinity

"Oh, Trinity," I responded. "Trinity means that you and I should love and respect each other."

"What did you say?" Ahmad asked, quite amazed.

"Trinity means that you and I should love each other," I continued. "The word 'Trinity' is not in the Bible. It is a term that entered Christian vocabulary about two hundred years after Jesus, when a North African theologian, Tertullian, suggested that 'Trinity' might be a good way to describe the Christian experience of God. So, if we can find a better way to explain God, that is all right."

Drawing from Augustine, the fifth-century North African theologian, and his reflections on the Trinity, I continued, "When we Christians say 'Trinity,' we are attempting to express God's love with inadequate human language. Trinity means that within

God himself there is communion, fellowship, loving relationship, and unity. Trinity means God is love; he reaches out beyond himself to meet us in loving service and invitation.

"God has revealed himself and his love for us in the life and ministry of Jesus the Messiah. God invites us to begin to participate in the same quality of self-giving love and fellowship that we meet in Jesus. Through the Holy Spirit of God, we are empowered to begin to love one another like Jesus loved."

"In summary, Trinity means that within God, there is loving fellowship. God invites us to love one another as he loves."

Ahmad listened very attentively. He was quite astonished. After a reflective pause, he commented, "That is very good, to love each other as God loves."

Thereafter Ahmad became my friend and advocate within the Muslim community in Eastleigh, but that conversation remains a prototype of deep perplexity that Muslims experience as they relate to Christians.

Persistent Distortions

There are real theological grounds for the Muslim concerns or objections about the Trinity or Jesus as the Son of God. Those theological objections should be addressed in the spirit of respect, dialogue, and witness.

However, not all of the objections are theological. Much of the Muslim objection to the Christian faith is rooted in distortions about what Christians believe. It is absolutely necessary to address distortions of Christian beliefs so that Muslims will understand what biblical faith teaches. It is impossible to dialogue with Muslims about matters of real theological concern as long as the Christian faith is discredited because of wrong perceptions about Christian beliefs.

Some of these distortions arise from the Arabian context in which the Muslim movement began. As noted in chapter 2, Muhammad preached in a milieu where some of the traditional Arabian gods married and had children. Some of the seventh-century chatter by Arabian Christians about Jesus as the Son of God dismayed Muhammad. It sounded to him like pagan polytheism, where gods married and begat children.

In the seventh century, some Arabian Christians did not

understand the Christian Trinity as Father, Son, and Holy Spirit. They, like many other Christians, referred to the virgin Mary as the mother of God. It is possible that for some Christians who did not have access to biblical scriptures, "Trinity" seemed to mean three divinities—Father, Mother, and Son. The qur'anic denial of the Trinity is a forthright objection to such polytheism. The Qur'an derided the Trinity as utterly reprehensible, because God would never have a consort and bear a son (Maida [The Table Spread] 5:75; Anam [Cattle] 6:100-1). Throughout the centuries, these distortions concerning the meaning of the Christian use of the term "Trinity" have persisted within the Muslim *ummah* in the form of the qur'anic frontal attack against polytheistic tri-theism.

However, nowhere does the Qur'an directly address the Christian belief in the Trinity as Father, Son, and Holy Spirit. In fact, one of the verses wherein the Qur'an objects to the notion that Jesus is an associate of God also refers to the Spirit of God and calls the Messiah the Word of God (Nisaa [Women] 4:171). These are statements that do not seem to lock the Muslim door absolutely against any dialogue in regard to trinitarian theology.

However, Islamic theology has developed independently of the witness of the Christian scriptures. Therefore, Muslims interpret the Qur'an only in the light of the Qur'an and the Hadith, with little or no thought as to what the Bible says about the Holy Spirit or the Messiah as the Word of God.

So, Muslims explain, "The Spirit of God is the angel Gabriel."

They add, "Jesus was created miraculously *by* the Word of God; he *is* not the Word of God."

God as Trinity or Jesus as the Son of God is not the only stumbling block. There are other distortions as well. For example, the Qur'an asserts that Christians believe that God is the Messiah. The Qur'an warns, "They indeed have disbelieved who say: Lo! Allah is the Messiah, son of Mary" (Maida 5:17).

However, biblical theology does not suggest any such notion, that God is the Messiah. That would be to say that when Jesus was on earth, the God of the whole universe was Jesus. Not so! Jesus the Messiah prayed constantly to God, his loving heavenly Father. He was dependent on God. He was not an independent god—that is the biblical witness. Jesus the Messiah lived in constant obedience to God and in fellowship with the Father. All that the Father commanded him, he did. When we see the Son we have met the Father (John 14:6-11). The New Testament witness is that the Messiah is God, but not that God is the Messiah.

Another distortion that is expressed repeatedly in the Qur'an is the notion that Christians ascribe a partner or partners to God. God has no associates, God is God alone, the Qur'an insists (Anam 6:22-23, 136-37, 163). One reference condemns those who believe in two gods (Nahl [The Bee] 16:51). Some of these references in the Qur'an are directed against pagan polytheism. However, some are addressed explicitly or implicitly to the Christians.

The distortions are persistent. For example, within the space of one year I visited four different mosques in four different cities. I was accompanied by Christian colleagues.

In each setting the imam said, "To say that God begat a son is the sin of *shirk*. That is ascribing an associate to God. That is the most damnable sin; there is no forgiveness for *shirk*. Anyone who says that God begat a son will go to hell."

In each setting the imam made it clear that he was concerned for us, and that was the reason he needed to warn us so forthrightly. In each case the imams asked our forgiveness if they had offended us. Yet they could not deviate from their responsibility to warn us of judgment if we persisted in our belief that Jesus is the Son of God.

Of course, Christians should not ascribe associates to God.[1] The God revealing himself fully in the Messiah in the New Testament is neither the theology of two gods, nor three gods, nor that of ascribing associates to God. These notions are distortions of biblical faith, and must be addressed wherever and whenever possible as the church meets the *ummah*.

Unless corrected, these distortions inoculate the Muslim community from having any interest in hearing the witness of the church concerning God who in the Messiah reveals himself as Redeemer and Savior. These misunderstandings prevent people from considering the Gospel that in the Messiah, God reconciles us to himself (2 Cor. 5:18).

Interpreting the Son of God

As noted above, a person cannot wait to address the Son of God perplexities until there is a solid trusting relationship between Muslim and Christian friends. It is the up-front and disturbing concern on the minds of Muslims, and it must be addressed forthrightly. The apostle Peter's counsel is appropriate:

> Do not be frightened. But in your hearts set apart Christ as Lord. Always be prepared to give an answer to everyone who asks you to give the reason for the hope that you have. But do this with gentleness and respect, keeping a clear conscience (1 Pet. 3:14-17).

One evening a surgeon, Dr. Ali, and I were leading a dialogue in the Front Street Mosque in Philadelphia. The group of about fifty was equally divided between Muslims and Christians.

"We totally reject that Jesus the Messiah is the Son of God!" Dr. Ali exclaimed most emphatically. "Ascribing associates to God is blasphemous."

"May I respond to your statement?" I asked.

"Of course," my good friend said.

For the next five minutes I attempted respectfully to give account of the faith of the Christian believer.

"Christians do not believe that God took a consort and fathered a son. Away with all such notions! Neither is it biblical to add associates to God. Nor do we believe in two Gods, or three gods."

"However, God himself has named the Messiah, 'My beloved Son.' Twice in the ministry of Jesus the Messiah, God spoke from heaven saying, 'This is my beloved Son.' God has spoken. Therefore, we do well to discern what God meant by declaring the Messiah to be his beloved Son.

"There is a window within the Qur'an itself that provides a glimpse into what God meant when he named the Messiah, 'my beloved Son.' The Messiah is referred to as *Kalimatuhu* (His [God's] Word) in the Qur'an" (Nisaa 4:171).

Dr. Ali objected, "Of course, the Messiah is the Word of God. However, that has nothing to do with Son of God. Rather it means that God spoke, and the Messiah was conceived in his mother's womb miraculously. Just as God's Word created Adam, so also God's Word created the Messiah within the womb of the virgin Mother."

I continued. "Thank you for explaining the Muslim interpretation of the qur'anic statement that Jesus is the Word of God. The

Injil (Gospel) also refers to the Messiah as the Word of God. This evening we invite you to hear the witness of the biblical scriptures on what it means for the Messiah to be the Word of God.

"As Muslims you sometimes talk about the Mother of the Book in the heavens (Ali 'Imran [The Family of Imran] 3:7; Rad [Thunder] 13:39; Az-Zukhruf [Ornaments of Gold] 43:4). You say that this book is God's eternal and uncreated Word inscribed on a guarded tablet. Of course, the guarded tablet is a metaphor. God's Word is always living, for God is always expressing himself. And his Word is always the true revelation of who God is, for God will not lie. There is no divergence between God and his Word.

"The witness of Jesus the Messiah, the biblical scriptures, and the church is that the Messiah is the in-human-form revelation of God's Word in fullness. God's living, creative, redeeming Word can never be captured on tablets; no indeed. Rather his life-giving Word has become human, and walked among us. If we want to know what God is like, let us meet the Messiah. The Messiah is the full revelation of the presence of God among us, for there can be no separation between God and his Word.

"'Son of God' means that he is the Word of God in human form. The name also means 'relationship.' The Messiah had a perfect loving relationship with God. In fact, he called God his Father. He said, 'I and the Father are one. If you have seen me, you have seen the Father' (as in John 14:8-10).

"Through the ministry of the Messiah we are invited to begin to discover God as our heavenly Father. Jesus the Messiah is *the* Son of God; his relationship with his Father in heaven was perfect. However, through the Messiah we are also invited into the family of God and become his sons and daughters. The Messiah is *the* Son of God; we are invited to become adopted sons and daughters into the family of God" (as in Eph. 1:5).

There was a long silence. Then the doctor said, "In that case, I could believe."

Several Gospels

However, conversations like these do not resolve all the objections to the Christian faith. When Muslims meet the New Testament, especially the gospels, other perplexities arise.

"Where is the gospel of Jesus the Messiah?" a Muslim scholar in a Nairobi mosque asked a group of us visiting Christians. "The New Testament contains gospels of four men, but there is no gospel of the Messiah. Apparently Jesus took the gospel with him when he went to heaven."

The confusion of the Nairobi scholar is pervasive among Muslims who are acquainted with the New Testament. Muslims observe that there is only one Qur'an, but there are four gospels, each through a different person. As they see it, the gospel of the Messiah is absent. Identifying that perplexity can open the door to explain the nature of the Gospel.

In Nairobi that day, one of our group responded, "In the Arabic language of the Qur'an, Jesus the Messiah is called (good news) from God (Ali 'Imran 3:45). Injil means 'evangel or good news or Gospel.' The Messiah is good news because he is the Injil or Gospel. Christians do not believe that Jesus the Messiah brought the Gospel because he is indeed the good news from heaven. He is the Word of God in human form. The Gospel is, therefore, not a book; the good news from God is the person of Jesus the Messiah.

"Matthew, Mark, Luke, and John each recorded their witness concerning this One who is the Gospel. The Messiah is so astonishing, that if there were only one witness, we would probably conclude that the account of the life and teachings of the Messiah was a human invention. However, not so when there are four witnesses. In any court of law, four witnesses is persuasive evidence.

"The Spirit of God inspired Matthew, Mark, Luke, and John as they each recorded their witness concerning the Messiah. We believe their writings are trustworthy accounts of the life, teachings, and ministry of Jesus the Messiah who is the Gospel."

These conversations are examples of dialogue that Christians and Muslims experience all over the world when they enter into an authentic commitment to hearing one another and begin to share with one another. The Christian needs to hear the reasons Muslims reject the Messiah as Son of God—both the distortions, as well as the theological objections. Only after the distortions are addressed can the theological concerns be explored. It is important for Muslims to hear what the New Testament means by Jesus as the Son of God; this is a secret known only to the church. It is only through the witness of the church and the New Testament scriptures that Muslims will ever learn of the meaning of the secret that Christians cherish: God in the Messiah reconciling us to himself.

The Gospel and the Qur'an

Comparing Jesus the Messiah to Muhammad distorts and confuses the respective understandings of the place of the Messiah within the Christian faith and Muhammad within the Muslim faith. One difference is that Muslims believe the Qur'an came through Muhammad, but we have observed that the Gospel did not come through the Messiah, because he is the Gospel.

"As Muslims, you believe that God revealed the Qur'an through Muhammad. Is that correct?" I asked a gathering at the Susquehanna Street Mosque in Philadelphia.

"That is correct," the imam said.

I continued, "Both Muslims and Christians agree that Jesus the Messiah was born of the virgin Mary. The Messiah, who is the Gospel, came into our world through the virgin. Muslims believe that the Qur'an came through the prophet Muhammad. The virgin was the human instrument through whom the Messiah came; Muhammad was the instrument through whom the Qur'an came."

What Is Truth?

The Messiah and the Qur'an are the respective truth centers for the church and the *ummah.* Both Jesus and the Qur'an make very radical truth claims.

Jesus said, "I am the way and the truth and the life. No one comes to the Father except through me" (John 14:6).

Jesus observed, "You diligently study the Scriptures because you think that by them you possess eternal life. These are the Scriptures that testify about me" (John 5:39). Jesus claimed to be the great divide between belief and non-belief (John 12:35-50).

The Qur'an says, "As for that which We inspire in thee of the Scripture [Qur'an], it is the Truth" (Fatir [The Originator of Creation] 35:31). The Qur'an claimed to be the criterion of all truth. It is the great divide between those who are sincere believers and those who are non-believers (Inshiqaq [The Rending Asunder] 84:20-25).

Regarding the ultimate criteria for truth, the Qur'an recited by Muhammad and Jesus the Messiah born through the virgin Mary are the comparison. The Messiah is the Word of God in human form. The Qur'an is the Word of God in a book form.

What difference does it make whether the Qur'an or the Messiah is the truth center? Some theologians urge that we nudge Jesus and the Qur'an aside, and that Muslims and Christians converse with one another only about God. In God we can find a common meeting ground, they surmise.

However, who is God? Is he a tyrant? Does he love us or hate us? Is he involved in human life or has he abandoned us? Does he reveal himself or only his will? What is the meaning of life and of our ultimate destiny? For all such questions and many more, we are driven into the arms of revelation. But then comes the question: Which revelation?

There is indeed convergence between biblical faith and qur'anic faith. Nevertheless, as Bishop Kenneth Cragg aptly states, within every convergence there is divergence. This is because ultimately the Messiah of the biblical scriptures and the Qur'an of Islam take us in different directions.

The message of biblical faith is that God in the Messiah enters personally into our sinfulness to redeem us from sin and death. God, in the Messiah, actively and personally and lovingly pursues us so that we might be reconciled to him, to one another, and to creation. The message of qur'anic faith is that God, the merciful and compassionate one, sends his will down to us. In submission to his will we find well-being. Jesus offers redemption; the Qur'an offers guidance.

Unity–Mission–Diversity

God is one (*tawhid*) and God as Father, Son, and Holy Spirit (Trinity)—these understandings of God emerge from the desire of Muslims and Christians to faithfully express their scriptures, their witness, and mission. The long faith journeys of the Muslim nation and the Christian church are a response to these different understandings of God and his nature. These faith commitments have exceedingly significant practical implications, implications related to diversity and unity on planet earth, not to mention within the communities of faith. These understandings also form the different commitments to mission that characterize the

Muslim nation and the Christian church. (Chapter 14 will explore the mission of these two communities.)

The Muslim *ummah* confesses the oneness of God (*tawhid*). Of course, Christians also confess that God is one.

Whenever a Christian is baptized, the church seals the covenant of baptism in the name of God the Father, God the Son, and God the Holy Spirit. The liturgies and worship of the church, the creeds and confessions of faith, proclaim that the Christian movement is a faith response to God who has revealed himself as Creator (Father), Redeeming Savior in the Messiah (Son), and present within us now (Holy Spirit), the One in Three, triune God. That is diversity and communion within the oneness of God.

God as Trinity is God who is personally involved in mission. God sent his Son! God sent his Holy Spirit! God who is love reaches out beyond himself. In his unity, God as Trinity does not just reveal his will. He loves the sinner, and personally seeks the sinner in order to redeem the sinner. That is the calling of the church. As God sent his Son into the world, God also sends the church into the world. Why? To love, serve, and seek lost people as the Messiah loved, served, and sought to redeem all sinners.

The confession that there is diversity united in self-giving love in God provides the theological foundations for allowing diversity within the church. The unity of the church is based on a self-giving loving commitment: God's self-giving love to us; our self-giving love for God; self-giving love for one another; self-giving love for sinners. The church confesses: one body (the church), one Spirit, one hope, one Lord, one faith, one baptism, one God and Father of all, and, therefore, diversity within the unity of the bonds of peace (Eph. 4:4-6). This is a unity that celebrates diversity. Trinitarian theology is a theology of self-giving, loving unity within diversity; that theology nurtures the global church in two directions: diversity within unity.

Muslims very frequently comment, "The church has tremendous diversity. But within the Muslim nation every congregation prays at the same times and in the same way, all over the world. Even the language of worship is the same everywhere. We are united as one worldwide Muslim nation."

This Muslim commitment to one way of worship is consistent with the Muslim theology of *tawhid*. Just as there is no diversity within God, so there is no diversity within his will, and worship patterns should reflect that reality. For example, as noted earlier, God's final will is revealed in an Arabic Qur'an. It cannot be translated, for translation would bring diversity into the revelation and into the Muslim *ummah*. That should not be.

In various ways Islamic renewal movements are attempts to establish the unitary will of the unitary God on earth. Within bounds there are diversities of interpretation as to how that will should be expressed. There are four Islamic schools of law that do reflect diversities within boundaries. (Chapter 12 will address Islamic law.) Nevertheless, the core commitment to implementing God's single will on earth is always there in all Islamic renewal movements.

The Iranian sociologist, Ali Shari'ati, has expounded on the theological foundations of the Iranian Islamic revolution. The commitment of that revolution is to establish the one will of the one God on earth and in time among all peoples. Shari'ati argues that any divergence from the unitary will of God is *shirk*, just as pernicious as ascribing associates to God. There is no secular arena—all arenas of life are sacred. The political, economic, cultural, domestic, private, and public domains need to express the *tawhid* of God's will.[2]

There is not much space for diversity within Shari'ati's kind of unitary framework. The unity of the Islamic movement must be enforced. Relaxation of pressure on people to conform to the unity of the will of God would permit intolerable diversity. It would erode the fundamental commitments to *tawhid*. However, that commitment is not easily implemented in the modern world with all its diversity; witness the on-going stresses within the Iranian revolution.

Muslim Questions to the Church

When Muslims view the church, they often critique the church for abandoning any commitment to *tawhid* as a commitment to the unitary will of God. This critique is twofold. It often reveals perplexity. The critique is often expressed as questions.

Why Is There So Much Diversity?

First, Muslims are surprised that there is so much cultural diversity within the Christian church. There are huge differences in practice. How can the Quakers, who have no liturgy or rituals, and the high Anglicans, with their incense and liturgy, all be considered as expressions of the Christian church? While Christians might feel that the diversities within the Christian movement are an expression of dynamism, rich variety, and vitality, Muslims are not so sure that Christian diversity is a good thing.

Why Don't Christians Follow Jesus?

The second critique is the observation that Christians often too easily succumb to schizophrenia, dividing life between pious worship and the gung-ho secular. For example, during the height of the hostage crisis in Iran (1979-81) a Christian acquaintance of mine, Charles Kimball, traveled to Iran with an American church delegation. They met with Ayatollah Khomeini, who was the spiritual leader of the Iranian Islamic revolution that was just getting underway at that time.

It was a terrible time in Iranian-American relations. Nevertheless, the ayatollah advised his American Christian visitors, "I have a message to the church in America: Follow Jesus! If the Christians in America would follow Jesus the Messiah, problems between Iran and the United States would be quickly resolved."

I suppose the ayatollah had an overly high regard for the influence of American Christians on international policy! However, just as the ayatollah advised the American church delegation in Iran, Muslims have often counseled me, "If you believe that Jesus is Lord, then act that way."

Occasionally, Muslims have chided me, "As Muslims we have always said that the teachings of Jesus are not practical. We believe that in contrast the Qur'an is practical. For example, Jesus taught that his disciples should not use the sword or get divorced. As Muslims we know that is an impossible ideal, so the Qur'an and Islamic law tell us how to fight, how to treat our enemies, and how to divorce in a proper way. Islam is practical, and so it is possible to live in submission to universals of Islamic law.

"The great inconsistency within the Christian church is that you claim with your mouths Jesus is Lord, but your lives reveal that you really believe that Jesus is not practical. Your lives show that you agree with Islam, that the teachings of Jesus are an impossible ideal. So you divide your lives into compartments, rejecting Jesus in some areas, and obeying him in convenient areas. You violate Christian *tawhid* by living divided lives."

That was Ahmad's concern when I met him several years after the conversation about the Trinity in Nairobi. Ahmad was now driving taxi in Washington, D.C. He took me to a restaurant offering Ethiopian *injera* and *wat*.

He said, "Christians say that Jesus is Lord. Yet I have not yet met any Christians who obey the teachings of Jesus. They obey Jesus the Messiah only when it is convenient. However, most certainly if Christians followed Jesus, this country would be transformed in wonderful ways. In fact, the church in America would be a blessing to nations everywhere."

Recall that several years before that Washington dinner, Ahmad had knocked on my door in agitation and concern in Eastleigh, Nairobi, because he was committed to supporting *tawhid*. He was disturbed because he was sure that Trinity was adversarial to *tawhid*. Now Ahmad was pleading with me to take Jesus seriously.

He implored, "If the law of the Messiah is love, then live that way! Christians loving as the Messiah loved would indeed bless all nations."

Readings from the Bible:
Matthew 28:18-20
Readings from the Qur'an:
Rum 30:30-32; Shura 42:13-15

Questions for Reflection and Discussion:
1. Comment on this statement: Some of the objections to the Trinity and Son of God by the Muslim *ummah* are based upon misunderstandings or distortions of Christian belief (Maida 5:75; Anam 6:100-1).
2. How might a Christian explain to a Muslim friend the meaning of the Messiah as the Son of God (John 1:1, 14; Nisaa 4:171)?
3. In what ways does *tawhid* influence Muslim reform movements such as the Iranian revolution?
4. The Muslim *ummah* often observes that the Christian church really agrees with the Muslim observation that the life and teachings of Jesus are impractical. Comment.

5. Christians pray for God's will to be done on earth as in heaven. Yet the Christian church experiences great diversity. The Muslim *ummah*, on the other hand, has far less diversity; for example, all Muslim formal prayers are similar. Explain the difference.

6. Comment on this statement: God as Trinity is God the missionary God.

— 11 —

Pilgrimage:
the *Hajj*—the Eucharist

Yusuf had a notable temper. He was the labor officer in the Somali town where we lived. I dreaded going to his office with employees at the school I was directing. Yusuf's tongue could cut.

Then the town chatterers spread the good news. Yusuf was going on the pilgrimage to Mecca.

Farah, our foreman, explained to me, "When Yusuf returns from the pilgrimage he will have a new name. He will be Hajji Yusuf. He will also have a new character. The whole town is delighted that Yusuf will gain a transformed name and character."

When Yusuf returned from the pilgrimage, he carried his new status of *hajji* with becoming dignity. As for his tempestuous temper, an instantaneous cure was not evident, but the villagers hoped for a gradual transformation.

The Pillars of Belief and Duty

The pilgrimage (*hajj*) that Yusuf took is one of the five pillars of Muslim faith, duty, and action. The five pillars are: (1) giving witness to the faith (*shahada*)—there is no God but Allah and Muhammad is the prophet of Allah; (2) submitting to God in worship and ritual prayer (*salat*); (3) giving alms to the poor (*zakat*); (4) fasting during the month of Ramadan (*sawm*); (5) the pilgrimage to Mecca (*hajj*).

Some Muslim theologians and communities also include a sixth pillar, that of striving in the defense of Islam (*jihad*).[1] All the pillars of duty are proclaimed in the Qur'an. Muhammad modeled all of these acts of faithfulness, although none of the rituals are fully developed within the qur'anic scriptures. Each of these acts of faith and duty has had its own development during the first several centuries of the Muslim movement.[2] This chapter explores only the fifth pillar, that of the pilgrimage.

The Pilgrimage to Mecca

Every year Muslims from around the globe make the pilgrimage to the Ka'bah in Mecca. They receive a new name: in East Africa the name is *hajji* (men) or *hajjiah* (women). In the 1930s as many as one hundred thousand pilgrims came to Mecca annually for the pilgrimage; today as many as three million people journey to Mecca and the adjunct pilgrimage locations during the five to nine days of pilgrimage. The pilgrimage, which begins on the eighth day of the month of Dhu al-Hijjah, has become the largest gathering of people for any event on earth.

When the pilgrims return home, in hundreds of languages and thousands of hamlets around the world the new *hajjis* and *hajjiahs* tell of their experiences in Mecca. Attentive little boys and girls listen to the stories and determine that they will also journey on the pilgrimage sometime.

The pilgrimage is only required for those who can afford the journey. However the Muslim theologian, Muhammad Hamidullah, comments:

> But which Muslim would not collect, little by little, the necessary amount for being one day able to visit the center of his religion, the Ka'bah or the House of God? The Qur'an (Ali 'Imran [The Family of Imran] 3:96) does not exaggerate when it says that this is the oldest house in the world dedicated by mankind to God and to the cult of monotheism. If one were to think only of Abraham—who according to the Islamic tradition, was but the restorer of the edifice erected originally by Adam—it would be older than the temple of Jerusalem constructed by Solomon.[3]

We shall trace the nine-day pilgrimage. This sojourn reveals core Islamic beliefs.

The Arrival in Mecca

All male pilgrims wear an *ihram* (a ritual two-piece white garment). The garment reveals that all Muslims are equal under God. *Ihram* is also a state of reverent dedication to God. The pilgrim must enter the state of *ihram* before arriving in Mecca. Pilgrims arriving by road will see a sign prohibiting non-Muslims from approaching Mecca. Indeed the *ummah* is distinct from all other communities on earth.

Most pilgrims converge in Jeddah, from whence they commence the forty-five mile journey to Mecca. As they make the journey they offer this prayer (the *talbiyyah*) continually,

> Here am I, O God, at Thy Command, here I am!
> Thou art without associates,
> Thine are praise and grace and dominion,
> Thou art without associates.
> Here I am![4]

The Ka'bah (The First House of God)

In Mecca, the pilgrims enter the Masjidal-Haram. This is the Sacred Mosque that can accommodate five hundred thousand people. The Ka'bah stands in the center of the Sacred Mosque. Muslims believe that this is where Adam first worshiped God. The Ka'bah is the first house of God that Adam built and Abraham and Ishmael rebuilt. Muhammad cleansed this house of idolatry, destroying the 360 deities of the Ka'bah when he began his prophetic preaching. Muhammad not only confronted the idolatry of idol worship, but he also preached against the injustices that were intertwined with these idolatrous practices, such as female infanticide.[5]

Within the wall of the Ka'bah is a sacred black stone. Muslims believe this stone came from the heavens at the time Adam and Eve descended to earth from paradise. They believe Abraham and Ishmael miraculously found this neglected stone, and placed it within the wall of the Ka'bah when they rebuilt the house of God.

Muhammad kissed this stone in his farewell pilgrimage just before his death. All pilgrims likewise kiss or point toward the stone as they circle the Ka'bah counterclockwise. The stone and the Ka'bah are on their left. The ritual and prayers are precise and detailed. Pilgrims circle the Ka'bah seven times.

The following comments from Muhammad Hamidullah help to clarify the role of the black stone and the Ka'bah in Islam.

> In the Hadith (Traditions), the Prophet has named the (black stone) the "right hand of God" (*yamin-Allah*), and for purpose. In fact one poses there one's hand to conclude the pact, and God obtains there our pact of allegiance and submission. In the qur'anic terminology, God is the king, and . . . in (his) realm there is a metropolis (*Ummal qurra*) and in the metropolis naturally a palace (*Bait-Allah, home of God*). If a subject wants to testify to his loyalty, he has to go to the royal palace and conclude personally the pact of allegiance. The right hand of the invisible God must be visible symbolically. And that is the *al-Hajar al-Aswad*, the Black Stone in the Ka'bah.[6]

The pilgrimage is a journey to the most sacred place in Islam. In a very special way Muslims believe that at the Ka'bah, there is the convergence of the revelation of God with the first, middle, and final prophets of Islam: Adam, Abraham, and Muhammad. For Muslims the pilgrimage to this most sacred of places is a sign of sealing the covenant of full submission to the will of God. The Ka'bah is not just a building that houses a black stone. It is rather, the first house of God, the center of the earth where the first human parents bowed in worship and submission to Allah.

The Footsteps of Hagar, Ishmael, and Abraham

For Muslims the pilgrimage is also a reenactment of Abraham's journey. Pilgrims pray at the Station of Abraham. They move on to the well of Zamzam. This is the place where the angel Gabriel miraculously provided water for Hagar and Ishmael. It is considered to be the purest water on earth. Pilgrims drink not only for refreshment, but also for cleansing.

From the well they move a short distance to the twin hills of al-Safa and al-Marwa. They walk back and forth between these hills remembering Hagar's distress when she walked between these hills praying for water for her son who was near death from thirst.

Muhammad's Last Pilgrimage

The pilgrims move on to the Plain of Arafat about ten miles from Mecca. In the center of the plain is the Mount of Mercy, where Muhammad preached his last sermon to one hundred thousand believers. In that message he instituted the pilgrimage.

As the Muslims gather at the mount, they hear a sermon pro-claimed with the same themes that Muhammad preached there on his last pilgrimage. The Mount of Mercy is also where Adam sought guidance and mercy from God.

The gathering of this vast congregation of two to three mil-lion people from around the world is the climax of the pilgrim-age. The preacher stands on the Mount of Mercy where Adam and Muhammad had once stood. The throngs stand together as one people to hear the Word of God proclaimed: God is one and has no associates; all Muslims are equal to one another.

Remembrance of Ishmael—the Feast of Sacrifice

After a time of rest, the pilgrims make their way to Mina after midnight, where three stone pillars stand as representations of devils. The pillars are a reminder that the devil tried to persuade Abraham not to sacrifice his son Ishmael. At Mina the pilgrims throw pebbles against the pillars as a demonstration of their opposition to the devil and his wiles.

After the pebble throwing at Mina, the pilgrims come out of *ihram*. They dress in the costumes of their native countries. It is now festival time. They buy sheep or other animals such as camels for the nighttime sacrifice and feasting. The sacrifice of these animals is in remembrance that God saved the life of Ishmael from sacrifice by providing a ram as a substitute.

Muslims around the world participate in this night of sacri-fice and feasting. The nations and peoples who comprise the Muslim nation are bound together in this Festival of Sacrifice ('Id al-Adha). This four-day festival begins on the tenth day of the month of pilgrimage (Duhl-Hijja). All Muslims cherish Abraham and Ishmael as prophets who together persevered and passed on the Islam upon which Muhammad and the Muslim nation have established their faith and practice. Not only was Ishmael saved from death by that substitute sacrifice, but the faith foundation of the Muslim nation was also preserved and thereby passed on to future generations. Gifts are shared and food is provided for the poor.

The final act of pilgrimage is to return to Mecca a final time for a last visit to the Ka'bah. Many pilgrims will extend their stay, perhaps visiting Medina as well. Such forays might be edifying, but they are not part of the requirements for pilgrimage.

Theology of the Pilgrimage

Profound theological themes are interwoven within the pilgrimage. Anthropologists of religion observe that in many faiths there is a place that represents the "navel of the earth." The navel is the link between divinity and humanity, the connection between heaven and earth. In Islam, the Ka'bah is that link.

The black stone in the Ka'bah is heaven's gift to Adam and all humanity. It represents the link between heaven and earth, between humanity and God, and the unity of all people. It is a symbol of Islam that God has sent down as a mercy for all people. The stone represents the unity of all prophets, for Adam, Abraham, and Muhammad all treasured that stone.

The stone represents the miracle of revelation; the stone came from heaven for Adam. It was lost, buried in the sand. Muslims believe that miraculously, Abraham and Ishmael found that stone, and it is now forever embedded in the first house of God, the Ka'bah.

The Abraham, Hagar, and Ishmael narratives prevail as organizing themes throughout the pilgrimage. The same is true of Muhammad's farewell pilgrimage and his last sermon proclaimed from the Mount of Mercy on the Plains of Arafat. Adam's legacy is interwoven as well. The pilgrimage is an explicit statement of Muslim solidarity with all God's prophets and people throughout the ages. It is also a statement of Muslim otherness from those peoples who do not submit to Islam.

The festival of sacrifice is noteworthy. Within the soul of the pilgrimage is the celebration of joyous remembrance that God saved Ishmael and the Muslim nation through the substitute sacrifice of a ram. This is a mystery within the soul of Islam. What is the meaning of the ram that was sacrificed in the place of a son of Abraham?

Is this a Sign?—a Ram Substituted for Abraham's Son

Christians invite Muslims to consider another sacrifice on a hill called Golgotha, just outside Jerusalem's walls. That is where, Christians believe, Jesus was crucified. Could it be that the Messiah, who is also called the Lamb of God, is the fulfillment of the mystery of the ram offered by Abraham in the place of his son?

That question confronted a group of us Muslims and

Christians during a late-night conversation in a Philadelphia mosque during the Ramadan month of fasting. The prayers continued for about two hours. It was approaching ten o'clock when we were able to gather in a circle for conversation.

The imam asked, "Have you noticed that we have offered extra prayers tonight? We are praying about two extra hours every night during the month of fasting. We hope that these extra prayers will compensate for our sins."

"Have you said enough prayers to fully compensate for your sins?" one of the Christians asked.

"We have no idea," the imam responded.

We said, "In the Torah of Moses, the people of God were commanded to sacrifice animals as sin offerings. What do these sacrifices mean? What is the meaning behind the sacrifice of a ram in the place of a son of Abraham?

"One of the names of Jesus the Messiah is Lamb of God. This means that the Messiah has taken our place through his sacrificial death on the cross. The New Testament reveals that the animals sacrificed in the Torah are signs pointing toward the ultimate sacrifice of the Messiah. He has taken our place. We are forgiven."

"That is impossible," the imam protested. "Each person must bear the consequence of his own sin. When the judge pronounces judgment, the guilty person must pay the consequence of his sin."

"That is true," we agreed. "However, if the judge himself steps down from his judge's bench and says, 'I will take your place,' then you are free. That is the meaning of redemption. In the Messiah God has entered the courtroom to redeem us by taking our place."

There was an awesome silence in the mosque that night as for a brief minute we considered the costly gift of forgiveness and redemption that God in the Messiah offers.

God the Merciful Intercessor

Redemption is at the heart of the Christian Gospel, but redemption is not a central theme in Muslim theology. Nevertheless, there are hints within Islam of a God who redeems. Noteworthy is the ram that God provided as a substitute for a son of Abraham. There is also an affirmation in the Qur'an that God himself is our intercessor.

The Qur'an states, "[Allah] mounted the throne. Ye have not, beside Him, a protecting friend or mediator [intercessor]. Will ye not then remember?" (Sajda [Adoration] 32:4).

Elsewhere we read:

> And when those who believe in Our revelations come unto thee, say: Peace be unto you! Your Lord had prescribed for Himself mercy [or inscribed upon himself the rule of mercy], that whoso of you doeth evil through ignorance and repenteth afterward thereof and doeth right, (for him) lo! Allah is Forgiving, Merciful. (Anan [Cattle] 6:54)

This last verse is the most Gospel-like statement in the Qur'an—God has inscribed the rule of mercy upon himself! In these verses God is described as our friend and merciful intercessor. In Islam God extends mercy to those who make the first move to God in repentance. There is mercy for the sinner who repents and submits to Islam, for God has prescribed mercy for himself.

Such qur'anic references are hints of Gospel-like understandings of God. Nevertheless, within the Gospel, we meet God in the Messiah seeking for and eating with sinners. He gives his life for sinners.

The religious authorities asked, "Why does [Jesus] eat with tax collectors and 'sinners'?"

Jesus responded, "I have not come to call the righteous, but sinners" (Matt. 9:11, 13).

In the New Testament, God is portrayed in a parable of a father and his two sons. In that parable, the father abandoned his dignity to run to embrace the lost and rebellious son when he saw him at a great distance down the road. He prepared a feast for the lost son. This father also pled with the sullen older son, who was still living at home, to also enjoy the feast of gracious bounty in the father's house, for the son who was lost had come home (Luke 15:11-32).

This parable is a revelation of God's self-giving love revealed in many ways, but supremely so in the sacrificial love of the Messiah (Luke 15:1-7). God in the Messiah seeks sinners and welcomes them. He even eats with sinners. The Messiah gives his life for the redemption of sinners. And that brings us again to the Feast of Sacrifice within Islam. What is the meaning of this mystery? Is this a sign that is fulfilled in the sacrificial, self-giving love of God revealed in the

Messiah? God provided the ram to redeem a son of Abraham from death by taking the son's place. The Gospel proclaims that in his sacrificial death on the cross, the Messiah has taken our place.

Pilgrimage with the Messiah

Christians do not go to a sacred place to commemorate an Abrahamic pilgrimage as the Muslims do during the Dhu al-Hijja. However, God does call all people of faith to follow him. This call, like that of Abraham, means that we need to "leave" the securities of place and family in order to follow God in faith. That leaving might not be a literal packing of bags and moving to another country, although God does call some people to do exactly that. However, whether God calls a person to another country or not, all people of faith discover that following God's call is a pilgrimage that demands ultimate loyalty, a loyalty that supersedes all other commitment.

In the Christian calendar there are commemorations that are both convergent and divergent with the Muslim pilgrimage: Palm Sunday, Good Friday, and Easter. We will explore these events, celebrations, and memorials within the Christian experience and against the backdrop of the Muslim pilgrimage to Mecca.

The Temple (The House of God)

Jesus the Messiah frequently came to the temple. In fact, his first recorded statement, given when he was twelve years old, was to his parents when they found him in the temple: "'Why were you searching for me?' he asked. 'Didn't you know that I had to be in my Father's house?'" (Luke 2:49). Jesus lived in faithfulness to the Jewish religious expectations related to the temple tradition and practices.[7]

Nevertheless, Jesus did challenge the injustices, hypocrisy, and dehumanization within the temple system. Furthermore, he acted as one who believed that his presence was the fulfillment of the faith that the temple represented. That conviction led him into collision with the temple authorities. Chapter 8 commented on Palm Sunday and the cleansing of the temple. Chapter 9 also described the developing conflict between Jesus and the temple system.

Within Jewish theology the temple was considered to be the House of God. At the time when King Solomon dedicated the first temple, the glory of God filled the temple (2 Chron. 6:1–7:10). Solomon's temple was destroyed by Babylonian invaders in 586 B.C. It was rebuilt under Zerubbabel's leadership and dedicated in 515 B.C. Just before and following the time of the Messiah, a major rebuilding and restoration of the temple was underway. Throughout the centuries, Israel made regular pilgrimages to the temple to commemorate Jewish festivals. A pervasive and costly temple cult had developed by the time of Jesus. For many in Israel, the house of God had become an ensnaring, costly, corrupting idolatry.[8]

Jesus entered the temple and drove out the corrupting merchants, proclaiming, "Get these out of here! How dare you turn my Father's house into a market" (John 2:16). Six centuries later, Muhammad cleansed another house of God, the Ka'bah in Mecca, of corrupting worship practices. On the face of it, the mission of Jesus and that of Muhammad in cleansing these respective houses of worship seem convergent. However, Jesus not only cleansed the temple of corruption, he also scandalized the authorities by declaring the temple to be an irrelevancy in the true worship of God. (Recall chapter 9.)

The Messiah Is the Temple

Within the tumult created as Jesus cleansed the temple, he further outraged the temple authorities by proclaiming, "Destroy this temple, and I will raise it again in three days" (John 2:19). On another occasion Jesus dismayed his disciples by predicting, "As for what you see here, the time will come when not one stone will be left on another; every one of them will be thrown down" (Luke 21:6).

Muhammad never declared himself to be the replacement of the house of God, the Ka'bah. In fact, the annual Muslim pilgrimage to the Ka'bah reinforces the utter significance for this first house of God for all Muslims.[9]

However, for Jesus, there was no need for a house of God built by human hands. Jesus believed that he was the replacement of the temple. Now that he had come, the temple was needed no more. He is the Temple of God.[10] That conviction was a key reason the religious authorities demanded his crucifixion.

In later Christian theology, the church—the body of the Messiah—is also the temple of God. The Messiah and his church replace the temple. The only house of God is the Messiah who is the fullness of the presence of God and the people of God among whom and within whom the Messiah dwells through the Holy Spirit (Eph. 2:19-22). Jesus said it clearly and bluntly, "For where two or three come together in my name, there am I with them" (Matt. 18:20).

The Temple Mount

If the Ka'bah in Muslim understanding is the first house of God, there are other Muslim sacred places as well. Noteworthy is the Temple Mount in Jerusalem where the Dome of the Rock Mosque is built. The introduction to this book observed that a core reality creating the current Israeli-Palestinian impasse over Jerusalem is that both Muslims and Israelis consider the Temple Mount to be a most sacred place. This is the very place that Jesus considered to be an irrelevancy.

During the Israeli siege of the Church of the Nativity in Bethlehem in the first half of 2002, Muslim friends told me of their incredulity that the two billion Christians on earth did not rise up in riotous outrage. How could Christians be so quiescent when one of their most sacred places was being so desecrated? They contrasted this with the faithful Muslim commitment to their holy places—witness the outrage and subsequent Palestinian *intifada* when Arial Sharon led a squadron of troops onto the Temple Mount when Muslims were gathered at the Dome of the Rock Mosque during Friday prayers, September 27, 2000.

Of course, Christians are dismayed and grieved when places of sacred memory are desecrated. That is an outrage. Yet Christians believe that the House of God is not made with human hands. All those who love God "become a dwelling in which God lives by his Spirit" (Eph. 2:22).

A Eucharistic Pilgrimage

This means that the Christian church does not need to take pilgrimages to a sacred place. There is no house of God built by human hands that Christians must visit. This is because the new House of God is not made of wood and stone, but rather it is the people of God. So the Christian pilgrimage does not lead one to a sacred place, but rather to following God wherever he leads. The pilgrimage is receiving and celebrating and sharing God's grace.

The eucharist (communion or mass) is a sign of the nature of the Christian pilgrimage. The word eucharist means "grace, joy, and gratitude." What is the source of grace and joy and gratitude in the eucharistic pilgrimage?

A Muslim Prayer: The Table

The Qur'an reveals yearning for a communion feast provided by God, a feast that Christians believe is fulfilled in the Eucharist. In the final portion of the *sura* called Maida (the Table Spread), the disciples of Jesus the Messiah plead,

> Is thy Lord able to send down for us a table spread with food from heaven? . . . We wish to eat thereof, that we may satisfy our hearts and know that thou has spoken truth to us, and that thereof we may be witnesses.
>
> Jesus, son of Mary, said: O Allah, Lord of us! Send down for us a table spread with food from heaven, that it may be a feast for us, for the first of us and for the last of us, and a sign from Thee. Give us sustenance, for Thou are the Best of Sustainers.
>
> Allah said: Lo! I send it down for you (Maida [the Table Spread] 5:112-15)!

This surprising prayer may well be a whimsical remembrance of the table at Mount Sinai where Moses and the seventy elders of Israel ate in the presence of the Lord (Exodus 24:11). However, according to Yusuf Ali, a respected Muslim commentator, this prayer relates to the Last Supper.[11] Within the concluding chapters of the Qur'an proclaimed during the time the community was developing its identity in Medina, there is this beseeching prayer: Lord, provide a feast from heaven. And God replies: It is provided! The feast of forgiving grace, the fellowship of the covenant; it is provided.

Let us reflect on the nature of that feast as fulfilled in Jesus the Messiah who broke bread and shared the cup with his disciples in anticipation of his crucifixion and resurrection.

Jesus and His Disciples Share in the Passover Meal

The evening before Jesus' betrayal, arrest, and crucifixion, he joined in a Passover meal with his disciples. Passover was a Jewish remembrance that God had saved the first-born sons in Israel from death in Egypt through the sacrifice of lambs at the time when God delivered Israel from enslavement to pharaoh. That evening, as Jesus and his disciples ate the Passover meal together, Jesus linked the meaning of Passover to his forthcoming sacrificial death on the cross and the future fulfillment of the kingdom of God.

Broken Bread and Crushed Grapes

Jesus took bread and a cup of wine and said, "I have eagerly desired to eat this Passover with you before I suffer. For I tell you, I will not eat it again until it finds fulfillment in the kingdom of God" (Luke 22:15-16).

He broke the bread, sharing it with his disciples and saying, "Take and eat; this is my body."

Then he shared the cup of wine, saying, "Drink from it, all of you. This is my blood of the covenant, which is poured out for many for the forgiveness of sins" (Matt. 26:27-28).

Local Christian congregations gather regularly and eat bread and drink wine together, commemorating Christ's sacrificial suffering and crucifixion.

Roy Hange, who has taught Christian theology in the Imam Khomeini Education and Research Institute in Qom, Iran, comments that a most distinctive surprise of the Gospel is the meaning behind the signs of the broken bread and crushed grapes of the communion service. These are signs of suffering and service. The grapes are broken and crushed, thereby becoming wine. That is the pilgrimage to which God calls the church. This is a journey with Christ into a world that does not comprehend the suffering, serving, and self-giving love of God. Yet in this pilgrimage of redemptive suffering, the church becomes a community of healing to the nations. The whole Christian life is that kind of pilgrimage.

Invitation

This Christian pilgrimage is an invitation to gather as sinners in the name of Jesus the Messiah, to receive anew his costly gift of forgiveness and grace, and to scatter in our multiple and diverse pilgrimages into the world. As the broken bread and crushed grapes give life to all who receive, so also the church offers life and healing to all who will receive the gift of God's grace in the Messiah.

Pilgrimage involves the senses. It is a journey with sights and smells and people. When Muslims return to their homes from the *hajj*, they reminisce on what they felt on that journey. The eucharistic pilgrimage for the Christian is also a journey filled with surprises. This includes the surprises of the touch of God's grace as the worshipers receive the signs of grace in the broken bread and the wine of the crushed grapes celebrating with joy the sacrifice of the Messiah for the redemption of sinners.

The church is also on a pilgrimage into the future. As Jesus shared the cup of wine at that last Passover supper with his disciples, he said, "I will not drink of this fruit of the vine from now on until the day when I drink it anew with you in my Father's kingdom" (Matt. 26:29). That statement anticipates the final chapter of history.

Readings from the Bible:
  John 2:12-22
Readings from the Qur'an:
  Baqara 2:196-203; Hajj 22:26-33; Maida 5:115-118

Questions for Reflection and Discussion:
  1. Reflect on the significance of Abraham and Ishmael in the commemorations enacted in the Muslim pilgrimage. What are the theological and spiritual themes that are enacted on this journey (Baqara 2:124-27; Saaffat 37:99-111)?
  2. How did Muhammad relate to the Ka'bah in Mecca (Baqara 2:124-128)? How did Jesus relate to the temple in Jerusalem (Luke 2:41-50; John 2:19-22; Luke 21:5-6; Eph. 2: 19-22)? What is especially astonishing about Jesus' pronouncements in regard to the temple?
  3. What do Muslims mean by the house of God (Maida 5:100; 2:26)? What is the New Testament understanding of the temple of God (Eph. 2:19-22)?
  4. What is the significance of the Feast of Sacrifice in Islam (Hajj 22:28)? What is the meaning of the eucharist in the life of the church (1 Cor. 11:23-28)?
  5. Is it appropriate for Christians to invite Muslims to consider the Feast of Sacrifice as a sign whose meaning is fulfilled in the sacrifice of the Messiah as the Lamb of God? Give reasons for your response.

— 12 —

Two Ways:
Shari'a—Holy Spirit

"THIS area of the city has come under the control of the Shari'a," my Muslim companions observed as they drove me into the heart of Birmingham, England. "Do you see the evidence?"

I did see evidence. A number of billboards were painted black. They told me that behind the black paint was either a scantily clad woman or a beer advertisement.

This was during six days of dialogues hosted by the Muslim Students' Association of the United Kingdom. At the end of a fervent week of public debates, my hosts drove me and the companions with whom I had been in these dialogues, to Heathrow Airport.

On the way, one of the dialogue team said, "Western society needs Islamic Shari'a. When that day comes, the West will be redeemed from its decadence."

"I disagree," I said. "I believe that Shari'a circumscribes the freedom of people in ways that are destructive of the God-given dignity and responsibilities of the person. And the church is always severely curtailed, as you can see from what is happening in Sudan and Nigeria."

"Oh, my no!" one of the team exclaimed. "Christians appreciate Shari'a, for it brings an end to decadence and protects the rights of the Christians."

"That is not how we Christians experience Shari'a. It always places the Christians and other minorities in an inferior status," I persisted.

There was a thoughtful silence. Then one of the team said, "I am flying to Canada today and not back to my childhood homeland of Pakistan. I have chosen to live in Canada, because neither I, nor any one of us in this car, want to live under Shari'a either."

That conversation was a revelation of a struggle within the global soul of Islam and the Muslim community. How can the Muslim community embrace the unchangeable Law of God in a world that perceives that law to be repressive and abusive of the rights and freedoms of the person?[1] The literal meaning of Shari'a is "the path to the watering hole." The intention of Shari'a is well-being and peace. What is the path to that well? What is the responsibility of the Muslim authorities to define and defend that path?

That was one of the concerns of a dialogue between Iranian and Mennonite theologians in October 2002. Several Muslim theologians from Qom, Iran, invested four days in conversation and dialogue with Mennonite theologians in Toronto, Canada. At the Muslims' request, the organizing theme of the dialogue was faith and modernity. They wanted to hear and learn from Mennonites who practice faith in a modernizing world. The Iranian Muslim revolution is in the cauldron of struggle: how does a Muslim state uphold Shari'a when the democratizing forces run counter to the Law of God? Those were the core concerns of our days together.

"The way that Jesus and the New Testament church believed and lived is all right for monks who are on the edges of society, but not for religious leaders who have political power and responsibility," was the comment of one of the Iranians in response to an Anabaptist presentation on pluralist culture and truth.

We will explore how Shari'a developed and then note modern responses to Shari'a. Then we will look at the mission of the Holy Spirit in Christian experience. A central concern is the way these commitments equip the Muslim nation and the Christian church for the challenges of modern pluralist societies.

The Development of Shari'a

Muslims believe that Islam is the perfect guidance for belief and practice. As mentioned repeatedly in previous chapters, Muslims believe that God has sent down Islam to humankind through the mediation of angels. Islam never changes. The Islam sent down to the first prophet, Adam, is the same Islam that God sent down through the middle prophet, Abraham, or the final prophet, Muhammad. Islam as revealed and clarified in the Qur'an is the final and perfect guidance.

This Muslim understanding of guidance is somewhat similar to the understanding of Torah (the Law of God) in the theology of Israel. The Torah is the soul of the Jewish scriptures, the first five books of the Bible. The Jewish people were very concerned that they obey all the laws of the Torah faithfully. So, after the temple was destroyed in A.D. 70, Jewish experts in the Law of God began the 350-year task of developing the Talmud, which defined how Jews should conduct themselves. The sixty-three volumes of the Talmud are viewed as a "fence around the Torah." It protects the Torah by defining how to live in order to obey the Torah faithfully.

In a similar way, Muslims have developed the Shari'a to define obedience to the Qur'an. In Jewish practice, the Talmud defines how to obey the Torah; in Muslim practice, the Shari'a defines how to obey the Qur'an. For both Jews and Muslims, the core commitment is to obey the Law of God in all its fullness.

However, what is the fullness of the Law of God? The Qur'an proclaims:

> It is not righteousness that ye turn your faces to the East and the West; but righteousness is he who [1] believeth in Allah [2] and the Last Day [3] and the angels [4] and the Scripture [5] and the prophets; [6] and giveth wealth, for love of Him, to kinsfolk and to orphans and the needy and the wayfarer and to those who ask, and to set slaves free; and observeth proper worship and payeth the poor-due. [7] And those who keep their treaty when they make one, and the patient in tribulation and adversity and time of stress. Such are they who are sincere. Such are the Allah-fearing (Baqara [The Cow] 2:177).

Muslims refer to this passage as the Seven Commandments of Islam. The five pillars of belief are included in the seven commandments and are listed here: All Muslims must believe (1) in God, (2) the final judgment, (3) angels, (4) scriptures, and (5) prophets. The passage also commands justice, righteousness, giving alms to the poor, and regular prayer. The entire Qur'an is that kind of book, a guide for belief and conduct. But how does a Muslim know that he has fulfilled these commands? For example, what is steadfast prayer and regular charity?

The Sunnah

Ah, it is the way Muhammad lived. He is the Seal of the Prophets, and surely he has obeyed all the commands of God in the right way. God gave Muhammad wisdom (*hikma*) to fully understand, interpret, and practice the revelation of God.

Therefore, all believers do well to follow the *sunnah* (way) of the Prophet. However, what is the *sunnah* of Muhammad? What is his way?

The Hadith

During the first two centuries of the Muslim era, that question led to the development of the Hadith (Traditions) The most monumental collection is by Bukhari, and includes 9,082 *hadiths* (when repetitions are excluded, there are 2,602 *hadiths* in Bukhari's collection[2]). Each *hadith* is a statement or episode regarding the way of the Prophet. Here is an example.

Uqba ibn Amir said, "Someone sent the Prophet a silk gown and he wore it during prayers but on withdrawing he pulled it off violently with a gesture of disgust and said, 'This is unfitting for Godfearing men.'"[3]

Other traditions had a distinctly political-theological intent. A famous example is a *hadith* defending the authority of Ali, the son-in-law of the Prophet whose reign as the fourth caliph was marred by violent conflict. This *hadith* was intended to counter the spread of fabricated *sunnah*. Note the typical chain of authority that is used to authenticate the validity of the *hadith*.

> Abu Bakr ibn abi Shayba told us that Ghundar told him on the authority of Shu'ba, and also that Muhammad ibn al-Muthanna and Ibn Bashshar both told him that Muhammad ibn Ja'far told him that Shu'ba also told him, on the authority of Mansur on the authority of Rib'I ibn Hirash who hear 'Ali, may God be pleased with him, giving a sermon in which he said that the messenger of God, may the prayers and peace of God be upon him, said, "Do not spread lies about me! Whoever spreads lies regarding me will enter the fires of hell."[4]

Over the decades following Muhammad, hundreds of thousands of *hadith* circulated. Bukhari's task was to determine which of these was authentic. That decision was based on the reliability of the chain of witnesses (*isnad*). Another scholar, Saheeh Muslim, carried forward a parallel effort to that of Bukahri. Tradition claims that Bukhari selected his 9,082 *hadiths* from six hundred thousand that he examined,[5] and that he did not even consider hundreds of thousands of others. His volume consists of ninety-seven books divided into 3,450 chapters.[6]

Systems of Shari'a

Alongside the concern for a trustworthy *sunnah* of the Prophet, other theologians were developing schools of law (the Shari'a). The Hadith was a tremendous help. The theologians drank from four streams of authority as they developed the Shari'a:

> First was the Qur'an.
> Second, the Hadith.
> Third, the art of *qiyas* (analogy).
> Fourth, the authority of *ijma* (consensus).

Developing systematic rules for living from the Qur'an and Hadith demanded insight and wisdom. Therefore the theologians developed the art of analogy and relied upon the consensus of the community as they strove to write the rules for Muslim believers. Consensus by the theologians has always been absolutely crucial within Sunni Islam. Even the decisions about which scriptures to include in the Qur'an ultimately rested upon the consensus of the theologians. They carried the responsibility to interpret God's divine guidance and apply this guidance to societies. This responsibility to interpret is called *ijtihad*. The responsibility to interpret is based squarely upon *figh*, that is insight and understanding that is derived from in-depth knowledge.

Through this process of consensus formation, the theologians developed schools of law. During the eighth and ninth centuries, the Sunni Muslims developed four schools of Shari'a: *Hanafi, Maliki, Shafi'i,* and *Hanbali*. Nuances are different, but the core is the same: The Qur'an and the *sunnah* of Muhammad provide the true highway through life. These systems define the four great families of Sunni Muslims. Shi'ite Muslims have developed other schools of law.

Although these schools of Shari'a project different nuances, they all seek to imitate the *sunnah* of their Prophet. Therefore any critique of Muhammad is felt at the deepest levels of Muslim personhood as a character assassination against all Muslims and as an attack against the whole Islamic edifice.

Muslim communities struggle with the challenges of change. *Bid'ah* (innovation) is prohibited. Sunni Muslims have generally believed that this means that since the tenth century the door of *ijtihad* was closed and there could be no further development in Shari'a. The Shi'ite Muslims, on the other hand, have never closed the door on *ijtihad*. These Muslims exercise the freedom for a continual interpretation and adaptation of Muslim practice generation by generation.

Shari'a defines for all Muslims those actions that are acceptable (*halal*) and those that are prohibited (*haram*). For example, eating flesh of an animal that has not been slaughtered in the prescribed manner is *haram;* feasting on an animal that has been slaughtered in the Muslim way is *halal.* Shari'a defines much of life into acceptable and unacceptable actions. A few violations of *haram* require penalties (*hadd*) if violated.

Shari'a and Proselytizing

Commitment to Shari'a means that people who convert to Islam must move from their culture into the Muslim culture. This is because Shari'a represents a vigorous commitment to define Muslim culture. That is the primary role of all Muslim schools of theology. All of the institutions of learning throughout the Muslim nation have a preeminent commitment to equipping leaders who are qualified to interpret and enhance Muslim culture as defined in Shari'a.

This means that whenever a person becomes a Muslim the process of proselytizing commences. By proselytizing I refer to a movement from one culture to another. The first step in the process is the confession of faith: there is no God but Allah, and Muhammad is the prophet of Allah. That simple confession sets in motion the process of absorption into Muslim culture and society. The premise is simple. Muhammad is the prophet of God. Therefore the believer must submit to the will of God as revealed in the Qur'an and follow the way of the prophet. That means submitting to Shari'a. It also means learning Arabic. Islamization assumes enculturation within the Muslim culture as defined by the Shari'a.

Shari'a and the Political Order

The Muslim ideal is that all areas of personal life and society come under the rule of law as defined by Shari'a. However, there have always been at least nuances of a two-track reality in the Muslim political-religious system. This is to say that the secular Muslim political authorities respect the Shari'a and the role of the *'ulama* (experts in Muslim law), while also administering affairs of state with the pragmatism that political realities demand. Although Muhammad was both prophet and statesman, most often throughout Muslim history the statesman and the *'ulama* have functioned within rather different spheres. In modern times these two-track realities have created enormous tensions within some expressions of the Muslim nation when Muslim renewal movements seek to bring the whole social and political order under the control and authority of the *'ulama*.

Modern Iran is an example. The Council of Guardians is committed to the Islamic revolution: All areas of public and private life must come under the unitary will of God as interpreted by the clerics, the Muslim theologians. The elected government, on the other hand, is opposed to the authoritarianism of the theological establishment and some of the restrictions on personal freedom they impose.

In November 2002, Iran hit a flashpoint. In the middle of the month, thousands of students were in the streets protesting the death sentence that the Islamic judiciary had passed on a college professor, Hashem Aghajari. According to Ali Akbar Dareini of the Associated Press, the professor's accusers claimed that in an address he said that "each new generation should be able to interpret Islam on its own." He criticized the clerical establishment for considering the interpretations of previous clerics as sacred and unalterable.[7]

President Mohammad Khatami criticized the death penalty, saying that the sentence "never should have been issued at all." A government spokesperson said this was in "collision course with national interests and no one supported such a verdict."[8] These forcefully stated objections contributed to the decision by the Islamic authorities to review the verdict. For the next months these different streams of authority in Iran could not resolve their differences and the fate of Professor Aghajari was not resolvable.

While Iran struggled, Nigeria, four thousand miles away, was in danger of becoming a pariah within the global community of nations. A woman named Amina Lawal had conceived a child out of wedlock and been sentenced to death. A year earlier Safiya Hussaini was sentenced to death for the same offense. She claimed that the father of her child was her former husband. That sentence was commuted because the conception happened before Shari'a was implemented in northern Nigeria. However, the sentence against Amina still stood. Unless the sentence was overturned, she was to die by stoning as soon as her baby was weaned. Although capital or corporal punishment for the most serious offenses, known as *hadd*, are demanded by Shari'a, these forms of retribution are generally not enforced or condoned by Islamic governments.

The implementation of Shari'a in twelve of Nigeria's northern states has taken these regions in directions that more modernist Islamic societies resist. The impetus for this movement seems to have been related to the election in Nigeria of a Christian president, Olusegun Obasanjo, in May 1999. The northern Muslims much preferred to live under the authority of Muslim leadership. The decision of the northern states to live under the fullest authority of Shari'a was a commitment to insulating these regions from Christian authority.[9]

Shari'a in the northern states also meant that the substantial Christian minorities were experiencing the circumscribing regulations of Shari'a in these regions. Of course, there were also tensions with the federal government, which is secular and pluralist. The death sentence on Amina Lawal was one such point of serious dissonance. The federal courts would never uphold such a judgment.

The global press highlighted several violent clashes between Muslims and Christians as the Shari'a program began to take hold in the northern states of Nigeria. Less world attention was given to the mass Christian prayer meetings across the country and the days devoted to prayer and fasting. The entire Christian community yearned for peace with their Muslim neighbors while also expressing forthright concern about the imposition of Shari'a. Many churches across Nigeria embraced a commitment to dialogue and pray.

For a thousand years, Muslims believed that "the path to the watering hole" was well-defined. The theologians still believe that, and all the reformers reinforce the fences along that path. However, modernity persistently and perniciously challenges those fences and the path itself.

Iranian students commented to a friend of mine, "The Iranian revolution has cleansed us of having any interest in Islam."

Others are grateful that in Iran, the true way of Islam is finally being upheld after many years of decadent influences foisted upon Iran by unbecoming alliances with the West. For these Muslims, Shari'a provides "a profound sense of stability and security."[10]

The crisis between the modernizing and conservative forces is not academic. It permeates most Muslim societies.

Now we will explore a different way, that of the Spirit of the Messiah.

The Holy Spirit

"I know nothing about the Holy Spirit," a Muslim theologian said during an evening of public dialogue on a university campus.

I replied, "The Holy Spirit is a precious gift. It is only the Holy Spirit that can reveal ultimate truth and convict of sin and convince a person to believe the Gospel."

"Do you mean that you cannot prove the Gospel to us Muslims? Islam is totally rational and logical, and so I have proved the truth of Islam tonight. Why don't you prove the Gospel?" my colleague prodded.

I said, "The Gospel is not illogical. In fact, for the believer the Gospel is the center that gives reason and purpose to all of life. But the Gospel is a total surprise—that Christ crucified is the power of God. Without the Holy Spirit, we would never naturally come to that conclusion."

"So you are saying that rationally and naturally, we cannot find the truth," my companion asked in astonishment.

"Yes. Unless the Holy Spirit opens our hearts to the truth we cannot believe the truth," I said.

"So how can we find the Holy Spirit?"

"Jesus said, 'Ask God for the Holy Spirit.' If we ask, God will not disappoint us," I said.

Muslims believe that Islam is natural and the person is fundamentally good. Therefore, people do not need the Holy Spirit in order to become believers in Allah or that Muhammad is the prophet of Allah. Logic and rationality are enough. Human will is able to discern the right way. This is the reason the Shari'a structure of Islam is so significantly dependent on *figh*, understanding based on knowledge.[11]

The Holy Spirit in Islam

However, although there is not much space for the Holy Spirit in Islamic theology, the Qur'an does refer to the Holy Spirit. In fact, God breathed his Spirit into Adam at the time of creation (Al-Hijr [The Rocky Tract] 15:29). Furthermore, the Messiah was the Spirit from God (Nisaa [Women] 4:171). Elsewhere we read that the Holy Spirit from God inspires believers (Bani Israil [The Children of Israel] 17:85-86).

Nevertheless, Muslim theologians are inclined to interpret the qur'anic references to the Holy Spirit in ways that depart from New Testament theology. Islamic theology is cautious about the Holy Spirit, in part because of a resistance to trinitarian theology. It is unusual for Muslim theologians to reflect on biblical scriptures. However, when they do so, they interpret the Bible in the light of the Qur'an, much like Christians who interpret the Old Testament through Jesus. There are several directions Muslim theologians go in regards to the Holy Spirit.

Some Muslim commentators observe that the Holy Spirit who "inspires" is the angel Gabriel, who brought revelation to Muhammad. In fact, some theologians suggest that all references to the Holy Spirit in the Qur'an are about the angel Gabriel.

However, Muslim commentator Abdullah Yusuf Ali observes that a careful exegesis does not support that notion. He believes that some references are to Gabriel, but not all. He writes that the Qur'an sometimes refers to the Holy Spirit as an expression of the mercy of God that is different from angels or books of revelation.[12]

Other Muslim theologians impose a qur'anic interpretation on the promises of Jesus about the Holy Spirit in John 14, 15, and 16. These theologians insist that these scriptures have nothing to do with the Holy Spirit, but rather are promises about the coming of the prophet Muhammad.

Jesus promised, "[He] . . . will teach you all things and will remind you of everything I have said to you. . . . I have much more to say to you, more than you can now bear. But when he, the

Spirit of truth, comes, he will guide you into all truth" (John 14:26, 16:12).

When Muslims read those scriptures, they rejoice, for they are confident that surely Jesus was prophesying the coming of the prophet Muhammad, who has brought to clarity and completion all that Jesus began to teach. Chapter 5 explored the manner in which some Muslim apologists go even further by insisting that the original texts actually did refer explicitly to Ahmad (Muhammad); however, there is no historical textual basis for such a conclusion.

Why do Muslims deflect from an engagement with the Holy Spirit of the New Testament? I will mention three reasons.

First, Muslims have full confidence in the ability of the person to find and believe the truth. The Qur'an and Muhammad's *sunnah* are clear witnesses to the truth. The signs of nature also reveal the truth. What more can the Holy Spirit add?

Second, the Holy Spirit, who is sent from the Father and the Messiah, creates a different kind of spirit in the disciple than the Spirit as described in the Qur'an. In one qur'anic *sura*, the Spirit strengthens the believers so that they will enter paradise (Al-Mujadilah [She that Disputeth] 58:22). This verse also proclaims an additional role: The Holy Spirit empowers the believers so that they will not love those who resist God or Muhammad (the Apostle), even if these nonbelievers are their own family.

In quite remarkable contrast, in the New Testament the first sign of the fruit of the Spirit in the life of a believer is love: "But the fruit of the Spirit is love" (Gal. 5:22).

The mission of the Messiah was to love sinners and non-believers; that is also true of the Holy Spirit. "God has poured out his love into our hearts by the Holy Spirit, whom he has given us. You see, at just the right time, when we were still powerless, Christ died for the ungodly. . . . God demonstrates his own love for us in this: While we were still sinners, Christ died for us" (Rom. 5:5-6, 8).

Third, Muslims have the Shari'a, "the path to the watering hole." What can the Holy Spirit add? The Shari'a describes the beliefs and practices that are required in order to submit to the will of God. There is less need for the Holy Spirit "to guide you into all truth" (John 16:13) when we have the Shari'a. Since we are fundamentally good, we do not need an inner transformation other than the choice to submit to the will of God as defined in the Shari'a. There is little theological space for the Holy Spirit in a Shari'a-centered system.

The Messiah and the Holy Spirit

The Holy Spirit anointed the Messiah for his ministry before the church was created. Even his birth to the virgin Mary was through the power of the Holy Spirit. The angel who came to Mary proclaimed, "The Holy Spirit will come upon you, and the power of the Most High will overshadow you. So the holy one to be born will be called the Son of God" (Luke 1:35).

Then when John baptized Jesus, the Holy Spirit came upon Jesus, descending from heaven like a dove (Luke 3:21-22). Thereafter Jesus was "full of the Holy Spirit" (Luke 4:1). And when his public ministry began, he commenced that ministry with a sermon in the synagogue in his hometown of Nazareth. He began that sermon with a scripture from the prophet Isaiah, which begins with this phrase, "The Spirit of the Lord is on me" (Luke 4:18). The whole life and ministry of Jesus the Messiah was empowered by the Holy Spirit.

During his time of ministry, Jesus occasionally made promises about the work of the Holy Spirit that would follow his crucifixion and resurrection. The ministries of the Holy Spirit in the life of the church, described above, are in harmony with the promises Jesus made about the Holy Spirit. Once when he was participating in the Feast of Tabernacles at the temple, he astounded the thousands who had gathered for the festivities with an amazing promise about the Holy Spirit.

> Jesus stood and said in a loud voice, "If a man is thirsty, let him come to me and drink. Whoever believes in me, as the Scripture has said, streams of living water will flow from within him." By this he meant the Spirit, whom those who believe in him were later to receive. Up to that time the Spirit had not been given, since Jesus had not yet been glorified (John 7:37-39).

Recall that Shari'a means the "path to the watering hole." And note that here, Jesus describes the Holy Spirit as the living water that flows from within all who believe in the Jesus Christ, the Messiah.

In the experience of the church, the Spirit is never in divergence from Jesus and glorifies the Messiah in all ways. The cross and resurrection are at the soul of the ministry of the Messiah. The Holy Spirit never departs from revealing the meaning of that center. In the Messiah crucified and risen, believers receive the gift of grace, forgiveness, and new life. The Holy Spirit enables believers to believe in the Messiah and to receive the gift of salvation.

The Holy Spirit implants fruitfulness in the life of the believer. The scriptures explain:

> But the fruit of the Spirit is love, joy, peace, patience, kindness, goodness, faithfulness, gentleness and self-control. Against such things there is no law. Those who belong to Christ Jesus have crucified the sinful nature with its passions and desires. Since we live by the Spirit, let us keep in step with the Spirit (Gal. 5:22-25).

The Holy Spirit in Christian Experience

Within Christian experience, it is the Holy Spirit who brought about the creation of the church (chapter 8). And in contrast to both Judaism or Islam, the Holy Spirit freed the early church from a need to have a fence around the law. In fact, for Christians, even the Torah itself underwent a radical reinterpretation as the Holy Spirit occupied the role of the law in the life of the church. Peter and Paul were at the center of the drama.

First, while Peter was awaiting his dinner on a rooftop in Joppa, he had a vision of a sheet coming from heaven filled with all kinds of animals, including those that the Torah forbade eating, such as swine.

A voice horrified Peter, proclaiming:

> "Get up, Peter. Kill and eat."
> "Surely not, Lord!" Peter replied. "I have never eaten anything impure or unclean."
> The voice spoke to him a second time, "Do not call anything impure that God has made clean" (Acts 10:13-15).

This happened three times. Then two messengers appeared at the house to invite Peter to come to the home of Cornelius, a Gentile centurion who lived thirty miles away, in Caesarea. An angel had instructed Cornelius to invite Peter.

When Peter arrived at the home of Cornelius, he found a

house full of guests eager to hear him. He rather rudely exclaimed, "You are well aware that it is against our law for a Jew to associate with a Gentile or visit with him."

Nevertheless, Peter shared the Gospel with Cornelius and his household. When the whole household believed, Peter was absolutely astounded that the Holy Spirit came upon everyone, just as had happened to the apostles on the Day of Pentecost when the Holy Spirit created the church. What could Peter do? He baptized all who believed, even though they were Gentiles and not circumcised as the Law of Moses commanded.

A few days later, back in Jerusalem, the leaders of the church called Peter to give account. They could not comprehend how Gentiles, who did not fully obey the rituals and practices of the Torah, could be included in the Christian movement. Peter told them the whole story, and when the Jerusalem church heard this astonishing evidence of the work of the Holy Spirit, "they had no further objections and praised God, saying, 'So then, God has granted even the Gentiles repentance unto life'" (Acts 11:18).

Surprising Freedom

But the issues of the Torah and the Holy Spirit didn't go away. Paul and his colleagues were commissioned by the church in Antioch to preach among the Gentiles. Churches formed in Asia Minor wherever they traveled. None of the Gentile men were circumcised. The Jewish leaders of the church were appalled, because the Gentile church was departing from the explicit regulations of the Law of Moses. So they convened a conference in Jerusalem to examine the relationship between the Torah and the Holy Spirit.

At that meeting, conservative Peter, who had always lived in obedience to the Torah, arose and said, "Now then, why do you try to test God by putting on the necks of the disciples a yoke that neither we nor our fathers have been able to bear? No! We believe it is through the grace of our Lord Jesus that we are saved, just as they are" (Acts 15:10-11).

The conference agreed and wrote, in a letter to all the Gentile churches, "It seemed good to the Holy Spirit and to us not to burden you with anything beyond the following requirements: You are to abstain from food sacrificed to idols, from blood, from the meat of strangled animals and from sexual immorality. You will do well to avoid these things" (Acts 15:28-29).

The decision to free the Gentile churches from the burden of the law was astounding and exceedingly bold, for it meant that the church would never have a cultural or ritual cohesion. Not only would the church become a community of amazing diversity, but the way in which the church handled the scriptures would be transformed. That decision involved the dialogical engagement of scripture, the community of faith, and the Holy Spirit. "It seemed good to the Holy Spirit and to us," the letter to the churches proclaimed.

The decision at the Jerusalem Conference meant that the church would never develop a comprehensive system to define Christian culture and conduct. The church would not develop a Talmud as in Judaism or Shari'a as in Islam. (A possible exception is canon law developed by the Catholic Church in the Middle Ages. This seems to me to be an aberration of the New Testament church.)

The Holy Spirit and Proselytizing

The decision at the Jerusalem Conference also meant that the faithful church in mission would not proselytize.[13] It would invite people to conversion, to commitment to Jesus the Messiah. However, there was no demand that new believers move from one religious culture to another. Gentile Christians did not need to adopt the Jewish culture that was based upon the Torah and the Talmud. They could remain Gentile.

Before the Jerusalem Conference, the assumption of all theologians was that everyone who wanted to become a participant in the covenant community of God had to become a proselyte to Judaism. However, after that Jerusalem Conference, no Gentile believer was expected to become a proselyte into a Christian culture. Quite to the contrary, the test of being a covenant member of the Christian church was just one thing: conversion—that is, a turning away from sin and commitment to Jesus the Messiah and the fellowship of the church.

A New Creation

The emphasis within the biblical accounts is for the Law of God to be inscribed within the person. One of the gifts of the Holy Spirit is to bring about that inner transformation. The Holy Spirit brings a new creation within the person. Some five hundred years before the coming of the Messiah, God promised through the prophet Jeremiah that a day would come when "I will put my law in their minds and write it on their hearts" (Jer. 31:33). Christians believe that this promise is fulfilled in the new creation work of the Holy Spirit within the soul of the believer.

A conversation with a student illustrates a Shari'a and a Holy Spirit understanding of the Law of God.

Abdi Muhammad stopped by my home, and after pleasantries, he asked, "Please give me a copy of the Christian Shari'a. I want to know what the rules are for a Christian."

I said, "The Holy Spirit is the rule for a disciple of the Messiah. The center of that rule is self-giving loving service for others, even one's enemy. The Sermon on the Mount in the Gospel according to Matthew is an example of how disciples of Jesus live when they are living in obedience to the Holy Spirit. You cannot write down all the rules on how to live in that way. However, the Holy Spirit provides a new creation within the person. Jesus referred to this new creation of the Holy Spirit as being born again."

On another occasion, I asked an illiterate older person, Abdullahi, who was a disciple of the Messiah, "How do you know the right way?"

He replied, "My heart is like a dull knife. The Holy Spirit is like a file. At night as I listen to the Holy Spirit, it files my heart and makes all things sharp and clean." This new creation of the Holy Spirit is a gift that frees. Paul says it this way: "Therefore, there is no condemnation for those who are in Christ Jesus, because through Christ Jesus the law of the Spirit of life set me free from the law of sin and death" (Rom. 8:1-2).

Readings from the Bible:
John 16:5-16; Galatians 5:16-26
Readings from the Qur'an:
Baqara 2:177; Al-Mujadila 58:22

Questions for Reflection and Discussion:
1. Account for the keen interest in "the law" within both Judaism and Islam. Give reasons why the New Testament goes against such inclinations.
2. Give reasons for the very minimal attention given to the

Holy Spirit in Islam.

3. The Holy Spirit in the Gospel is rooted in the life and ministry of Jesus the Messiah. Consider the significance of this reality in understanding the differences between the work of the Holy Spirit in Islamic theology and Christian theology.

4. How do *sunnah* and Shari'a in Islam relate to the formation of Islamic culture and the political order?

5. What is the difference between a convert and a proselyte? Critique and assess this statement: The Holy Spirit converts people and Shari'a proselytizes people.

6. Consider the remarkable decisions of the Jerusalem Conference in freeing the church to embrace cultural diversity. How did that conference define the center of the Christian movement? How did it define Christian ethics? How did the conference work at the issues of biblical interpretation in cross-cultural church growth? (Acts 15)

7. In what ways does an Islamic approach to Shari'a influence political developments in predominantly Muslim societies? Account for the tension between modernizing influences and Islamic theologians.

Prayer: *Salat*—Fellowship

"ABDI" is a favorite name among Muslims. *Abd* in Arabic means "servant." All faithful Muslims are committed to being servants of God. This is the reason faithful Muslims prostrate before God with hands and forehead on the ground at least seventeen times daily. Faithful Muslims invest almost an hour daily in obligatory ritual worship (*salat*).

Muslims seek to submit to the true religion (*din*) revealed by God. That true *din* is Islam, which can be simply summarized in five (or six) pillars of faith and five (or six) pillars of duty. The whole commitment is submission to the true *din* as the servants of God.

Salat is the practice of ritual prayer that expresses this commitment to submit to God. The ritual prayers of *salat* are a persistent sign among Muslims of their commitment to submit every area of life to God's revealed will, the Qur'an. Thus the specific five-times-daily acts of *salat* are a visible sign of the believers' commitment, a total way of life to submit to the beliefs and practices of Islam and the will of God. *Salat* and the final judgment are intertwined. The specific acts of *salat* and a total life lived in the submission that *salat* represents will be significant when God determines our destiny at the final judgment.

An incident in a mosque illustrates this.

After the evening *salat* was completed, the imam urged the congregation to contribute money for the repair of the mosque. "A final judgment is coming," he reminded the worshipers. "Imagine this tragedy. You decide not to give to this need. You leave this mosque and a car hits you and kills you. On the final judgment day this good deed of giving to the mosque is not on your balance scales of good and bad. What a tragedy! I urge you; do not leave this place without giving for this need."

This chapter explores the specific ritual of *salat*, as well as the broader meaning of *salat* as a commitment to total submission to the will of God. First, we explore *salat* as submission to both the pillars of belief and the pillars of duty in Islam. Then we reflect on *salat* as the specific action of submission to God in ritual prayer. For the faithful Muslim every aspect of life is *salat*—that is, humble submission to the will of God as revealed in the Qur'an.

The Pillars of Belief

The pillars of *iman* (belief) were briefly noted in the previous chapter. The required beliefs for a Muslim are outlined in one verse in the Qur'an, much as the Jewish confession of faith is summarized in the *Shema*: "Hear, O Israel: The Lord our God, the Lord is one." The response is, "Love the Lord your God with all your heart and with all your soul and with all your strength" (Deut. 6:4-5).

The Qur'an commands five core belief commitments. The key verse is: "O ye who believe! Believe in Allah and His messenger and the Scripture which He hath revealed unto His messenger, and the Scripture which He revealed aforetime. Whoso disbelieveth in Allah and His angels and His scriptures and His messengers and the Last Day, he verily hath wandered far astray" (Nisaa [Women] 4:136).

This verse summarizes the pillars of Islamic *iman*:

1. Belief in one God
2. Belief in the prophets of God (Every people group have had their prophet/s, but Muhammad is the final seal of all the prophets.)
3. Belief in the books of revelation (noted in chapter 6):
   The *Suhuf* (Pages) of the prophet Abraham, which are lost
   The *Taurat* (Torah) of the prophet Moses
   The *Zabur* (Psalms) of the prophet David
   The *Injil* (Gospel) of Jesus the Messiah
   The Qur'an of the prophet Muhammad.
4. Belief in angels. This is an essential belief because it is the angels who are the messengers who bring revelation to the prophets.
5. Belief in the Last Day and the final judgment.

Muslims quite frequently include a sixth pillar of belief, that of *qadar* (determinism), the irresistible sovereignty of God and his will. The Qur'an proclaims, "And ye will not, unless (it be) that Allah willeth, the Lord of Creation" (At-Takwir [The Overthrowing] 81:29).

A *hadith* (tradition) describes these six beliefs in this way. Gabriel asked the Messenger of God what is the nature of true belief. Muhammad replied, "*Iman* (faith) is to believe in Allah, His Angels, His Books, His Messengers, the Last Day, and to believe in *qadar* and what it brings of good or bad."[1]

Wherever a non-Muslim asks a Muslim, "What do you believe?" the answer from any knowledgeable Muslim is always the same: We believe in God, the prophets, the books, angels, and the final judgment. Most will also include determinism. This is true of all Muslims, whether Sunni or Shi'ite, whether they live in Mecca or Nairobi or Teheran or New York City. Our exploration in previous chapters has included perspectives on these beliefs. Here we highlight the role of the final judgment in regard to these beliefs. All Muslim beliefs are anchored in the fear of and respect for the final judgment.

The Final Judgment

Fear of the final judgment pervades the Qur'an. That day will come suddenly and unexpectedly, like lightning. A trumpet will sound proclaiming that the last day has come. The heavens will be torn apart, and the earth pulverized to dust.

On that last day, God will decide whether a person is cast into hell with the demons or invited into paradise. Hell is described in horrible imagery: fire, sparks flying upward, suffocating smoke, boiling water, devils, hot faggots in the stomach, and sinful people. Paradise is portrayed as a place of pleasure and beauty: fruit trees and streams, wide-eyed virgin maidens, rich carpets, plush cushions, pavilions, abundant wine (Al-Ghashiyah [The Overwhelming] 88:9-16; Al-Wagi'ah [The Event] 56:11-24). Each person's book, where his good and wrong deeds are recorded, will be opened, and God will examine our beliefs and actions.

Those who have believed that God has associates (*shirk*), will be damned. That is the worst sin, for it is polytheism. Judgment will also fall on those who separate God from his messengers, or who reject some messengers and accept others. (Ali 'Imran [The

Family of 'Imran] 3:84-87; Fat-h [Victory] 48:8-10). The good and evil deeds will be placed on the opposite sides of a balance scales. If the good deeds outweigh the wrongful deeds and beliefs, it is hoped that God will extend mercy (Muminun [The Believers] 23:101-4; Anbiyaa [The Prophets] 21:47).

Many Muslims believe that at the final judgment, Muhammad will be an intercessor. The Qur'an says that there is no intercessor, except by permission (Ta-Ha 20:109). A twelfth-century *sufi* theologian, al-Ghazali, comments that Muhammad will ask permission to intercede. He will come forward at the last judgment and exclaim, "I am the right one (to intercede) insofar as God allows it for whomever He wills and chooses." Then God will respond, "O Muhammad, lift your head and speak, for you will be heard; seek intercession and it will be granted."[2]

The next chapter explores the Christian and Muslim views of history. For now we only note that this fifth pillar of belief, the final judgment, is at the center of all Muslim considerations of the meaning of history. That is what Islam is essentially about, submitting to the will of God in the hope that the merciful Allah will have compassion on the day of judgment.

The Pillars of Duty

The spirit of *salat* is also expressed in submission to the pillars of duty. Chapter 11 reviewed these pillars briefly and explored the implications of right duty for the later development of Muslim Law (Shari'a). The pillars are: the confession of faith (*shahada*), prayer (*salat*), fasting (*sawm*), alms (*zakat*), and the pilgrimage (*hajj*). Most Muslims add a sixth, striving in the way of Allah (*jihad*). Each of these statements of duty is a profound insight into Islamic spirituality.

Submission in Prayer

Just as the final judgment is key to understanding the pillars of belief, so the submission in ritual prayer (*salat*) is the core to understanding the full-orbed commitment to right conduct as commanded in the pillars of duty. The ritual symbolism of prayer unlocks much of the meaning and attraction of Islam. We explore *salat* recognizing that the spirit of contrition before God that *salat* commends is really the soul of Islam.

A Mennonite Christian, Evan Bontrager, tells of several weeks when he bowed in prostration before God with his face to the floor five times a day. He did this to explore the spirituality within the Muslim ritual.

> During prayer I brought my head all the way to the floor and spread my arms and hands. I was physically and verbally submitting to God's will. I committed myself to being a servant. Each day became fuller. The prostration became more natural but never lost its significance. I prayed each morning just after dawn, then at noon, mid-afternoon, after dusk, and just before going to bed. I talked to God as I seldom had. I found a rhythm and common prayers of submission. I saw the benefit of a memorized prayer, as taught in Islam. . . . I am a different Christian. I learned the humble strength of submission. I submit to the desire to live as Christ to the full glory of God.[3]

Christian monastic orders have for many centuries practiced forms of ritual prayers that are signs of full submission to God. Christian disciplines of prayer and fasting affirm the spiritual values that so many Muslims experience in these regular disciplines. Prostration before God and fasting has not been only a Muslim practice.

Muslims are required to pray five times daily. The muezzin calls the community to prayer. This call and invitation (*adhan*) is proclaimed from the minaret, unless Muslims are a minority community and the neighborhood prohibits the five bold resonating invitations to come and pray. The *adhan* consists of the central and nonnegotiable core of Islamic faith and mission: I give witness. Allah is most great. Muhammad is the apostle of Allah. Come and worship. Experience well-being.

Promptly the congregation gathers for prayer. Or if people cannot gather, they can worship individually wherever they are. Ritual ablutions are required before each time of prayer. Each prayer requires a certain number of *rak'ahs* (prayer cycles): early dawn—two *rak'ahs*; noon—four *rak'ahs*; mid afternoon—four *rak'ahs*; just after sunset—three *rak'ahs*; at bedtime—four *rak'ahs*. Each of these seventeen *rak'ahs* is performed according to a precise ritual. The *salat* begins with a statement of intention (*niyya*), and then consists of seven steps.

1. Placing open hands on each side of the face while saying the *takbir*: *Alahu akbar* (God is most great). This ritual is a rejection

of the devil and the detractions of the world as the worshiper faces toward the Ka'bah. The *mihrab* (niche) in the wall of every mosque shows the *qiblah* (direction) of the Ka'bah and hence the direction for prayer.

2. Placing the right hand over the left on one's chest, and uttering prayers glorifying God. The concluding commitment is "I take refuge with God from the accursed devil." Then the worshiper recites the prayer recorded in Al-Fatiha (the first *sura* of the Qur'an), referred to as the perfect prayer. This is recited while standing. Often other *suras* of the Qur'an are also recited.

3. Bowing at the hips, while still standing, and uttering another *takbir* (God is most great.).

4. Standing up straight.

5. Going down on the knees and falling prostrate until the forehead, both hands, both knees, and toes are on the ground.

6. Rising to a sitting position while repeating another *takbir*, with both hands on the knees.

7. Prostrating again while reciting the *takbir*. The worshiper then stands saying a *takbir*, and the *rak'ah* has concluded.

These seven steps comprise one *rak'ah*. Each of the next *rak'ahs* begin with the second step. After the prayer cycles are completed, the worshipers recite the *shahada*: "There is no God but Allah, and Muhammad is the prophet of Allah." They will turn the head to the right and the left, recognizing the guardian angels who are at hand. They also greet one another with the peace of Islam.

After the ritual prayers, worshipers may sit with hands open and palms up as they bring their petitions to God. These prayers of requests (*du'a*) do not need to be in Arabic, but all ritual prayers must be in Arabic.[4] In the *du'a* prayers, worshipers will often raise their eyes and, with palms up and open, sit in quiet intercession to the merciful and compassionate God they have worshiped in the submission of *salat*.

A man always stands in front of the worshipers to lead the prayers. He might be an *imam*, but that is not a requirement, at least in Sunni congregations. Women are always separated from the men to avoid any distraction. Some Muslims will make up *rak'ahs* that they have missed at the set times for prayer; they might do that in the evening in the mosque. Before or after the formal congregational prayers, one will observe individuals repeating *rak'ahs* standing alone in different locations in the mosque. Muslims have frequently told me that some of the worshipers say extra *rak'ahs* to compensate for wrongdoings.

The Congregation

It is best for Muslims to gather in the *masjid* (place of prostration or mosque) for the times of prayer. If it is not convenient to go to the mosque for each of the five daily prayer times, the devotee can pray anywhere. On Friday, however, all Muslims within an area are urged to meet together for the noon prayer. That is when the homilies are delivered. Most communities have one large mosque designated as the "Friday mosque" where all the Muslims from the region meet for the weekly gathering and to hear the sermon. Of course, men and women do not meet together for these times of worship; sometimes there is a separate mosque for women, but most often women meet in a room separated from the main assembly.

Relationship with God

Faithful Muslims are committed to submitting to all the duties that *salat* requires. The Muslim theologians specialize in Islamic law so as to clarify for the entire Muslim community the details that are required to faithfully submit to the Law of God. What about theology? Can we know God? Can we have a relationship with God? That question has inspired the *sufi* quest among Muslims. Although orthodoxy perceives that God is unknown and essentially unknowable in a personal relationship, the *sufi* quest seeks to know God by becoming absorbed into God. Occasionally the relationship between orthodoxy and sufism is a rough ride.

For example, a Syrian Muslim doing her Ph.D. in Islam at Temple University once addressed a daylong seminar for Christian students. I was the teacher in charge. On her chalkboard, she had placed "Allah" at the top and "man" at the bottom. As she worked through the pillars of faith and duty, she mentioned occasionally that we cannot know God personally. Each time she said that, she made a horizontal line between the words "Allah" and "man." By the end of her several-hour lecture, that white line had become an inch thick, a rather dramatic, and, it seemed, intentional way of making the point that in her Sunni orthodox faith, she was committed to submitting to God's will, but did not presume to know God personally.

Sufi Mysticism

The *sufi* mystics pursue a way around that kind of orthodox spirituality that emphasizes submission, but does not seek union with God. The *sufis* long for power, the power that they believe is found in mystical union with God. The *sufi* quest does not go in the direction of an "I-thou" relationship with God that is at the soul of Christian theology; rather, *sufis* seek a loss of ego identity within the divine (*fana'*). Orthodox Muslims emphasize the qur'anic teaching on *tanzil*, which implies that there is no fellowship between God and man. However, the *sufis* point out that in the Qur'an, some people are friends of God, *awliya*. Abraham was *Khalil-Allah* (an intimate friend [*wali*] of God). So the *sufis* seek a submission to God that cultivates a friendship that they perceive as mystical union with the divine (Maida [The Table Spread] 5:53-54; Yunus [Jonah] 10:62).

How can the worshiper achieve absorption (*fana'*) into God? There are several themes that *sufi* spirituality emphasizes. This exploration is not adequate to probe those spiritual streams in depth. However, for several years our family lived across the street from a *sufi* mosque in Eastleigh, Nairobi. I will comment on that particular community. There were four significant themes: the spiritual leader; the founding saint of the order, who served as intercessor for the community; the remembrance of God and the saints; and the participation in the mysteries of the community that introduced the worshiper into mystical absorption or union with the divine.

The *sufi* movement exists as communities within the all-encompassing Muslim *ummah*. All such *sufi* communities are known as *tariqas* (paths or orders). Spencer Trimingham comments:

> The basis of the religious orders in Islam is the belief that the believer who desires to attain communion with God needs the guidance of one who is experienced in the "path" thereto, one who has been blessed by God on earth by special virtue (*baraka*), and who can act as an intermediary between the disciple and God. The founders of the *tariqas* were such guides, and their spiritual descendants inherit their *baraka* and continue their functions to this day.[5]

The spiritual guide of the *sufi* order in the Eastleigh community possessed the symbols of his initiation and ordination into
the Qadiriyya order. The community believed he possessed the
blessing and power that came from his intimate relationship and
learning from a saint who was in the direct line of spiritual
authority and power of the founding member of the order, Abd
al-Qadir al-Jilani. The founding leader of the order had received
his intimate insights from a line of spiritual authorities who went
right back to the prophet Muhammad.[6] Sufis refer to this line of
authority and blessing as a chain or linkage (*sisila*) that directly
connects the local saint with the power and blessing and mystery
of the founding leader.

The devotees of the Qadiriya sheikh in Eastleigh, Nairobi
would meet in the mosque with their leader every Thursday
night. Between times they met in the home of the sheikh. These
meetings always consisted of repeating the name of God over and
over again in a hypnotic chant. This is the remembrance of God
(*dhikr*). They would also repeat the name of Muhammad and the
founder of their order. They would intersperse these eulogies of
chanted remembrances with pauses for drinking tea and chewing
a mildly euphoria-enhancing drug known as *kat*. They waved
flags. They wafted incense. The goal of the worship was the loss
of a sense of personhood so as to become absorbed into the
Universal.

The Quest for an Intercessor

Once I accompanied a friend, Farah Ali, on an annual pilgrimage to the grave of an ancestral *sufi* saint. Every Somali clan
has a *sufi* saint, and the annual pilgrimages to the grave are a time
to renew clan solidarity and participate in the mystical powers of
the dead saint. We went to the saint's grave, where people were
wailing and praying as they took handfuls of dirt from the grave
and sprinkled the dirt on their bodies.

As we began the journey home, Farah explained, "We are sinners, and so God does not hear our prayers. That is why we go to
the grave of our *sufi* saint, for he is one of us. He intercedes for us
to Muhammad, who takes our requests to God. We know this is
not good Islam, for in Islam there is no intercessor.[7] But we have
no other way."

I said, "I can understand your concern. However, there is one intercessor whom God has appointed. He is the Messiah. God has appointed the Messiah to be our intercessor."

"Amazing!" Farah said. "Tell me more."

Farah was not at peace with his *sufi* piety, partly because of the tension with mainstream Islamic Sunni orthodoxy. For him it was a necessary piety, yet it was a piety that he and many of his fellow Muslims believe contradicts the core commitments of Islam.

On another occasion, this time in central Java, my hosts took me to the grave of a *sufi* saint, and explained his miraculous and intercessory powers. They told of the hundreds of thousands of pilgrims who come to this grave.

"Is this good Islam?" I asked.

"Do not ask that question!" my host said. "We all know that this is not the Islam we should follow."

Nevertheless, in spite of some ambivalence about the *sufis*, their piety infuses Sunni Islam. Sufism is a response to a desire for contact with the Creator.

Augustine, a fourth century Christian and North African theologian, observed that our hearts are restless until we find our rest in God. In his *Confessions,* he prays, "How, then, do I look for you O Lord? For when I look for you, who are my God, I am looking for a life of blessed happiness. I shall look for you so that my soul may live."[8] *Sufis* assert that they are on a quest for that rest and happiness.

The Messiah and the *Sufi* Quest

A remarkable gift of the spirituality of the way of the Messiah is that the quest of the *sufis* for contact with God is fulfilled. The Messiah is the intercessor, appointed by God. Through his life and ministry we are invited into the family of God as friends, as his sons and daughters. This is a relationship that does not obliterate personhood, but rather affirms the integrity of the person in the "I-thou" relationship of intimacy and communion with God. The Holy Spirit fills the believer with the presence and power of God, bringing about inner transformations, a new creation. All of this happens within the experience of the community of faith bonded together; not in the hidden mysteries of a spiritual leader, but through the bonding unity of the Spirit.

The *sufi* stream of spirituality in the Muslim community responds to a felt spiritual need. The witness of the church is that in the Messiah and through the Spirit of God, these spiritual needs are fulfilled in ways that free and affirm the integrity of the person. The Gospel invites us into communion with God, not absorption into the Universal.

Abraham and Faith

Although the *sufi* way invites the devotee into an experience of mystical piety, the *sufis* do not critique the need to submit to all dimensions of Islamic *salat*. All faithful Muslims, whether *sufi* or orthodox, Shi'ite or Sunni, practice *salat* and the implications of *salat* as defined in the Shari'a. I was impressed by this reality in the fall of 2000 when I was the guest of the Muslim Student Association of the United Kingdom for one week. These were busy, overloaded students. They were living in a secularized, fast-moving industrial society. Yet they would not let anything short-change their times for *salat*.

One evening the topic for dialogue with the students was Abraham. I developed the theme, "Abram believed the Lord, and he credited it to him as righteousness" (Gen. 15:6). It was challenging for Abraham to believe God. Abraham faltered in some tests of faith. He missed the way; he sinned. Yet he wanted to believe. And in the believing, he learned to know God as his faithful friend. That walk of faith opened Abraham's life to the surprise of grace. His walk of faith is the forerunner of the faith and grace we are invited into through the life and ministry of Jesus the Messiah. We are saved by grace; even faith is a gift from God. By grace we experience the forgiveness of our sins, and we learn to know God as our loving heavenly Father. We cannot "earn" that favor; this is a gift of God, his unmerited favor.

My Muslim colleague emphasized that Abraham prostrated himself with his face to the ground, as do all Muslims. He called God by his true name, Allah, and never as Yahweh. Abraham and Ishmael cleansed the Ka'bah of its idolatries, and established the faith of Islam at the Ka'bah. They restored the house of God at the Ka'bah, and worshiped God in the right way. My companion gave an invitation to all Christians in the audience to follow Abraham's example and prostrate with face to the ground in prayer, for that is the only right way to pray. He challenged them to call God by his only true name, Allah. They should face the house of God, the Ka'bah, in prayer, recognizing that Abraham, the father of faith, prostrated himself before God at the Ka'bah.

It is evident that the mission of Abraham as the father of faith is a journey that invites vigorous dialogue. What is faith? What is submission to God? What is true worship? Is it a duty performed to God? Do right acts of worship attract the mercy of God? Or is worship a joyful celebration of God's grace and a responsive commitment to glorify God?

The Meaning of Worship

When I was living in Somalia, the fellowship of believers in the Messiah had a series of very searching conversations on the meaning of worship. American Mennonite missionaries and Somali Christians explored together the nature of worship as revealed in Jesus the Messiah. Muslims sometimes comment that when Christians meet for worship, their singing sounds as though they are having a party. That is true—a party celebrating God's grace in the Messiah. We focused on the essence of Christian worship and the symbols within a Somali Muslim context that would communicate that center meaningfully to the Muslim community and within the believers' fellowship. These were some of the suggestions that emerged from those conversations.

Worship on Sunday is a sign that the small emerging congregations in Somalia are linked with a worldwide fellowship of believers who also meet on Sunday. It is important to have a place that is reserved just for worship. This place reminds us that God is holy; we should remove our shoes when entering this place as a sign that we are meeting the Holy One. It would be good for the leaders to dress as clergy who are leading the congregation in worship, much as the imams wear attire symbolizing their leadership role in the community. Some formal liturgy should be implemented like, for example, reciting the Apostle's Creed and the Lord's Prayer at each service. It would be good to chant the Lord's Prayer as a sign of the mystery of prayer. The formal reading of scripture should happen at each worship gathering.

Baptism is a witness that a person has joined the new covenant community. Communion should be observed regularly as a celebration of the sacrifice of the Messiah, the Lamb of God, for our redemption. A liturgy of confession of sins should be included in the worship time. The church should practice the liturgy of foot washing, following the example of the Messiah who washed his disciples' feet. This is important in a Somali setting, for the servant theme in washing another's feet runs powerfully against cultural values. But the Messiah has come to turn the proud into servants.

Believers should stand for prayer, not bow and prostrate. Slaves prostrate. Believers in the Messiah become daughters and sons of God. Children stand to talk with their father; they do not prostrate. Furthermore, in Islam prostration, is always toward the Ka'bah. But the Messiah our Lord is risen, and his Spirit lives among us and with us. There is no direction towards which to prostrate. Christians should stand for prayer as a sign of meeting their Lord in face-to-face relationships. Singing should be an important dimension of all worship. Somali songs with alliteration and local music and idiom enrich the worship as more songs are written.

Spirit and Truth

Such conversations happened in a variety of settings, but for a period of several months a group met every Saturday to explore the meaning of worship. That group reveled in the conversation Jesus had with the Samaritan woman at Jacob's well near Sychar in Samaria (John 4:1-26). The woman thought that there was a right place and way to worship: Jews worshiped in Jerusalem, Samaritans worshiped at the mountain.

Jesus countered:

> Believe me, woman, a time is coming when you will worship the Father neither on this mountain nor in Jerusalem. You Samaritans worship what you do not know; we worship what we do know, for salvation is from the Jews. Yet a time is coming and has now come when the true worshipers will worship the Father in spirit and truth, for they are the kind of worshipers the Father seeks. God is spirit, and his worshipers must worship in spirit and in truth (John 4:21-24).

"Salvation is from the Jews," Jesus insisted in his conversation with the Samaritan woman.

Indeed, the Gospel and the church are nonsense when severed from the story of Israel and their scriptures. The church stands within the authority of the biblical scriptures. The church is a continuation of the covenant people of the Old Testament. The Messiah fulfills, but does not abrogate, the former scriptures. The church is birthed and nurtured through the witness of the biblical scriptures, and these scriptures are interpreted and applied by the church. The Bible and the church are complementary.

"Spirit and truth!" we pondered in those Somali meetings on the meaning of worship.

Place is an irrelevance—neither on the sacred Samaritan mountain nor at the Jewish temple. Nor, Jesus would surely insist, facing the Ka'bah. The only quality of true worship is spirit and truth. There can be no hidden sin. Worship requires utmost integrity. True worship, therefore, includes confession of sin. Spirit refers to communion and presence. We know God, and God knows us. We commune with God in worship.

The Samaritan woman responded to all of this by observing, "When [the Messiah] comes, he will explain everything to us."

Jesus astounded her, "I who speak to you am he" (John 4:25-26).

Two Prayers

We conclude this discourse on *salat* and worship with two prayers: the *Fatiha* of Islam, which faithful Muslims recite at least seventeen times daily, and the Lord's Prayer of the church, which Jesus taught his disciples. These two prayers are a powerful statement of the soul of worship in the Muslim community (the peace of submitting to the will of God) and the heart of worship within the Christian church (the joy of knowing God as our heavenly Father).

The *Fatiha*:

> In the name of Allah, the Beneficent, the Merciful.
> Praise be to Allah, Lord of the Worlds,
> The Beneficent, the Merciful.
> Master of the Day of Judgment,
> Thee (alone) we worship; Thee (alone) we ask for help.
> Show us the straight path,
> The path of those on whom Thou hast favored; Not (the path) of those who earn Thine anger nor of those who go astray (Al-Fatiha [The Opening] 1:1-7).

The Lord's Prayer:

> Our Father in heaven,
> hallowed be your name,
> your kingdom come,
> your will be done
> on earth as it is in heaven.
> Give us today our daily bread.
> Forgive us our debts,
> as we also have forgiven our debtors.
> And lead us not into temptation,
> but deliver us from the evil one.
> [For yours is the kingdom and the power and the glory forever.
> Amen.] (Matt. 6:9-13)

Reading from the Bible:
Matthew 6:9-13
Reading from the Qur'an:
Al-Fatiha 1:1-7

Questions for Reflection and Discussion:

1. What is the meaning of *salat* in Islam? What is the meaning of worship in Christian experience? What value is there in ritual worship?

2. Compare the Lord's Prayer and the *Fatiha*. Comment on the statement: Christians can pray the *Fatiha*; however, Muslims would not pray the Lord's Prayer.

3. Comment on this statement: The biblical book of Hebrews presents the Messiah as a priest and intercessor in ways that relate very meaningfully to a *sufi* understanding of the need for an intercessor (Hebrews 7:1–8:6; Ta-Ha 20:109; Anam 6:51, 70). Imagine a dialogue between a *sufi* and a Christian on the theme of "intercessor."

4. Reflect on the inner meaning of four different experiences of worship: 1) seventeen *rak'ahs* in *salat*, performed at five different times throughout the day; 2) the continuous repetition of the name of God and the founding saint of the order in a *sufi* gathering; 3) a Sunday worship gathering in a Catholic church; 4) a Sunday worship gathering in a traditional Protestant church.

5. What does it mean to worship God in spirit and in truth (John 4: 21-25)?

6. Comment on this statement: The *sufi* quest is to have contact with God within a Muslim experience through absorption into the Universal. The life and ministry of the Messiah and the presence and work of the Holy Spirit offers the gift of knowing God personally. Consider the differences between these two kinds of spirituality. Is there a possibility that the *sufi* movement among Muslims can be a bridge that helps Muslims understand the nature of the Christian Gospel?

— 14 —

Global Mission:
the *Ummah*—the Church

HALF the people on earth are either Muslim or Christian. That reality is a revelation of the energetic missionary nature of these two global communities: the Muslim *ummah* and the Christian church.

As missionary movements, the *ummah* and the church are in competition. I mentioned in the preface that some years ago, Badru D. Kateregga and I wrote a dialogue, with Badru representing the Muslim faith and I the Christian witness.

Badru has told me that in his global travels speaking in Muslim audiences, he holds up this dialogue book and says:

> David has been in Lithuania developing a Christian university. I am in Uganda developing a Muslim university. We know that we are in competition, for I give witness to the Muslim faith, and he is committed to the mission of the church. Nevertheless, we are very good friends. The way we relate to each other is a model of the way all Christians and Muslims should relate.

Mission Communities

Sadly, too often the relationship between these two missionary communities has not been as respectful as the fraternity that Badru idealizes. The modern relationship challenges and global mission commitments have roots that reach deep into the early histories of the Christian and Muslim movements.

Recall that within one century of the emergence of the Muslim movement, half the world's Christians came under Muslim rule. A Muslim assumption has been that these early victories were the precursor to the whole Christian world, and in fact, the whole world, becoming Muslim. That has not happened.

Growth Patterns

Except where there have been sustained pressures to become Muslim, there has not been a worldwide movement of Christians into Islam. There are individual conversions, but substantial movement of Christians toward Islam has almost always happened only in regions where Muslims could impose prolonged political control. As noted previously, the *dhimmi* arrangement to protect the church also included forms of pressure to induce Christians to become Muslims. In most regions where the church has existed under Muslim rule, over the centuries the membership in the churches has declined as Christians became Muslims.

However, not all Islamic growth is dependent on political power. In recent years thousands of African-Americans from Christian backgrounds have joined the Muslim movement in the United States. A factor contributing to this movement is racism in the United States. Of course, the mission of the *ummah* is not only to the Christian communities. The Muslim mission is global and to all people. In that spirit Muslim traders and missionaries have spread the Muslim faith into non-Christian areas of Asia and Africa quite effectively, even in the absence of political power.

Nevertheless, whenever possible, Muslims have sought political power to assist in fulfilling the mission of the Muslim *ummah*. Sometimes this has taken on a *jihadist* militant expansion of the Dar al-Islam. Noteworthy are the eighteenth- and nineteenth-century West African *jihads* that extended Muslim military power and authority over vast regions of sub-Saharan West Africa.[1]

The church has also experienced considerable growth, especially during the last century. For example, in 1975 the number of Muslims and Christians in Africa became equal for the first time since the Muslim conquests of North Africa in the seventh and eighth centuries. Twenty-five years later there were fifty-five million more Christians in Africa than Muslims (380 million African Christians and 325 million African Muslims). At the beginning of the twenty-first century the African Christian community is growing annually by 10.75 million and the Muslim community by 8.25 million.[2] The African experience is part of a global pattern of Muslim and Christian growth.

Worldwide, there are nearly twice as many Christians as Muslims. In 1900 there were 200 million Muslims and 558 million Christians. In 2000, there were 1.2 billion Muslims and two billion Christians. Christianity gained more members during that century, but the Muslim population increased at a faster rate.[3] However, a larger birthrate among Muslims is a more significant reason for that growth than are conversions into Islam. Sometimes Muslims have embraced militancy and even military power in order to discourage the growth of the church, as in southern Sudan.

Mission of the Muslims

The Muslim mission is twofold: *da'wah* and *dawlah*. *Da'wah* is witness and invitation. This mission of the Muslims is expressed five times daily as the *adhan* (call to prayer) is proclaimed from hundreds of thousand of minarets around the world.

> God is most great, God is most great.
> I bear witness that there is no god except God:
> I bear witness that Muhammad is the Apostle of God.
> Come ye unto prayer.
> Come ye unto good.
> Prayer is a better thing than sleep.
> Come ye to the best deed.
> God is most great. God is most great.
> There is no god except God.[4]

There is no compulsion in this mission. It is a witness boldly and confidently proclaimed. It is a forthright invitation. The one who hears this witness and invitation must decide whether to come or to remain distant.

Dawlah is the second dimension of Muslim mission. This is the political and territorial mission of the *ummah*. Chapter 9 explored this political dimension of the Muslim mission. This is the commitment to establishing the Dar al-Islam whenever and wherever possible. Ideally the Dar al-Islam does not coerce people into becoming Muslims. However, the mission of political Islam is to assure that the integrity of the *ummah* is protected. *Dawlah* is the commitment to using the instruments of political power to bring all areas of life under the authority of Islam.

Historical realities challenge both the *dawlah* and the *da'wah* dimensions of the Muslim mission. Movements such as the Taliban in Afghanistan that sought to embrace a pure Islam are maligned by much of the world. The grandeur of the Golden Age of Islam withered a millennium ago. When there is space for the church to grow, it most often does grow. Poverty and illiteracy plague huge areas where Islam has suzerainty. (We also recognize that several hundred million Christians, especially in some regions of Latin America and Africa, are also impoverished.)

The *ummah* is not functioning very effectively as a witness over the nations, yet that is its mission. Ways must be found to rectify the situation. And, indeed, a way to regain the mission momentum of the Muslim nation is at hand. There is hope for the Muslim missionary enterprise. A number of Arab nations in the Middle East have enormous oil revenues. They are heavily engaged in global Muslim missions.

A special focus, at present, is the countries of the former Soviet Union where there had been a Muslim tradition. Within the wreckage of former communist societies, Muslim missionaries are awakening people who have been traditionally Muslim to the possibilities that Islam offers. At this juncture, throughout these regions, the church and the *ummah* are both vigorously missionizing. Muslim missionaries are experiencing considerable positive response in many of these formerly Muslim communities.

The global Muslim *ummah* is experiencing growth. As the twenty-first century commenced, the number of professing Muslims around the world was increasing by twenty-seven million per year![5]

Mission of the Christians

Forty days after the resurrection of Jesus, he met with his disciples on a hilltop. He told them:

> But you will receive power when the Holy Spirit comes on you; and you will be my witnesses in Jerusalem, and in all Judea and Samaria, and to the ends of the earth (Acts 1:8).

He also gave them the great commission:

> All authority in heaven and on earth has been given to me. Therefore go and make disciples of all nations, baptizing them

in the name of the Father and of the Son and of the Holy Spirit, and teaching them to obey everything I have commanded you. And surely I will be with you always, to the very end of the age (Matt. 28:18-20).

These were the last pronouncements and commands of Jesus before his ascension into heaven. For the next several hundred years, the church moved outward in mission in obedience to this command and expectation of Jesus. As noted in chapter 1, after Constantine the Western church experienced a transformation wherein the church and the political order were understood to be the presence of the kingdom of God on earth. This was understood as Christendom. This is very similar to the Dar al-Islam of the Muslims.

However, for Western Christians, that grand vision has waned. Instead of Christian Europe blazing the way forward for the whole world into the *eschaton* (the future), the modern church in Europe experiences a pervasive malaise. Not only has Islam presented a persistent challenge to the global mission of the church, but in modern times secular movements such as Marxism have confronted the Western church with forthright rejection of the Gospel. In Marxist societies, that rejection has included tremendous persecution and millions of martyrs. And we cannot forget the Holocaust—right in the heartland of Christendom, Nazi Germany attempted to eradicate the Jewish race. How could such evil take root in a Christianized civilization? History has cruelly disappointed Western Christian visionaries.

However, the malaise of the Christian movement in Western Europe is not a characteristic of the church in most other regions of the world. Globally the church is experiencing remarkable renewal and growth. There is confidence and hope. One would be hard put to identify any time in history when churches have grown more rapidly than in some of the post-communist societies of Eastern Europe and the former Soviet Union. The church in China is also experiencing unprecedented growth. According to *Operation World*, at the turn of the century there were nearly one hundred million professing Christians in China, with church growth approaching seven million new believers annually. At the dawn of the twenty-first century the global church was growing by twenty-eight million adherents annually.[6]

Every year tens of thousands of Christian missionaries serve around the world. They are sent from churches everywhere, not just from the wealthy churches of the West. At the beginning of the twenty-first century there were ninety-eight thousand missionaries serving internationally and more than two hundred thousand missionaries serving cross-culturally within their own countries. Korea was one of the leading missionary sending countries, with eleven thousand missionaries serving internationally.[7]

The Purpose of History

Why do Muslims and Christians invite people to believe in Islam or the Gospel? Why do these movements commission missionaries to serve around the world? Why do Muslim or Christian business travelers chat about their faith and invite people to believe wherever they go? Why do Christian or Muslim immigrants invite their neighbors to become believers?

The missionary vision of the Muslim nation and the Christian church is rooted in their understandings of the purpose of history. These respective understandings of history are in many ways a summation of this exploration of the beliefs and mission of the Muslim nation and the Christian church What is the meaning of history and, therefore, what is the purpose of the Muslim or the Christian movement? We will now explore Muslim and Christian responses to these questions.

Islam and History

In the Muslim understanding, history is like a set of parentheses. As described in chapter 3, Adam and Eve were originally created for paradise, not for earth. However, when Satan deceived Adam, God sent them to earth. Many Muslims believe this time on earth is for a period of testing.[8] When the testing period is concluded, history will end with the final judgment. Some will be damned in hell and others invited into paradise. We live on earth within the parentheses of coming from paradise at the dawn of human history and returning again to paradise at history's conclusion. In the meantime history hangs, as it were, between the parentheses.

When God sent Adam and Eve down to earth, they lived in the Plains of Arafat around the Ka'bah, the first house of God. While on earth, they and their progeny have the responsibility to serve as God's *khalifa,* caretakers. In his mercy God sent down his guidance to instruct humankind on how to function as responsible caretakers. That guidance is Islam. This guidance comes to us through prophets, Adam being the first. Every people have a prophet; perhaps there have been as many as 124,000 prophets of God throughout human history.[9]

The essence of the guidance has never changed; it is always Islam. People might forget or even attempt to change the guidance. That cannot happen. The guidance transcends history, for it is a sent-down guidance. It is noncontingent. It is inimitable. "It has no relationship in its form to the passage of historical time. It literally descended from heaven, having been written on the pre-existent divine tablet."[10]

It is the inimitable nature of the Qur'an that makes the Arabic Qur'an untranslatable. In the past, peoples have been careless about the guidance that God has sent down. They neglected, forgot, and even sought to change the guidance. But the mission of the Muslims is to preserve the final revelation, the Qur'an, from any innovation. Every word is an exact replica of the original heavenly copy.

This noncontingent understanding of revelation means that historical events have no essential connection with the Muslim scriptures.[11] For example, as noted earlier, if a verse in the Qur'an states that the Messiah was not crucified, any historical evidence to the contrary is irrelevant. Historical events cannot supersede the authority and truth of the Qur'an, which transcends history. Neither history nor human experience informs the content of scripture. A noncontingent Qur'an transcends human experience

How does this sent-down understanding of revelation affect a people's view of human responsibility in regards to history and creation? How does it affect the significance of history? If what we do does not affect either God or his revelation, then is who we are and what we do of any real significance? In that case, the only significant reality is God's sent-down guidance. It is not, therefore, surprising that the study of Islamic law supersedes all other disciplines in islamized societies.[12] Muslims are certain that the Law of God is good news.

Historian William Cantwell Smith observes:

> Once and for all a final, clear statement of His truth and His justice was sent down; a messenger was chosen who would deliver

it, interpret it, live it, with undeviating precision; a community was launched on its career that would preserve the message with a scrupulous fidelity, would carry it in triumph to the ends of the earth, and would obey it to the fullest implication of its practical outworking.[13]

The purpose of history, then, is to test each person's response to the Law of God. This testing time is between the parentheses of a paradise lost and the paradise that is to come (or, alternatively, hell for those who fail the test). Judgment is a dominant theme throughout the Qur'an. The day of accounting is coming; paradise or hell awaits all humanity at that hour when the sojourn of human history on earth ends.

During this time of testing on earth all people should submit to Islam, the guidance of a merciful God. The mission of the *ummah* is to give witness to that guidance and urge people everywhere to submit to the perfect Law of God as revealed in the Qur'an and the Hadith and defined in the Shari'a.

However, do most Muslims faithfully submit to Islam? Alas, there are too many compromises. Addressing that reality is the work of the Muslim reformers—they assist the Muslims during their sojourn on earth so that they will be faithful to Islam. Today the global Muslim *ummah* is exposed to reform movements that seek to lead Muslims into the glories of an earlier era, when Muslims were more faithful than they are today. These reforms are threefold:[14]

1. Militant and *jihadist* movements teach that the current situation is disastrous and can only be corrected by violent confrontation with the non-Islamic Dar al-Harb (Regions of War) and confrontation with hypocritical Muslims who are trying to change Islam. They view the eras of Islamic glory to be when Muslims were truly faithful to the model community established by Muhammad at Medina. The use of violence at Medina to establish, purify, and extend Islam is normative and must apply to the modern situation (al-Qaida is an example).

2. Conservative reformers teach that the great eras of Islam happened when the *ummah* faithfully followed the *sunnah* and Qur'an and applied these instructions through the faithful practice of the Shari'a. Modern adaptations and applications are at times necessary, but the foundations are firm and must not be debated (the Arabian Wahhabiyya are an example).

3. Progressives rather cautiously urge that the spirit of the Qur'an needs to be the source of modern secularist Muslim society. The Hadith, *sunnah,* and *Shari'a* entrap the *ummah* in patterns that are not applicable to the modern world.

All these reform movements agree on the following:

1. Islam is the faith for the oppressed, the people at the margins, in contrast to the Western Christian movement that has become the faith of the oppressors. (Note that Muslims have not always perceived that Western Christianity is the oppressor. This is a perception that has been developing over the last century.)[15]

2. Muslims must work to extend Islamic authority throughout the earth.

3. In order to regain the glory and power of the Muslim nation, Muslims must return to the core commitments of Islamic faith and practice.

The reformers struggle with issues of diversity. Islam does recognize diversity; every people have had a prophet. Yet now that the Qur'an has been revealed, all sincerely believing people will want to submit to Islam in the hopes of acquiring paradise when the final judgment comes. Different reformist streams work with issues of diversity in different ways; however, all agree that submitting to Islam is the path for peace in the present and the way toward the future when the believer hopes for paradise.

Another comment from Smith:

> Collectively and singly they [the Muslims] have sought both Paradise beyond this world and within history, a kind of society which, they believe, is proper to personal preparation for that Paradise and at the same time proper to the mundane scene itself, correct both for the individual for the next world and for the community for this. . . . The meaning of history lies in the degree to which these become actualized . . . it is an endeavor to integrate temporal righteousness in this world with a timeless salvation in the next.[16]

This means that every dimension of life needs to be brought into submission to Islam. That was the role of the caliphate in Sunni Islam and the imamate in Shi'a Islam. Theologian and Islamist Kenneth Cragg elaborates:

> Islam exists to be not only a way of devotion, but a form of government. It expects the rule of God, not only over, but as the

kingdom of men. The potential identity between them was the original keynote and the perpetual ambition of Muslim history.[17]

The unity of all of life under the rule of Islam is the ultimate mission of the Muslim nation. How far will that mission be realized when judgment day comes as the end of history?

Badru Kateregga comments that Muslim theologians are divided on the extent that the Muslim nation will spread before the final judgment. Some theological streams believe the Muslim *ummah* will become universal, and others believe that there will be a falling away of faith before the final judgment.[18]

G. E. von Grunebaum observes:

> The yearning for a political and spiritual renascence implies the conviction that human affairs tend to improve, that change tends to be for the better. This belief runs counter to the general feeling of traditional Islam that sees its history as a perpetual decline. The "best" Islam was that obtaining in the days of the prophet Muhammad, the next best that practiced by his immediate successors. The world deteriorates and Islam with it.[19]

However, as the parentheses of history nears its conclusion, Jesus the Messiah will return to earth. There is an obscure verse that contributes to this belief. "And lo! verily there is knowledge [for Jesus is a sign] of the Hour. So doubt ye not concerning it, but follow Me. This is the right path" (Zukhruf [God Adorns] 43:61). The theologians point out that Jesus cannot be a sign of judgment unless he is present. It is the Hadith that further elaborates on his second coming mission.

Some streams of Shi'ite Islam believe that Jesus will return with the Twelfth Imam, who has vanished. What will Jesus do? These Shi'ites believe that he will appear with the Twelfth Imam at Jerusalem and every eye will see them. The imam and Jesus will together command the Muslims and Christians to get along.

Most Sunnis believe that Jesus will destroy all the pigs and crosses and correct the errors of the Christians. He will restore Islam and in that way prepare the earth for the final judgment. Jesus will then die a natural death and be raised up with all others for the final judgment.

In the light of all of this, what is the mission of the Muslims? Recently I asked that question to two Muslim theologians.

First, a Shi'ite Iranian theologian, now living in Germany,

commented, "The Dar al-Salaam is present wherever Muslims are welcome and respected. Since we Muslims experience peace in Germany, there is no need for Muslims to seek political power. Our mission is to witness to Islam. Yet every people have their own prophets, and so God intends diversity. Everyone does not need to become a Muslim. That would be boring."

A few weeks later I asked a Sunni Indian/Guyanan/Canadian Muslim theologian, an effective teacher of Islam and a global traveler, "What is the mission of the Muslims in North America?"

This Sunni Muslim responded, "Our mission in North America is to witness to the truth of Islam and invite people to submit to Islam. At present our Muslim community in North America is too small to have much political authority. However, eventually we will have the critical mass to gain political power. Then we will establish the Dar al-Islam across North America."

These two comments are windows into the diversity within the global Muslim community today as the Muslim vision for mission meets the realities of modernity and a pluralist world. Yet the core remains the same for all faithful Muslims: The mission of the Muslim nation is to bear witness that there is no God but Allah and Muhammad is the prophet of Allah.

The Gospel and History

The biblical narrative describes history as beginning in a garden and being consummated in a glorious city in the *eschaton*. The city comes from heaven to earth; it is the bride of the Messiah, who is the church. In this city the curse of sin is no more. This is to say that history is the real arena of God's real actions, and all of history is moving toward the fulfillment of God's kingdom on earth and in heaven. That is why the core of biblical revelation is God's acts in history. Much of the Bible is the history of Israel as they journeyed and sometimes stumbled forward into God's future in response to God's call.

Several weeks after the attacks in New York and Washington, D.C., my wife and I were visiting churches in Karaganda, Kazakhstan. I was interviewed on a local radio station. The listening audience was mostly secularized Muslims.

My interviewer said, "We believe that your country is not really concerned about the well-being of the poor nations. As a

Christian what are your comments on that statement and the U.S.–led war on terrorism?"

"Nations are inclined to act in self-interest," I responded. "Thus nothing surprises me when nations go to war. But the way of the nations is not the kingdom of God that Jesus the Messiah has inaugurated and that will be fulfilled when he returns in the concluding drama of history. The core ethical commitment of the kingdom of God is to love, even the enemy, as Jesus loved. And that is the calling of the church, to be a community who reveals the presence of the kingdom of God by loving and serving among the nations as Jesus did.

"I pray for my nation, and I seek to give witness that justice and righteousness is the will of God for my nation and all nations. But my first loyalty is to the kingdom of God, and that kingdom is a total surprise, for it is a people from every tribe and nation and language who are reconciled and forgiven. How I wish I could meet Osama bin Laden and embrace him and tell him that I am an ambassador of the King who loves him. I would invite him to repentance, forgiveness, and reconciliation."

The center of the Gospel is that God in the Messiah reconciles us to himself in his suffering love revealed in the cross and resurrection. God planted the seed of the promise of that reality among humankind at the beginning of the human story. When Adam and Eve turned away from God, sinfulness and death became our human experience. Nevertheless, God personally entered the garden where Adam and Eve lived. He looked for them and called them. When he found them hiding behind a bush, in his enormous grief he gave a promise: A son born to the woman would be wounded by the serpent (evil powers), but he would crush the head of evil.

That drama in the garden is the kernel of all biblical understanding of meaning and purpose in history. The biblical narrative is the story of God acting in human history to redeem a people who will glorify him and be a light to the nations. Israel was the beginning, a people of covenant with God; they were called to be a blessing and light to the nations. In the Messiah, all peoples are invited into the family of God. Christians believe that the church is the extended family of God that reaches out to all nations so as to include people from every tribe, language, and nation.

Not only Israel, but all people are created to glorify God and enjoy fellowship with him forever. Our rebellion and sinfulness tragically distorts that purpose. But God has not abandoned us. He meets us personally, and he reveals himself within our history as the One who is our "Wounded Healer."[20] What we do affects God, and in the Messiah crucified our sin has collided with God. In the Messiah God suffers for us, dies for us, and redeems us. In his sacrificial death, we are forgiven; the church is a fellowship of forgiven sinners.

All who believe become the new temple of God, for the temple of God is the people of God, wherein God lives. There is no other house of God than the people of God. There is, therefore, no further need for a physical temple. The sacred center is only this: the Spirit of the risen Messiah present, among, and within his people as they gather in his name (Eph. 2:19-22; Matt. 18:20). This is to say that the church wherein the Holy Spirit dwells is the incarnational presence of God on earth. God lives among his people!

Jesus was committed to justice. Wherever his kingdom comes, there is hope for the poor and oppressed. The church is called to be an extension in our communities and around the world of the Messiah's commitment to justice and peace (*shalom*). The kingdom the Messiah is establishing is universal and voluntary. It is also nonviolent. There is no place for force in this kingdom. It is a kingdom of peace for all who will receive it. The cross is the ethical way of the kingdom of God and the way of the faithful church who are communities of the kingdom.

The pilgrimage of the church includes the rhythm of gathering in the name of Jesus. The gathered worshipers occasionally break bread and share the cup as a sign of the covenant of redemption and forgiveness that Christ offered on the cross as he cried out in forgiveness for those who were crucifying him. Broken bread and crushed grapes are the signs of the covenant established by Jesus, a covenant of repentance, of being crushed in sacrificial love for one another and for our enemies, and of self-giving service.

The Holy Spirit creates the church and empowers the church with new life. Ezekiel, one of the Old Testament prophets, saw a vision of a river flowing into the desert from the altar and the temple in Jerusalem (Ezek. 47:1-12). Trees with fruit and leaves for healing grew along the river banks. The stream flowing from the altar and into the desert in Ezekiel's vision is a metaphor for the Holy Spirit who proceeds from God and the crucified and risen Messiah.

The desert in the vision is the world. The streams of life flow from the altar and the temple into the desert. The Holy Spirit flows from the inner being of the disciples of Jesus Christ the Messiah. This is a life-giving river in every desert that it touches; trees grow along its banks and bear fruit. I suppose the healing leaves on the trees are righteous people, and the fruit of the trees is the fruit of the Spirit of the Messiah: love, joy, peace, patience, kindness, goodness, faithfulness, gentleness, and self-control (Gal. 5:22).

This is the mission of the church: to be river-channeling communities until every desert in the world is touched with this life-giving stream who is the Holy Spirit. This is a mission of joy, for wherever people meet in Jesus' name and celebrate his grace, there is joy. It is a community of hope, of the future, for it looks forward to the day when God's will is fulfilled on earth as it is in heaven. The church is a community among communities. It exists in the world, but it is not of the world. It is called to be a community of "salt" and "light" (Matt. 5:13-16). It influences, but does not control.

The Messiah commanded his disciples to "go and make disciples of all nations" (Matt. 28:19). There is a spirit of persistent urgency that pervades the New Testament. All peoples must hear the Gospel. The mission of the church is to carry this good news from people to people. In the scriptures, there is eschatological urgency about the mission of the church. The end of history is consummated as every people group has heard the Gospel. History leans forward in expectancy of that day when "the earth will be filled with the knowledge of the glory of the Lord as the waters cover the sea" (Hab. 2:14)

Jesus said, "And this gospel of the kingdom will be preached in the whole world as a testimony to all nations, and then the end will come" (Matt. 24:14).

Christians believe that as the Gospel is received and believed and becomes present within one people group after another, the kingdom of God is extended. This happens as churches are formed and grow with believers who are true disciples of Jesus.

As the church moves from people to people, that is one very important way for the kingdom of God to grow.

Many Christian churches, including the Anabaptists, the Christian church movement I affiliate with, identify with the Muslim concern that the community of faith should express the *tawhid* (unity) of God and his will on earth. The New Testament expression of *tawhid* is the community of believers who are disciples of Jesus the Messiah. When believers walk in the way of the Messiah, they live in the harmonious unity, fellowship, and self-giving love of God. The church, as described above, is an authentic sign of the presence of the kingdom of God on earth. This is a repentant and forgiven community. It is a community that submits to God. It is a fellowship of people who live by his grace and the empowerment of the Holy Spirit. It is a people who pray and yearn to become a people wherein God's will and kingdom come "on earth as it is heaven" (Matt. 6:9-13).

The fulfillment of God's kingdom in the New Testament is always in contrast to those forces and persons who oppose the kingdom. Even the grand vision in the concluding chapters of the Bible of the wondrous eternal city includes the warnings of judgment for all who reject redemption. Outside the city of God are the wicked and unrepentant (Rev. 21:27, 22:11, 15). Jesus warned that those "goats," who do not care for the poor and hungry and prisoners and sick, will be cast into eternal fire prepared for the devil (Matt. 25:31-46). It is evident that even in the final judgment, God will not force his kingdom of righteousness upon anyone. Judgment awaits those who reject God's kingdom and his persistent invitation to be reconciled and redeemed.

During the fall of 2002 I spoke in an Iranian Shi'ite mosque to a congregation of several hundred who were celebrating the birthday of the Twelfth Imam. As mentioned above, these Shi'ites believe the Twelfth Imam will return at the conclusion of history with Jesus. The imam in the local mosque asked me to speak on the second coming of Jesus the Messiah.

This is what I shared: "The ministry of the Messiah was hope for the poor and the oppressed. He healed all who came to him. However, he did not complete his mission of establishing justice and peace on earth. This is the calling of the people of God, to carry on that commitment. Even the way we relate to animals should reveal a commitment to loving care for God's creation and for one another.

"We are confident that these efforts are not useless, for a day will come when the Messiah will return to fulfill the kingdom of God forever. And all people will see him.

"What will we see? We will see outstretched hands that have been wounded by the nail marks of his crucifixion. Every eye will see the wounded Messiah who seeks to embrace and redeem all of us. We will mourn as we see what our sins have done to Jesus (Rev. 1:7). In his wounded hands we will see how much God loves us. That is how his kingdom comes: through redemptive love. And God has given to the Messiah crucified and risen all authority to bring history to its rightful conclusion.

"When the Messiah returns to earth all creation will be redeemed, for there will be a new heaven and a new earth. His kingdom of righteousness and peace will be established forever, and all who love him will reign with him forever" (Rev. 5:9-10, 21:1-5; 22:1-5).

Both the Muslim nation and the Christian church anticipate the concluding drama of history. In both of these communities, Jesus the Messiah is significantly involved in bringing history to its rightful conclusion.

Thus we discern, as we have so often in this journey with Muslims and Christians, that in unique ways Jesus persists in insisting that his presence be recognized. Yet the mission of Jesus in the end times within the Muslim expectation and the Christian anticipation is very different. He both unites and divides. He exerts his authority in ways that surprise both Christians and Muslims. His persistent presence is unavoidable.

Why is that so?

Readings from the Bible:
   Ezekiel 47:1-12; Revelation 22:1-7
Readings from the Qur'an:
   Qaf 50:16-45

Questions for Reflection and Discussion:
   1. Compare the understanding of the mission of the community of faith in the Qur'an and the New Testament.
   2. Compare the Muslim understanding of the meaning of history with that of the biblical scriptures.

3. Compare the mission of the Messiah's second coming in Isalm and in the New Testament.

4. There is conversation today about a possible "war of civilizations." What is the basis for such notions? How should the church respond?

5. Each Christian community has a special gift of grace that it offers in mission. What might an Anabaptist gift be? A Catholic gift? A Pentecostal gift?

6. Are there gifts that the Muslim community offers the church? Are there ways that the Muslim community challenges the church to greater faithfulness?

7. What have you learned about the Muslim nation that has surprised you? In what ways has the Islamic alternative to the Gospel helped to clarify the meaning of the Gospel? How has your appreciation of the Gospel been deepened as you have explored the Muslim alternative to the Gospel?

8. What have you learned about the mission of the church that has surprised you?

— 15 —

Concluding Comment

BOTH the Muslim nation and the Christian church are people who seek to be committed to the Word of God. Both are communities of witness.

The Muslim witness is that the Word of God is most fully revealed in a sent-down revelation inscribed in Arabic scripture (Yusuf [Joseph] 12:2).

The Christian witness is that "The Word became flesh and lived for a while among us. We have seen his glory, the glory of the one and only, who came from the Father, full of grace and truth" (John 1:14).

The Muslim commitment is to become a faithful witness over the nations, calling all people to submit to Islam and experience the peace of submission to the eternal will of God. The mission of the Muslims is to submit every area of life to the will of God.

The Christian commitment is to give witness that God is most fully revealed in Jesus—a baby in a manger in Bethlehem, a refugee in Egypt, a carpenter in Nazareth, an itinerate teacher, a man crucified between two thieves, the resurrected Messiah breathing his peace upon his frightened disciples. The calling of the church is to commend this Messiah in whom we are reconciled to God.

I believe that in times like these, when the nations are in turmoil, it is vitally necessary for communities of faith to be present everywhere to give witness to the conviction that God's kingdom is not established with the clenched fist, or the indifference of folded arms, but rather in a man crucified on a hill called

Golgotha, that "Christ crucified [is] . . . the power of God and the wisdom of God" (1 Cor. 1:23-24).

This kind of witness is a surprise, and is most effectively expressed in communities who actually demonstrate that suffering love does triumph over evil, communities who live in the confidence that God has exalted the crucified and resurrected Messiah, giving "him the name that is above every name" (Phil. 2:9). I believe that such communities of faith and hope, who love and serve in the spirit of the Messiah, are a healing, reconciling, and inviting presence among the nations, including the Muslim nation.

Notes

Preface

1. Messiah is the Semitic way of expressing the Greek name, *Kristos* (Christ). The biblical name, Messiah, means "the Anointed One." The Qur'an recognizes Jesus as the Messiah, and for this reason we use the Semitic name, Messiah, throughout this book.
2. Badru D. Kateregga and David W. Shenk, *A Muslim and a Christian in Dialogue* (Scottdale: Herald Press, 1997), 205-6.
3. *Confession of Faith in a Mennonite Perspective* (Scottdale: Herald Press, 1995). This confession was a churchwide process that preceded the integration in North America of the Mennonite Church and the General Conference Mennonite Church. It provides a contemporary interpretation of faith and practice of North American Mennonite Church Anabaptists.

Chapter 1: Different Journeys

1. Jimmy Carter, *Keeping Faith: Memoirs of a President* (New York: Bantam Books, 1982), 273-403. A book that is contributing to thoughtful conversation in some circles committed to Middle East peacemaking Karl-Josef Kuschel, *Abraham: Sign of Hope for Jews, Christians, and Muslims* (New York: Continuum, 1995).
2. W. Montgomery Watt, *Muhammad Prophet and Statesman* (New York: Oxford University Press, 1961), 94.
3. Ibid., 213.
4. W. H. C. Frend, *The Early Church* (London: Hodder & Stoughton, 1971), 93, 164.
5. Samuel Hugh Moffett, *A History of Christianity in Asia: Beginnings to 1500*, vol. 1 (Maryknoll, N.Y.: Orbis, 1998), 138.
6. Theodoret, *Ecclesiastical History I*, quoted in Moffett, 144.
7. Eusebius, *Life of Constantine*, 4:56, quoted in Moffett, 138.
8. Arend Theodoor van Leeuwen, *Christianity in World History, The Meeting of Faiths East and West*, translated from Dutch by H. H. Hoskins (New York: Charles Scribner's Sons, 1964), 210.
9. Ibid., 211.
10. Alex Awad, "Learning to Live with Muslims," *The Mennonite* (19 November 2002): 8-10.

11. Badru D. Kateregga and David W. Shenk, *A Muslim and a Christian in Dialogue,* (Scottdale, Pa.: Herald Press, 1997), 108-9.

12. Andrew Rippin, *Muslims: Their Religious Beliefs and Practices* (London: Routledge, 2002), 63-65.

13. H. A. R. Gibb, *Muhammedism* (New York: Oxford University Press, 1969), 3-5.

14. Van Leeuwen, *Christianity in World History,* 254.

15. Gibb, *Muhammedism,* 8.

16. Van Leeuwen, *Christianity in World History,* 255.

17. Gibb, *Muhammedism,* 9.

18. Ibid.

19. Paul Crawford, "A Deadly Give and Take," *Christian History* 21, no. 2 (August 2002): 24.

20. Gregory Miller, "From Crusades to Homeland Defense," *Christian History* 21, no. 2 (August 2002): 31-34.

21. Cornelius J. Dyck, *An Introduction to Mennonite History* (Scottdale: Herald Press, 1993), 39, 57-59.

22. Myron S. Augsburger, *Pilgrim Aflame* (Scottdale: Herald Press, 1967), 252-68.

23. Bernard Lewis, *What Went Wrong? Western Impact and Middle Eastern Response* (New York: Oxford University Press, 2002).

24. Ibid., 1-63.

25. Charles M. Sennott, *The Body and the Blood, the Holy Land's Christians, and the Turn of a New Millennium* (New York: Public Affairs, 2001), 323-26.

26. Ibid., 334-35.

27. Awad, "Learning to Live with Muslims," 8-10.

28. Sennott, *The Body and the Blood,* 22.

29. Ibid., 22-23.

30. Ibid., 252.

31. Ibid.

Chapter 2: Out of Arabia

1. Andrew Rippin, *Muslims: Their Religious Beliefs and Practices* (New York: Routledge, 2001), 236-38.

2. Badru D. Katerrega and David W. Shenk, *A Muslim and a Christian in Dialogue* (Scottdale, Pa.: Herald Press, 1997), 69.

3. Kenneth Cragg, *Muhammad and the Christian: A Question of Responses* (Maryknoll, N.Y.: Orbis, 1984), 36.

4. W. Montgomery Watt, *Muhammad Prophet and Statesman* (New York: Oxford University Press, 1969), 117-118.

5. Cragg, *Muhammad and the Christian,* 90.

6. Philip K. Hitti, *History of the Arabs,* rev., 10th ed. (New York: MacMillan, 2002).

7. John P. Kealy and David W. Shenk, *The Early Church and Africa* (Nairobi: Oxford University Press, 1975), 168-88.

8. J. W. C. Wand, *A History of the Early Church to A.D. 500* (New York: Methuen & Co., 1965), 157.

9. Ibid., 223.
10. "Three Phases of Christian-Muslim Interaction," *Christian History* 21, no. 2 (August 2002): 26.

Chapter 3: In the Garden

1. Badru D. Kateregga and David W. Shenk, *A Muslim and a Christian in Dialogue* (Scottdale, Pa.: Herald Press, 1997), 40.
2. C. K. Leaman, *Biblical Theology: Old Testament,* vol. 1 (Scottdale, Pa.: Herald Press, 1971), 65.
3. Rene Girard, *I See Satan Fall Like Lightning,* translated by James G. Williams (Maryknoll, N.Y.: Orbis, 2002) and Girard, *Violence and the Sacred,* translated by Patrick Gregory (Baltimore: Johns Hopkins University Press, 1981).
4. Kateregga and Shenk, *A Muslim and Christian*, 42-43.
5. An imam is the leader of the prayers in the mosque, or a person who is recognized as a leader of the Muslim community. In the Shi'ite community the imam is the leader who traces his genealogy to Muhammad.
6. Muhammad Hamidullah, *Introduction to Islam* (Paris: Centre Culturel Islamique, 1969), 134.
7. Hamidullah, (cf. Ibn Hisham), 135.
8. Lesslie Newbigin, *Honest Religion for Secular Man* (London: SCM, 1966) and Arend Theodoor van Leewen, *Christianity in World History*, translated by H. H. Hoskins (New York: Charles H. Scribner, 1964), 324-33.
9. Moroslav Volf, *Exclusion and Embrace* (Nashville: Abingdon, 1996), 35-166.

Chapter 4: Sons of Abraham

1. Abdullah Yusuf Ali, *The Holy Qur'an: Text, Translation, and Commentary* (Beirut: Dar Al Arabia, 1958), Commentary and Notes, no. 4101, p. 1205.
2. "Ibrahim," *Encyclopedia of Islam,* vol. 3, new ed. (Leiden: Brill, 1960), 980-81.
3. David W. Shenk, *Global Gods* (Scottdale, Pa.: Herald Press, 1999), 48.
4. Ali, *The Holy Qur'an*, 52.

Chapter 5: Leaders

1. Some biblical scholars do not view Genesis 3:15 as a promise concerning the redemptive work of the Messiah. However, the mainstream of Catholic theology and some other communities of biblical scholars believe that this passage is fulfilled in the life and ministry of Jesus the Messiah.
2. Israel means "he who strives with God." Although God is always faithful, the people of the covenant have not always been faithful. Their journey has often been a story of their struggle with God.

3. Abdullah Yusuf Ali, *The Holy Qur'an: Text, Translation and Commentary* (Beirut: Dar Al Arabia, 1958), 1540, note 5438.

4. Mani formed a third-century Persian Christian syncretistic and heretical movement known as Manichaeism. He taught that he himself was the Holy Spirit promised by Jesus. The church as a whole rejected such notions. However, the idea was in circulation as a Christian heresy, several centuries before Muhammad, that the promise by Jesus to send the Holy Spirit was a prophesy about the coming of a prophet.

5. H. A. R. Gibb, *Mohammedanism* (New York: Oxford University Press, 1969), 92, 98.

6. Andrew Rippin, *Muslims: Their Religious Beliefs and Practices* (New York: Rutledge, 2001), 50.

7. Ibid.

8. Ali, *The Holy Qur'an*, 1393, note 4877.

9. Kenneth Cragg, *Muhammad and the Christian* (Maryknoll, N.Y.: Orbis Books, 1984), 75.

10. From Al-Ghazali, *Ihya' 'Ulum al-Din*, vol. 2 (Cairo: al-Maktabe al-Tijara al-Kubra, 1965), 381, quoted in Kees Wagtendonk, "Images in Islam, Discussion of a Paradox," in *Effigies Dei: Essays on the History of Religion*, edited by Dirk van der Plas (Leiden: E. J. Brill, 1987), 123.

11. J. S. Trimingham, *The Sufi Orders in Islam* (Oxford: Clarendon Press, 1971), 161.

12. Cragg, *Muhammad and the Christian*, 70.

13. Tarif Khalidi, *The Muslim Jesus* (Cambridge, Mass.: Harvard University Press, 2001).

14. Ibid., 24-26.

15. Ibid., 34.

16. Ibid., 15.

17. Ibid.

18. Cragg, *Muhammad and the Christian*, 10.

19. *Ra'd* (Thunder) 13:38. Ali, *The Holy Qur'an*, footnote 1861.

20. Khalidi, *The Muslim Jesus*, 45.

Chapter 6: Scriptures

1. Kenneth Cragg, *Muhammad and the Christian* (Maryknoll, N.Y.: Orbis Books, 1984), 134-35.

2. Emil Fackenheim, *The Presence of God in History: Jewish Affirmations and Philosophical Reflections* (New York: New York University Press, 1970), 8-14.

3. N. T. Wright, *The Challenge of Jesus: Rediscovering Who Jesus Was and Is* (Downers Grove, Ill.: InterVarsity Press, 1999).

4. Cragg, *Muhammad and the Christian*, 134-35.

5. Ibid.

6. Badru D. Kateregga and David W. Shenk, *A Muslim and a Christian in Dialogue* (Scottdale, Pa.: Herald Press, 1997), 67.

7. Nahl (The Bee) 16:103. Tarif Khalidi, *The Muslim Jesus* (Cambridge: Harvard University Press, 2001), 20-21. The Satanic verses are the exception, where unawares, Satan slipped a small portion into the recitation that was a compromise with polytheism. This was later corrected by the angelic messenger. See Najm (The Star) 16:19-23; Haff (The Pilgrimage) 22:52-3. George W. Baswell Jr., *Islam: Its Prophet, Peoples, Politics, and Power* (Nashville: Broadman & Holman Publishers, 1996), 45.

8. W. F. Albright, *From the Stone Age to Christianity* (Maryknoll, N.Y.: Orbis Books, 1984), 11-17.

9. Sean Kealy, *The Changing Bible* (Nairobi: KUC, n.d.), 87.

10. Bible societies and Christian communities sometimes offer Muslims biblical scriptures based specifically on those portions of the Bible that the Qur'an affirms: the Torah, the Psalms, and the Gospels.

   Using those principles, some years ago a team in Somalia and Kenya developed the *People of God* study course for Muslims, a study based especially on the three portions of biblical scriptures that the Qur'an recognizes. Bible societies published the scripture portions to accompany the course.

   Rather than inviting participants to study the Bible, students are invited into a study of the *Taura*t (Torah) of the prophet Moses. When they complete that course, they study portions of the *Zabur* (Psalms) of the prophet David and then the *Injil* (Gospel) of Jesus the Messiah. The course is mostly narrative. That is attractive, for the Qur'an alludes to the biblical narratives as sketchy illustrations, but not as full story accounts.

   The unifying theme throughout is the Messianic secret. Who is the Messiah and what is his mission? The course has been translated or is being translated into some forty languages. Thousands of Muslims enroll in the course annually. Their open reception to the course is surprising.

   Another way to make connections with Muslim interest in the Bible is biblical narratives. A few years ago, a team in the Middle East developed a Bible storybook for children with a picture and a story for every day of the year. Tens of thousands of these books have been published and are circulating widely in the region.

11. This translation is from *The Meaning of the Glorious Koran: An Explanatory Translation by Mohammed Marmaduke Pickthall* (London: George Allen and Unwin, Ltd., 1961).

Chapter 7: Revelation

1. Andrew Rippin, *Muslims: Their Religious Beliefs and Practices* (New York: Routledge, 2001) 33-34.

2. Badru D. Kateregga and David W. Shenk, *A Muslim and a Christian in Dialogue* (Scottdale, Pa.: Herald Press, 1997), 150.

3. Kenneth Cragg, *The Event of the Qur'an: Islam in Its Scriptures* (Oxford: Oneworld Publications, 1994).

4. Ibid., and Kenneth Cragg, *Muhammad and the Christian* (Oxford: Oneworld Publications, 1999).

5. Hans Kung, et al., *Christianity and World Religions: Paths to Dialogue with Islam, Hinduism, and Buddhism,* translated by Peter Heinegg (New York: Doubleday, 1986), 28-36.

6. Rippin, *Muslims,* 240-41.

7. Lamin Sanneh, *Translating the Message: The Missionary Impact on Culture* (Maryknoll, N.Y.: Orbis Books, 1989), 211-14.

8. Rafiq Zakaria, *The Struggle within Islam: The Conflict Between Religion and Politics* (New York: Penguin, 1989), 284.

9. Ibid., 285.

10. Ibid.

11. Ibid.

12. Ibid.

13. Ibid., 290.

14. Ibid., 288-89.

15. John Alembillah Azumah, *The Legacy of Arab-Islam in Africa* (Oxford: Oneworld Publications, 2001), 63-108.

16. Rippin, *Muslims,* 288.

17. Ibid.

18. Sanneh, *Translating the Message,* 157-209.

19. Kwame Bediako, *Christianity in Africa: The Renewal of Non-Western Religion* (Maryknoll, N.Y.: Orbis Books, 1995), 39-58, 172-188.

20. J. T. K. Daniel and R. E. Hedlund, *Carey's Obligation and India's Renaissance* (Serampore: Council of Serampore College, 1993), 153-298.

21. Ibid., 153-75.

Chapter 8: Power

1. Badru D. Kateregga and David W. Shenk, *A Muslim and a Christian in Dialogue* (Scottdale, Pa.: Herald Press, 1997), 71-72.

2. Abdullah Yusuf Ali, *The Holy Qur'an: Text, Translation, and Commentary* (Beirut: Dar Al Arabia, 1968), 691-93.

3. W. Montgomery Watt, *Muhammad: Prophet and Statesman* (New York: Oxford University Press, 1961), 82-228.

4. Tarif Khalidi, *The Muslim Jesus* (Cambridge, Mass.: Harvard University Press, 2001), 14.

5. Muhammad Kamil Husain, *City of Wrong,* translated by Kenneth Cragg (Oxford: Oneworld Publications, 1995).

6. Lamin Sanneh, *Piety and Power: Muslims and Christians in West Africa* (Maryknoll, N.Y.: Orbis Books, 1996), 73, 123-24.

7. C. J. Lyall, *Translations of Ancient Arabian Poetry* (London: 1930), 5, in Kenneth Cragg, *Muhammed and the Christian* (Maryknoll, N.Y.: Orbis Books, 1984), 39.

8. Kenneth Cragg, *Muhammad and the Christian* (Maryknoll, N.Y.: Orbis Books, 1984) 39-42.

Chapter 9: Holy Cities

1. N. T. Wright, *The Challenge of Jesus: Rediscovering Who Jesus Was and Is* (Downers Grove, Ill.: InterVarsity, 1999), 123.
2. Wright, *The Challenge of Jesus*, 110.
3. John Foster, *Church History: the First Advance, A.D. 29-500* (London: Society for Promoting Christian Knowledge, 1972), 35.
4. William G. Young, *Handbook of Source Materials for Students of Church History up to 650 A.D.* (Madras: The Diocesan Press, 1969), section 63.
5. Foster, *Church History*, 35.
6. George W. Braswell Jr., *Islam: Its Prophet, Peoples, Politics and Power* (Nashville: Broadman & Holman Publishers, 1996), 127.
7. Javid Iqbal, "Democracy and the Modern Islamic State," in *Voices of Resurgent Islam*, edited by John Esposito (New York: Oxford University Press, 1983), 252-60.
8. Jacqueline Hoover, "Pre-Islamic Arabia." Lecture from excerpts of Robert G. Hoyland, *Arabia and the Arabs* (New York: Routledge, 2001), 229-47.
9. Kenneth Cragg, *Muhammad and the Christian* (Maryknoll, N.Y.: Orbis Books, 1984), 32.
10. Bernard Lewis, *The Political Language of Islam* (Chicago: Chicago University Press, 1969), 29.
11. Bernard Lewis, *What Went Wrong?: Western Impact and Middle Eastern Response* (New York: Oxford University Press, 2002), 36-37.
12. Hamideh Mohagheghi, "The House of Islam." Lecture at the *Theologische Studientage der AMG*, Heiligenstadt, October 6-10, 2002.
13. Ibid.
14. Alfred Guillaume, *Islam* (New York: Penguin, 1979), 46.

Chapter 10: One God

1. That statement needs qualification. At least in popular Catholicism, as well as some other Christian communities, the honor bestowed on the virgin Mary or the saints might verge on the ascribing of associates that Islam decries. This Muslim objection is a concern that the church might wisely hear.
2 Ali Shari'ati, *On the Sociology of Islam*, translated by Hamid Algar (Berkeley, Calif.: Mizan Press, 1979).

Chapter 11: Pilgrimage

1. Andrew Rippin, *Muslims: Their Religious Beliefs and Practices* (New York: Routledge, 2001), 97-98.
2. H. A. R. Gibb, *Mohammedanism* (New York: Oxford University Press, 1969), 66-67.
3. Muhammad Hamidullah, *Introduction to Islam* (Paris: Centre Culturel Islamique, 1969), 64.

4. Mohamed Amin, *Pilgrimage to Mecca* (Nairobi, Kenya: Camerapix, 1978), 20.
5. Badru D. Kateregga and David W. Shenk, *A Muslim and a Christian in Dialogue* (Scottdale, Pa.: Herald Press, 1997), 69.
6. Hamidullah, *Introduction to Islam*, 66.
7. E. P. Sanders, *The Historical Figure of Jesus* (London: The Penguin Press, 1995), 33-48.
8. Donald B. Kraybill, *The Upside-Down Kingdom* (Scottdale, Pa.: Herald Press, 1978), 65-94.
9. The Muslim nation has a geographical center, the Ka'bah. The Christian church has no geographical center. A global missions scholar, Andrew Walls, observed at a consultation (December 6-8, 2002) at the Overseas Ministries Study Center in New Haven, Connecticut, that the Muslim nation has never experienced decline in the regions closest to its origins, which is also its geographical center. This is in contrast to the Christian church, which has experienced numerical decline in the regions closest to its origins. Does the absence of a Christian geographical center contribute to the reality that the church experiences great vitality on the frontiers of the movement, while historical centers often experience malaise and decline?
10. N. T. Wright, *The Challenge of Jesus* (Downers Grove, Ill.: InterVarsity Press, 1999), 110.
11. Abdullah Yusuf Ali, *The Holy Qur'an: Text, Translation and Commentary* (Beirut: Dar Al Arabia, 1958).

Chapter 12: Two Ways

1. Andrew Rippin, *Muslims: Their Religious Beliefs and Practices* (New York: Routledge, 2002), 8-9.
2. Frederick Mathewson Denny, *An Introduction to Islam* (New York: Macmillian, 1994), 161.
3. H. A. R. Gibb, *Mohammedanism* (New York: Oxford University Press, 1969), 74.
4. Rippin, *Muslims*, 47.
5. Denny, *An Introduction to Islam*, 161.
6. Gibb, *Mohammedanism*, 78-79.
7. Ali Akbar Dareini, "Iran President Chides Death Sentence," from the Associated Press (13 November 2002).
8. Ibid.
9. John Alembillah Azumah, *The Legacy of Arab Islam in Africa* (Oxford: Oneworld Publications, 2001), 191-95.
10. Denny, *An Introduction to Islam*, 197.
11. This is not to say that Muslims do not struggle with the paradoxes of human freedom and the sovereignty of God, which is also true of Christian theologians. But exploring those theological nuances would take us beyond the purpose of this book and chapter. For a further exploration of those issues refer to Jon Hoover's Ph.D. dissertation, *An Islamic Theodicy: Ibn Taymiyya on the Wise Purpose of*

God, Human Agency, and Problems of Evil and Justice, Centre for the Study of Islam and Christian-Muslim Relations, University of Birmingham, United Kingdom, 2002. Also see Jon Hoover, "A Typology of Responses to the Philosophical Problem of Evil in Islamic and Christian Traditions" (Unpublished paper presented at a Mennonite-Shi'i dialogue: Toronto, October 24-26, 2002).

12. Abdullah Yusuf Ali, *The Holy Qur'an: Text, Translation and Commentary* (Beirut: Dar Al Arabia, 198) 1605, footnote 5677.

13. The difference between proselytism and conversion was discussed at a conference on this theme at the Overseas Ministries Study Center in New Haven, Connecticut, December 6-8, 2002. The consensus in that conference was that proselytes abandon their culture as they move into the religious culture of the missionizing community. Converts remain in their culture but have converted to a new center in their lives. In Christian experience the convert is one who is committed to the Messiah but remains rooted in her indigenous culture.

Chapter 13: Prayer

1. *Tradition* by Saheeh Muslim.
2. Jane Idleman Smith, ed., *The Precious Pearl: A Translation from the Arabic* (Missoula, Mont.: Scholard Press, 1979), 59-60.
3. Evan Bontrager, "My Participation in Ramadan," *The Mennonite* (19 November 2002): 11.
4. Muhammad Hamidullah, *Islam in a Nutshell* (Philadelphia: Ayesha Begum Hyderabad House, Inc., 1990), 12-53.
5. J. Spencer Trimingham, *Islam in Ethiopia* (New York: Barnes and Noble, 1965), 232.
6. The spiritual authority comes down from Muhammad through a direct spiritual chain, from leader to leader. This understanding of spiritual authority within the *sufi* orders seems to have some analogies with the Christian churches who believe in the apostolic succession of spiritual authority.
7. Muslims are ambivalent about the role of intercessors. On the one hand, there is no need for intercessors. On the other hand, God might appoint an intercessor or intercessors; that is his prerogative (Baqara 2:255). Muslim tradition believes that Muhammad has been given that role. See Kenneth Cragg, *The Call of the Minaret* (New York: Oxford University Press, 1964), 113.
8. Saint Augustine, *Confessions*, translated by R. S. Pine-Coffin (Baltimore: Penquin, 1961), 226.

Chapter 14: Global Mission

1. John Alembillah Azumah, *The Legacy of Arab-Islam in Africa* (Oxford: Oneworld Publications, 2001), 63-79.
2. Patrick Johnstone and Jason Mandryk, *Operation World: When We Pray God Works* (Waynesboro, Ga.: Paternoster Publishing, 2001), 18-21.

3. David B. Barrett and Todd M. Johnson, "Annual Statistical Table on Global Mission," *International Bulletin* 25:1 (January 2002), 25.
4. Kenneth Cragg, *The Call of Minaret* (Maryknoll, N.Y.: Orbis Books, 1985), 26.
5. Johnstone and Mandryk, *Operation World*, 2.
6. Ibid., 160.
7. Ibid., 747, 749.
8. Badru D. Kateregga and David W. Shenk, *A Muslim and a Christian in Dialogue* (Scottdale, Pa.: Herald Press, 1997), 44.
9. Ibid., 64.
10. Andrew Rippin, *Muslims: Their Religious Beliefs and Practices* (New York: Routledge, 2001), 236.
11. Ibid., 238-45.
12. H. A. R. Gibb, *Mohammedanism* (New York: Oxford University Press, 1969), 9.
13. Wilfred Cantwell Smith, *Islam in Modern History* (Princeton: Princeton University Press, 1957), 14.
14. Dudley Woodberry, "Justice and Peace," *Christian History* 21:2 (August 2002), 44.
15. Ibid., 45.
16. Smith, *Islam in Modern History*, 22.
17. Kenneth Cragg, *Sandals at the Mosque* (New York: Oxford University Press, 1959), 124.
18. Kataregga and Shenk, *A Muslim and a Christian in Dialogue*, 111.
19. G. E. von Grunebaum, *Islam Essays in the Nature and Growth of a Cultural Tradition* (New York: Barnes and Noble, 1961), 227.
20. Henri J. M. Nouwen, *The Wounded Healer* (New York: Image Books, 1979).

Glossary

Muslim Terms

Abbasid	The golden age of Islam when the dynasty of Abbasid caliphs based in Baghdad ruled from the eighth to thirteenth centuries
abd	Servant or slave of God
adhan	The call to prayer
Ahl al-Kitab	The people of the book—Christians and Jews
Allah	The word for God in Arabic.
Aya/ayat	Sign or signs. Each verse in the Qur'an is a sign of God's revelation, as is creation.
baraka	Blessing
bid'ah	Change or innovation that is prohibited
Buraq	The winged horse-like creature that took Muhammad from Mecca to Jerusalem in his miraculous night journey
Dar al-Harb	The region of war that is not yet under Muslim rule
Dar al-Islam	The region that has come under Muslim rule
Dar al-Salam	The region under Muslim rule, which is the region of peace
da'wah	The invitation to become a Muslim
dawlah	Extension of Muslim political control over a region

dhikr	Remembrance. The mystics chant the name of God in devotional remembrance.
dhimmi	Protected communities that are under Muslim rule, especially referring the Christians and Muslims
din	Religion
du'a'	Informal prayers of petition to God. These prayers are not obligatory and can be offered in a language other than Arabic.
fana'	The *sufi* quest for passing away through absorption into divinity
Fatiha	The opening prayer of the Qur'an that Muslims repeat in every cycle of ritual prayer
fatwa	A legal decision made by legitimate Muslim authority
fiqh	The science of Muslim law
hadd	Restrictions that require specific penalties if violated
Hadith, *hadith*	Set of Muslim traditions (or a single tradition from that collection) that is a source of authority and guidance in addition to the Qur'an
hajj	The annual pilgrimage to Mecca that is one of the Five Pillars of Duty in Islam
halal	That which is permitted
hanif	Arabians who worshiped the God of Abraham
haram	That which is forbidden
hijrah	The migration of Muhammad from Mecca to Medina in 622. This is the beginning of the Muslim era.
Iblis	Satan, who is the originator of all evil
'Id al-Adha	The four-day feast at the climax of the pilgrimage to Mecca when Muslims remember the Abraham-Ishmael legacy and the sacrifice of a ram as a substitute for the offering of a son of Abraham (Ishmael in Muslim understanding)

'Id al-Fitr	The three-day feast at the end of the Ramadan month of fasting, when Muslims celebrate the gift of the Qur'an
ihram	The consecration of the pilgrims on the *hajj*
i'jaz	The doctrine that the Qur'an cannot be imitated because of its miraculous qualities
ijma'	Developing of consensus in matters of ritual and legal practice
ijtihad	Exerting personal effort and in-depth expertise in interpreting and applying the meaning of the Qur'an
imam	The leader of the prayers. Among the Shi'a Muslims the leader of the community is also sometimes referred to as the *imam*.
iman	Faith or belief
Injil	The Gospel which means good news. The book of the Gospel that was revealed through Jesus the Messiah.
'Isa	The name for Jesus in the Qur'an
Islam	The faith that Muhammad preached. The term means submission; peace is linked to this submission. Those who submit to Islam are called Muslims.
'isma	The belief that Muhammad was without sin
isnad	The chain of authority through which the episodes or sayings in the *Hadith* were validated
isra'	The night journey that Muhammad took from Mecca to Jerusalem
jahiliyya	The time of ignorance in pre-Islamic Arabia prior to Muhammad
jihad	Striving in the way of Allah for the protection of Islam. This is often considered to be the sixth pillar of Muslim duty.
jinn	Spirits, some of whom are good and others who are evil

Ka'bah	The House of God in Mecca that encompasses the sacred black stone
khalifa	All humanity have the responsibility to serve God on earth as his khalifa or vicegerents. Also the head of the Muslim community after Muhammad's death.
mihrab	The niche in the mosque that shows the direction to face in prayer
mi'raj	The ascension of Muhammad into the heavens where he received instructions as to how often Muslims should pray
Muslim	A believer in Allah who submits to Islam
nabbi	A prophet of God
qadar	Predestination
qadi	A Muslim judge who interprets Muslim law
qiblah	The direction in which Muslims pray
qiyas	The use of analogies in coming to decisions
rak'ah	The prayer cycle of standing, bowing, and kneeling that is included in the ritual prayers
rasul	A prophet of God through whom God reveals scripture
salat	The ritual prayers that are mandatory five times daily. Also commitment to submit every area of life to God as a constant posture of worship.
sawm	Fasting during the month of Ramadan
shahada	The witness: There is no God but Allah and Muhammad is his prophet.
Shari'a	The Muslim schools of law that are based on four streams of authority: Qur'an, *sunna*, *ijma*, and *qiyas*.
Shi'a	The branch of Islam that have believed that the son-in-law of Muhammad, 'Ali b. Abu Talib, and his heirs are the only legitimate leaders of the Muslim community. Ten percent of the Muslim nation are Shi'a and they are mostly Iranian.

shirk	The unforgivable sin of ascribing associates to God
shura	Consultation leading to a decision
sisila	The chain of spiritual authority through which the saints of the *sufi* mystics gain insight into spiritual mysteries
sufi	Mystical communities who seek union with the divine
sunnah	The way of the prophet Muhammad
Sunnis	The mainstream of Orthodox Islam who are in contrast to the Shi'a communities
sura	A chapter in the Qur'an
takbir	Voicing the expression: God is most great (*Alahu Akbar*)
tariqa	An order of a *sufi* community
Taurat	The book of revelation that came through Moses that the Qur'an recognizes as being scripture. This is the Torah or the first five books of Moses known as the Pentateuch.
tawhid	The oneness of God and his will
'ulama	Those who are experts in Islamic law
Umayyads	The first caliphs (661-750)
ummah	The Muslim community
Wahhabiyya	The disciples of an Arabian reformer, Ibn 'Abd al-Wahhab (d. 1787). This reform is the official policy of Saudi Arabia; the movement exerts significant influence on the modern global Muslim movement.
wali/awliya	Friend or friends of God. This spirituality provides impetus for the *sufi* mystical movement.
Zabur	The Psalms revealed through the prophet David that Muslims believe to be revealed scripture
zakat	Giving alms, one of the five pillars of Muslim duty

Zamzam — The well adjacent to the Grand Mosque in Mecca from which Hagar drew water for her thirsty son Ishmael

Christian Terms

Anabaptist — A Bible study renewal movement among West European Christians that began in the early sixteenth century. They taught the separation of church and state and believed that military service was contrary to the teachings and practice of Jesus. They rejected infant baptism but practiced adult baptism upon confession of faith and evidence of conversion.

apostolic succession — A belief in Catholic and Orthodox churches that the authority of the bishops derives from the succession of spiritual authority from the apostles of Jesus. This doctrine is also held by the Episcopal church.

apostles — Leaders of the early church, most of whom had been with Jesus

ascension — Forty days after Jesus rose from the dead following his crucifixion, his disciples saw him ascend into heaven. Just before his ascension he commanded them to go into all the world as his witnesses.

atonement — Sacrifice for the forgiveness of sins

baptism — A sign with water that is a witness that the person is included in the Christian church. Churches that practice only adult baptism do so when the person has decided to believe in Jesus the Messiah. Churches that practice infant baptism view baptism as a sign of God's grace that forgives us and that invites all people including the child into the fellowship of the church.

bishop — A church leader who is responsible for a group of churches.

Catholic	One meaning is the universal church. Another meaning refers to the Roman Catholic Church, the largest fellowship of churches with more than one billion members.
Christ	The English rendition of the Greek word *Kristos*, which means the Messiah or the Anointed One
Christendom	Western church where church and state have united. It is a sort of Christian expression of the Muslim *Dar al Islam*.
church	The fellowship of believers in Jesus the Messiah
Council of Nicea	A church council that convened in A.D. 325 at Nicea to discern Christian beliefs including what Christians should believe about the nature of Jesus the Messiah. The council wrote a confession of faith, known as the Nicene Creed, that Orthodox, Catholic, and Protestant churches embrace.
Constantine	Western Roman Emperor who made Christianity legal within the empire (A.D. 313). He tried to bring about unity of church and state.
covenant	A binding agreement between persons. God has initiated covenant relations with people and promises blessing for all who are committed to his covenant.
deacon	A person whose responsibility in the church is to assist the bishop or priest.
disciple	A follower or learner. Jesus had twelve disciples who were especially involved in his ministry.
El or *Elohim*	The name for God used by Abraham. The Arabic Allah as a name for God is the same as the Hebrew *El* or *Elohim*.
eucharist	Gratitude, thankfulness for God's grace revealed through communion in Jesus the Messiah. Regularly most Christian congregations share broken bread and wine together in a solemn commemoration of the life, crucifixion, and resurrection of Jesus the Messiah.

elder	A minister or leader in a congregation in the early church
epistles	Letters that are included in the New Testament that apostles wrote to churches
eschaton	The future when Jesus the Messiah returns, the final judgment happens, and the kingdom of God is fulfilled and established forever
fruit of the spirit	The new creation within a person that fills the person with fruits of the Holy Spirit such as love, joy, and peace
garden of Eden	The garden where Adam and Eve first lived
Gospel	The good news of the life, ministry, teaching, crucifixion, and resurrection of Jesus the Messiah
gospels	The four accounts of the life and ministry of Jesus the Messiah that are included in the New Testament: Matthew, Mark, Luke, John
great commission	Jesus' last command to his disciples before his ascension to go into all the world and make disciples of all nations
Holy Spirit	The Spirit of God who continues the work of Jesus the Messiah by convicting people of truth and empowering those who believe to live in the way of the Messiah
I AM	The name God revealed to the prophet Moses at the burning bush. Theologians sometimes refer to this name with the Hebrew term, *Yahweh.*
Immanuel	God with us, a name that the angel announced for Jesus when the angel told the virgin Mary that she would give birth to Jesus
incarnation	In the flesh. This refers to the belief that God revealed himself fully in the person of Jesus of Nazareth, the Son of Mary.
Jerusalem conference	A meeting of the leaders of the early church to discern how Gentile believers should relate to Jewish culture and the Old Testament practices. The meeting decided

that Gentiles may be free to continue within their culture but to abstain from some of the wrongful practices of their society. This meeting is described in Acts 15.

Jesus

The biblical name for the Messiah. The name means "Yahweh saves. "

Joseph

The man who married the virgin Mary, the mother of Jesus. He was a carpenter; Jesus also worked as a carpenter in his early years.

kingdom of God

Wherever the rule of God prevails. Christians believe that Jesus is the revelation within history of the fullness of the rule of God. His kingdom has begun now but will be fulfilled at the conclusion of history when Jesus the Messiah returns.

Lamb of God

One of the names for Jesus the Messiah. This refers to the sacrificial death of Jesus on the cross. There is a sign of the meaning of Jesus as the Lamb of God in most religions, because they have the practice of offering animals as a substitute sacrifice, like the ram offered in place of a son of Abraham. Christians believe that all people are sinners who deserve the judgment of God, but Jesus as the Lamb of God has taken our place and so we can be free of judgment and forgiven.

Messiah

God's Anointed One. Jesus is the Messiah.

Mount Sinai

The mount where God revealed the Ten Commandments to Israel and invited them to become his covenant people

Nazareth

The childhood home of Jesus

New Testament

The second division of the Bible, written after the birth of Jesus the Messiah

Old Testament

The first division of the Bible, written before the birth of Jesus the Messiah

Orthodox Church

This church has many similarities to the Roman Catholic Church, from which it separated in 1054. These churches are mostly east of the predominantly Catholic and Protestant churches of Western Europe.

Passover   Jewish solemn commemoration of God's deliverance of Israel from slavery in Egypt during the time of the Pharaohs. Moses led the people as God worked miracles to bring about their freedom. The night of their deliverance is called Passover, because on that night the angel of death smote homes throughout Egypt, but the Israelite homes, which had the blood of a lamb daubed on the door posts, were preserved from harm.

Paul   At one time persecuted Christians until the risen Messiah met him in a vision. Thereafter Paul became a believer in the Messiah and then a leader in the church, with special concern for including non-Jewish people in the church. He wrote a number of the epistles in the New Testament.

Pentecost   The annual Jewish Feast of Harvest. It was at this feast after Jesus had risen from the dead that the Holy Spirit came upon the disciples of Jesus with great power and the church was created.

Peter   A disciple of Jesus who became one of the key leaders of the church. He had a special role in extending the church among non-Jewish people.

people of Israel   The people who became the covenant community of the Old Testament. They trace their origins to Abraham and Isaac.

pope   The head of the Roman Catholic Church

prophet   A person who proclaims the Word of God and calls people to repentance. In biblical times God sometimes revealed scriptures through prophets.

Protestant   A Christian movement that separated from the Catholic Church early in the sixteenth century. The Protestants emphasized biblical authority and that salvation is the gift of God's grace.

Psalms   A portion of the Old Testament that consists mostly of poetry. David was one of the primary authors of these poems.

redemption	To pay whatever is necessary to rescue a person from harm or destruction, as to pay the price to have a person released from prison. Jesus has paid the price necessary for the redemption of humankind from the death and destruction that sinfulness and Satan brings upon us.
repentance	To make a U-turn, to turn from our self-centered, sinful ways to follow the Messiah
sacrifice	In most religions people offer animal or food sacrifices to their gods in hope of having their sins forgiven. The New Testament describes Jesus as the Lamb of God who is the sacrifice for our sins.
salvation	Forgiveness of sins and eternal life. Well-being and peace.
Satan	Similar to Iblis in Islam. He is a deceiver.
Savior	A name for Jesus, who saves us from our sin and offers forgiveness, fullness of life now, and life eternal in heaven.
second coming	Jesus promised that he will return at the final judgment, when the dead will be raised to life and the kingdom of God fulfilled forever. At that time there will be a new heaven and a new earth.
Sermon on the Mount	Teachings of Jesus about righteousness that he gave to his disciples on a mount
Son of God	The Messiah in whom God revealed himself fully and who had a perfect relationship with God
Temple	The Jewish place of worship that was first built by King Solomon
Ten Commandments	Commandments about right conduct that God revealed to Moses at Mount Sinai
testament	An agreement. The Bible consists of the Old Testament and the New Testament.
Torah	The first five books of the Bible

Trinity

A way that Christian try to express their experience of God as one in the unity of the loving fellowship of Creator, Savior, and Spirit (Father, Son, and Holy Spirit)

virgin Mary

The mother of Jesus

Yahweh

An attempt to express God as the I AM who revealed himself to Moses at the burning bush

Annotated Bibliography
Of Material in English on Islam
and Christian-Muslim Relations

Introductions to Islam

Abdalati, Hammudah. *Islam in Focus*. Indianapolis, Ind.: American Trust Publications, 1975. Reprinted. A basic guide to Islamic beliefs and practices for Muslims.

Chittick, William C., and Sachiko Murata. *The Vision of Islam*. St. Paul: Paragon House, 1994. Examines Islam from a *sufi* theosophical perspective.

Denny, Frederick Mathewson. *An Introduction to Islam*. 2nd ed. New York: Macmillan, 1994. A widely-used college textbook that tries to touch on everything.

Endress, Gerhard. *An Introduction to Islam*. New York: Columbia University, 1987. Focuses more on history than religion.

Esposito, John L. *Islam: The Straight Path*. 3rd ed. New York: Oxford U.P., 1998. Sympathetic introduction by a non-Muslim.

Hamidullah, Muhammad. *Introduction to Islam*. Kuwait: International Islamic Book Center, n.d. A traditionally minded introduction to Islam as it is to be believed and practiced. More extensive than the book by Hammudah Abdalati listed above.

Jomier, Jacques. *How to Understand Islam*. Trans. from French by John Bowden. London: SCM Press, 1989. An easy-to-read introduction to Islam for Christians.

Miller, Roland E. *Muslim Friends, Their Faith and Feeling: An Introduction to Islam*. St. Louis: Concordia, 1996. From a Christian perspective.

Rahman, Fazlur. *Islam*. 2nd ed. Chicago: University of Chicago Press, 1979. By a modernist Pakistani intellectual.

Renard, John. *Seven Doors to Islam: Spirituality and the Religious Life of Muslims*. Berkeley: University of California Press, 1996, and the companion volume *Windows on the House of Islam: Muslim Sources on Spirituality and Religious Life*. Berkeley: University of California Press, 1998.

Rippin, Andrew. *Muslims: Their Religious Beliefs and Practices*. 2nd ed. London: Routledge, 2001. Strongly analytical with a reconstructivist approach to Islamic origins.

Robinson, Neal. *Islam: A Concise Introduction*. Washington, D.C.: Georgetown University, 1999. Gives some attention to questions Christians ask.

Schimmel, Annemarie. *Deciphering the Signs of God: A Phenomenological Approach to Islam*. Edinburgh: Edinburgh U.P., 1994.

Waines, David. *An Introduction to Islam*. Cambridge: Cambridge U.P., 1995. A solid historical introduction.

Life of Muhammad

Guillaume, A. *The Life of Muhammad: A Translation of Ishâq's Sîrat Rasûl Allâh*. Karachi: Oxford University, 1955. (13th printing in 1998). Translation of the classic Arabic work on Muhammad's life.

Haykal, Muhammad Husayn. *The Life of Muhammad*. Trans. I. F. al-Faruqi from the Arabic. London: Shorouk International, 1983. Originally published in 1935. Written by a modernist Egyptian Muslim.

Lings, Martin. *Muhammad: His Life Based on the Earliest Sources*. Cambridge: The Islamic Texts Society, 2001. The best access in English to the traditional way Muslims tell the story.

Rodinson, Maxime. *Mohammed*. Trans. Anne Carter from the French. London: Penguin, 1971.

Watt, W. Montgomery. *Muhammad, Prophet and Statesman*. London: Oxford U.P., 1961.

The Qur'an in English

Ali, Abdullah Yusuf. *The Holy Qur'an*. Lahore, 1937. Many reprints. A good translation by a Muslim in older English. Used widely by Muslims.

Arberry, A. J. *The Koran Interpreted*. London, 1955. Known for its literary excellence among scholars in Islamic studies, but the verse numbering system is no longer widely used.

Dawood, N. J. *The Koran*. London: Penguin, 1956. Many reprints. By a non-Muslim. The easiest to read using contemporary English.

Fakhry, Majid. *The Qur'an: A Modern English Version*. Reading, UK: Garnet Press, 1997. A solid contemporary English translation.

Pickthall, Mohammed Marmaduke. *The Meaning of the Holy Qur'an*. Many reprints. By a British Muslim using older English.

Qur'anic Studies

Cragg, Kenneth. *The Event of the Qur'an: Islam in Its Scripture*. Oxford, UK: Oneworld, 1994.

Cragg, Kenneth. *The Mind of the Qur'an*. London, 1973.

Gätje, Helmut. *The Qur'an and Its Exegesis*. Trans. by Alford T. Welch. Oxford, UK: Oneworld, 1996. An anthology of classical Qur'an commentary. The best available access to this genre.

Hawting, G. R., and Abdul-Kadar A. Shereef, eds. *Approaches to the Qur'an*. London and New York, Routledge, 1993.

Muslim-Christian Research Group (GRIC). *The Challenge of the Scriptures.* Maryknoll, N.Y.: Orbis, 1989. Insights worked out in dialogue with Muslims.

Nelson, Kristina. *The Art of Reciting the Qur'an.* University of Texas, Austin, 1985. A technical study on perhaps the most central aspect of the Qur'an for the average Muslim.

Parrinder, Geoffrey. *Jesus in the Qur'an.* Oxford, UK: Oneworld Publications, 1995. Originally published 1965. Examines all the qur'anic texts pertaining to Mary, Jesus, Christians, and Christianity.

Rahman, Fazlur. *Major Themes of the Qur'an.* Chicago: Bibliotheca Islamica, 1980. An important work of qur'anic theology.

Rippen, A., ed. *Approaches to the History of the Interpretation of the Qur'an.* Oxford, UK: Clarendon Press, 1988.

Sherif, Faruq. *A Guide to the Contents of the Qur'an.* Reading, UK: Garnet Publishing, 1995.

Sells, Michael. *Approaching the Qur'an: The Early Revelations.* Ashland, Ore.: White Cloud, 1999. An excellent but incomplete place to begin study of the Qur'an. Includes a CD-ROM with Qur'an recitation.

Watt, W. Montgomery. *Introduction to the Qur'an.* Edinburgh: University of Edinburgh Press, 1970. The best overall introduction to technical issues in qur'anic scholarship.

Tradition (Hadith)

Ali, Maulana Muhammad. *A Manual of Hadith.* London: Curzon Press, 1977. Some *hadith* in English pertaining mostly to religious law.

Burton, John. *An Introduction to the Hadith.* Edinburgh: Edinburgh U.P., 1994. Introduction by a non-Muslim to both the history and the content of the Hadith.

Graham, William. *Divine Word and Prophetic Word in Early Islam.* The Hague: Mouton, 1977.

Siddiqi, M. Z. *Hadith Literature: Its Origin, Development, and Special Features.* Cambridge: Islamic Texts Society, 1993. Good introduction by a Muslim. Includes some criticism of Western scholars' approaches to the Hadith.

Islamic Law

Al-Misri, Ahmad ibn Naqib. *Reliance of the Traveler: A Classic Manual of Islamic Sacred Law.* Rev. ed. Trans. and ed. Nuh Ha Mim Keller. Beltsville, Md.: Amana, 1994. Translation of a fourteenth-century Sunni text. The best way to see what Islamic law traditionally was and what it still is by and large.

An-Na'im, Abdullahi A., ed. *Islamic Family Law in a Changing World: A Global Resource Book.* London: Zed Books, 2002. A country-by-country survey of personal status laws.

Cook, Michael. *Commanding the Right and Forbidding the Wrong in Islamic Thought.* Cambridge: Cambridge U.P., 2000. A massive historical study on the question of one's responsibility for promoting the good of the other in Islamic thought.

Coulson, N. J. *A History of Islamic Law.* Edinburgh: Edinburgh U.P., 1964.

Esposito, John L. *Women in Muslim Family Law.* Syracuse, N.Y.: Syracuse U.P., 1982.

Hallaq, Wael B. *A History of Islamic Legal Theories: An Introduction to Sunnî Usûl al-Fiqh.* Cambridge: Cambridge U.P., 1997.

Kamali, M. H. *Principles of Islamic Jurisprudence.* 2nd ed. Cambridge: Islamic Texts Society, 1991.

Masud, Muhammad Khalid, Brinkley Messick, and David S. Powers. *Islamic Legal Interpretation: Muftis and Their Fatwas.* Cambridge, Mass.: Harvard University, 1996. Good introduction to the *fatwa* genre with numerous examples.

Omrun, Abdel Rahim. *Family Planning in the Legacy of Islam.* London: Routledge, 1992. Comprehensive in its coverage of the issues.

Pearl, David. *A Textbook on Muslim Personal Law.* London: Croom Helm, 1987. From British/South Asian contexts.

Schacht, Joseph. *An Introduction to Islamic Law.* Oxford: Oxford U.P., 1964.

Weiss, Bernard G. *The Spirit of Islamic Law.* Athens, Ga.: The University of Georgia, 1998. The easiest access to the theoretical aspects of Islamic law.

Islamic Legal Perspectives on War, Peace, and Human Rights

Abu Sulayman, Abdul Hamid A. *Towards an Islamic Theory of International Relations.* Rev. ed. Herndon, Va.: The International Institute of Islamic Thought, 1993.

'Alwani, Taha Jabir al-. *The Ethics of Disagreement in Islam.* Herndon, Va.: The International Institute of Islamic Thought, 1994.

Johnson, James Turner, and John Kelsay. *Cross, Crescent, and Sword: The Justification and Limitation of War in Western and Islamic Tradition.* New York: Greenwood Press, 1990.

Johnson, James Turner. *The Holy War Idea in Western and Islamic Traditions.* University Park, Pa.: The Pennsylvania U.P., 1997.

Kelsay, John and James Turner Johnson, ed. *Just War and Jihad: Historical and Theoretical Perspectives on War and Peace in Western and Islamic Traditions.* New York: Greenwood Press, 1991.

Kelsay, John. *Islam and War: The Gulf War and Beyond.* Louisville, Ky.: Westminster/John Knox, 1993.

Khadduri, Majid. *War and Peace in the Law of Islam.* New York: AMS, 1979. Originally published, Baltimore: Johns Hopkins University, 1955.

Mawdudi, Abul A'la. *Human Rights in Islam.* Nairobi: The Islamic Foundation, 1976.

Mitri, Tarek, ed. *Religion, Law and Society.* Geneva: WCC Publications, 1995.

Peters, Rudolph. *Jihad in Classical and Modern Islam*. Princeton: Markus Wiener, 1996. Translations of basic texts and helpful interpretative essays. Good bibliography.

Peters, Rudolph. *The Doctrine of Jihad in Modern History*. Gravenhage: Mouton, 1979.

Qutb, Sayed. *Islam and Universal Peace*. Riyadh: International Islamic Publishing House, 1991.

Watt, W. Montgomery. *Islamic Political Thought*. Edinburgh U.P., 1968.

Women in Islam *(see also Islamic Law, above)*

Abu-Lughod, Lila. *Veiled Sentiments: Honor and Poetry in a Bedouin Society*. Berkeley: University of California Press, 1986.

Afkhami, Mahnaz. *Faith and Freedom, Women's Human Rights in the Muslim World*. London: I. B. Tauris Publishers, 1995.

Ahmed, Leila. *Women and Gender in Islam: Historical Roots of a Modern Debate*. New Haven, Conn.: Yale U.P., 1992. Latter part of book has a lot on Egypt.

El Saadawi, Nawal. *The Hidden Face of Eve: Women in the Arab World*. London: Zed Books, 1980.

Glaser, Ida, and Napoleon John. *Partners or Prisoners? Christians Thinking About Women and Islam*. Cumbria, UK: Solway, 1998.

Jawad, Haifaa A. *The Rights of Women in Islam: An Authentic Approach*. London: Macmillian Press, 1998.

Khan, Maulana Wahiduddin. *Women in Islamic Shari'ah*. New Delhi: Al-Risala Books, 1995. A defense of traditional Islamic family law.

Macleod, Arlene, Elowe. *Accommodating Protest: Working Women, the New Veiling, and Change in Cairo*. New York: Columbia U.P., 1991.

Mernissi, Fatima. *Beyond the Veil: Male-Female Dynamics in Muslim Society*. Rev. ed. Indianapolis: Indiana U.P., 1987.

Mernissi, Fatima. *The Harem Within: Tales of a Moroccan Girlhood*. London: Doubleday, 1994.

Nazlee, Sajda. *Feminism and Muslim Women*. London: Ta-Ha, 1996. A short defense of traditional Islamic views on women in the face of feminism.

Sachiko, Murata. *The Tao of Islam: A Sourcebook on Gender Relationships in Islamic Thought*. Albany, N.Y.: State University of New York Press, 1992. From a *sufi* theosophical perspective.

Shaltut, Mahmoud. *The Quran and Women*. Cairo: International Islamic Center for Population Studies and Research, n.d.

Stowasser, Barbara Freyer. *Women in the Qur'an, Traditions, and Interpretation*. New York: Oxford U.P., 1994. Survey of women in Islam's traditional sources.

Wadud-Muhsin, Amina. *Qur'an and Woman*. Kuala Lumpur: Penerbit Fajar Bakti, 1992. An attempt at a more egalitarian reading of the Qur'an.

Yamani, Mai. *Feminism & Islam: Legal and Literary Perspectives*. Reading, UK: Ithaca Press, 1996.

Islamic Creed, Theology, and Philosophy

'Abduh, Muhammad. *The Theology of Unity*. Translated from Arabic by Ishaq Musa'ad and Kenneth Cragg. London: George Allen & Unwin, 1966. 'Abduh (d. 1905) was a leading Egyptian modernist.

Caspar, R. *A Historical Introduction to Islamic Theology: Muhammad and the Classical Period*. Rome: Pontificio Istituto di Studi Arabi e Islamici, 1998. Trans. of 1987 French edition. In a field without a solid introduction, this is the next best thing. It also includes Christian theological reflection on the life of Muhammad.

Fakhry, Majid. *A History of Islamic Philosophy*. 2nd ed. New York: Columbia U.P., 1983.

Fakhry, Majid. *A Short Introduction to Islamic Philosophy, Theology and Mysticism*. Oxford: Oneworld, 1997. The easiest place to begin in these subjects.

Goodman, L. E. *Avicenna*. London: Routledge, 1992. Introduces the most important philosopher in Islamic history.

Leaman, Oliver. *A Brief Introduction to Islamic Philosophy*. Cambridge: Polity, 1999.

Martin, Richard C. and Mark R. Woodward with Dwi S. Atmaja. *Defenders of Reason in Islam: Mu'tazilism from Medieval School to Modern Symbol*. Oxford: Oneworld, 1997.

Watt, W. Montgomery. *Islamic Creeds: A Selection*. Edinburgh: Edinburgh U.P., 1994.

Watt, W. Montgomery. *Islamic Philosophy and Theology*. 2nd ed. Edinburgh: University of Edinburgh Press, 1985. Enlarged from 1962 ed.

Islamic Mysticism (Sufism)

Andrae, Tor. *In the Garden of Myrtles: Studies in Early Islamic Mysticism*. Trans. Birgitta Sharpe from the Swedish. Albany, N.Y.: State University of New York Press, 1987.

Awn, Peter J. *Satan's Tragedy and Redemption: Iblîs in Sufi Psychology*. Leiden: E. J. Brill, 1983. A fascinating study of a dark figure.

Baldick, Julian. *Mystical Islam: An Introduction to Sufism*. London: I. B. Tauris, 1989. A revisionist history of Sufism.

Chittick, William C. *Imaginal Worlds: Ibn 'Arabî and the Problem of Religious Diversity*. Albany, N.Y.: State University of New York Press, 1994. An introduction to the basic ideas of one of the most important mystics in Islamic history.

Haeri, Fadhlalla. *The Elements of Sufism*. Shaftesbury, Dorset, UK: Element, 1990. An easy entry into Sufism by a *sufi sheikh*.

MacCarthy, R. J., trans. *Al-Ghazali's Path to Sufism*. Louisville, Ky.: Fons Vitae, 2000. A translation of al-Ghazali's famed personal account of his conversion to Sufism.

Nasr, Seyyed Hossein, ed. *Islamic Spirituality: Foundations*. New York: Crossroad, 1985, and *Islamic Spirituality: Manifestations*. New York: Crossroad, 1991. The first volume is on Qur'an, Hadith, and early Sufism, etc. Second volume on *sufi* orders, literature, and art. Good work but articles of uneven quality.

Nicholson, Reynold A. *Studies in Islamic Mysticism*. Surrey, UK: Curzon Press, 1994. Contains some valuable translation of classical *sufi* writings.

Padwick, Constance. *Muslim Devotions: A Study of Prayer-Manuals in Common Use*. Oxford: Oneworld Publications, 1996. Basic Muslim prayers in English translation.

Schimmel, Annemarie. *And Muhammad Is His Messenger: The Veneration of the Prophet in Islamic Piety*. Chapel Hill, N.C.: The University of North Carolina Press, 1985.

Schimmel, Annemarie. *Mystical Dimensions of Islam*. Chapel Hill, N.C.: The University of North Carolina Press, 1975. The best single introduction to Islamic mysticism.

Smith, Margaret. *Readings from the Mystics of Islam*. London: Luzac, 1950.

Trimingham, J. Spencer. *The Sufi Orders in Islam*. Oxford, Clarendon, 1971; reprint 1998. An indispensable history of *sufi* brotherhoods.

Shi'ism

Daftary, P. *The Isma'ilis: Their History and Doctrine*. London: C.U.P., 1990. On the Isma'ili (or Sevener) branch of Shi'i Islam.

Halm, Heinz. *Shiism*. Trans. Janet Watson from the German. Edinburgh: Edinburgh U.P., 1991. A comprehensive historical introduction.

Momen, Moojan. *An Introduction to Shi'i Islam: The History and the Doctrines of Twelver Shi'ism*. New Haven, Conn.: Yale, 1985. Excellent background on the Twelver (or Imamiyya) branch of Shi'ism.

History of Islam

Al-Faruqi, R. Isma'il, and Lois Lamya' al-Faruqi. *The Cultural Atlas of Islam*. New York: Macmillan, 1986. A strongly apologetic Muslim perspective.

Esposito, John, ed. *The Oxford History of Islam*. Oxford, UK: Oxford U.P., 2000.

Holt, P. M., Lambton, A. K. S., and Lewis, B., eds. *The Cambridge History of Islam*. 2 vol. Cambridge: Cambridge U.P., 1970.

Hourani, Albert H. *A History of the Arab Peoples*. London: Faber, 1991. Excellent overview that is especially strong on the modern period.

Lapidus, Ira M. *A History of Islamic Societies*. 2nd ed. Cambridge: Cambridge U.P., 2002. An excellent general history of the Islamic world.

Riley-Smith, Jonathan, ed. *The Atlas of the Crusades*. London: Times Books, 1991.

Robinson, Francis, ed. *The Cambridge Illustrated History of the Islamic World*. Cambridge: Cambridge U.P., 1999.

Rodinson, F. *Atlas of the Islamic World Since 1500*. New York: Facts on File, 1982.

Smart, Ninian. *Atlas of the World's Religions*. Oxford, UK: Oxford U.P., 1999. Colorful and informative maps in the section on Islam.

Islam in the USA

Haddad, Yvonne Yazbeck, and John L. Esposito. *Muslims on the Americanization Path?* Oxford, UK: Oxford University, 2000.

Smith, Jane I. *Islam in America*. New York: Columbia University, 1999. An excellent and balanced introduction.

Islam in Africa

Haynes, J. *Religion and Politics in Africa*. London: Zed Books, 1996.

Hisket, Mervin. *The Course of Islam in Africa*. Edinburgh: Edinburgh U.P., 1994.

Hiskett, Mervin. *The Development of Islam in West Africa*. London: Longman, 1984.

Kritzeck, J., and W. H. Lewis, eds. *Islam in Africa*. New York: Van Nostrand, 1969.

Levtzion, Nehemia, and Randall L. Pouwels, eds. *The History of Islam in Africa*. Athens, Ohio: Ohio U.P., 2000. Extensive collection of essays.

Rasmussen, L. *Christian-Muslim Relations in Africa*. London: I. B. Tauris, 1993.

Sanneh, Lamin. *The Crown and the Turban: Muslims and West African Pluralism*. Boulder: Westview Press, 1997.

Stamer, P. Josef. *Islam in Sub-Saharan Africa*. Königstein, Germany: Aid to the Church in Need, 1995. Brief and deals with the question of a Christian response.

Modern Trends in Islam

Abu Rabi`, Ibrahim M. *Intellectual Origins of Islamic Resurgence in the Modern Arab World*. Ithaca, N.Y.: State University of New York Press, 1995.

Ahmed, Akbar S. *Postmodernism and Islam. Predicament and Promise*. London: Routledge, 1992. Looks at the search for an Islamic identity in the contemporary world.

Algar, Hamid. *Islam and Revolution: Writings and Declarations of Imam Khomeini*. Berkeley, Calif.: Mizan Press, 1981.

Arkoun, Mohammed. *Rethinking Islam: Common Questions, Uncommon Answers*. Trans. and ed. by Robert D. Lee from the French. Boulder, Colo.: Westview Press, 1994. An open and liberal presentation of Islam.

Choueiri, Youssef M. *Islamic Fundamentalism*. London: Pinter, 1997.

Cole, Juan. R. I., and Nikki R. Keddie, eds. *Shi'ism and Social Protest*. New Haven: Yale U.P., 1986.

Donohue, John J., and John L. Esposito, eds. *Islam in Transition: Muslim Perspectives*. New York: Oxford U.P., 1982. An anthology of texts from fifty modern Muslim thinkers.

Eshtashtami, Anoushiravan. *After Khomeini: The Iranian Second Republic.* London: Routledge, 1995.

Esposito, John L., and Azzam Tamimi. *Islam and Secularism in the Middle East.* New York: New York U.P., 2000.

Esposito, John L., and John Voll. *Islam and Democracy.* Oxford: Oxford U.P., 1996.

Hourani, Albert. *Arabic Thought in the Liberal Age, 1798-1939.* London, 1962.

Kepel, Gilles. *Muslim Extremism in Egypt: The Prophet and Pharaoh.* Berkeley: University of California Press, 1992.

Kurzman, Charles. *Liberal Islam: A Sourcebook.* New York: Oxford U.P., 1998. A wide-ranging anthology.

Kramer, Martin. *Arab Awakening & Islamic Revival.* New Brunswick: Transaction Publishers, 1996.

Lewis, Bernard. *The Shaping of the Modern Middle East.* New York: Oxford U.P., 1994.

Moussalli, Ahmad S., ed. *Islamic Fundamentalism: Myths and Realities.* Reading, UK: Garnet Publishing, 1998.

Moussalli, Ahmad S. *Moderate and Radical Islamic Fundamentalism: The Quest for Modernity, Legitimacy, and the Islamic State.* Jacksonville: University of Florida Press, 1999.

Mitchell, Richard P. *The Society of the Muslim Brothers.* New York: Oxford U.P., 1993. First published in 1969. Development of the Brotherhood in Egypt.

Voll, John O. *Islam: Continuity and Change in the Modern World.* 2nd ed. Syracuse, N.Y.: Syracuse U.P., 1994.

Zeberi, Kate. *Mahmud Shaltut and Islamic Modernism.* Oxford: Clarendon Press, 1993. Shaltut (d. 1963) was rector and a leading thinker at al-Azhar University. An engaging account.

Ziad, Abu-Amr. *Islamic Fundamentalism in the West Bank: Muslim Brotherhood and Islamic Jihad.* Bloomington: Indiana U.P., 1994.

Christian-Muslim Relations—History

Daniel, Norman. *Islam and the West: The Making of an Image.* Oxford: Oneworld Publications, 1993. New material added since this classic first published in 1960.

Gaudeul, Jean-Marie. *Encounters and Clashes: Islam and Christianity in History.* 2 vol. Rome: Pontificio Istituto di Studi Arabi e Islamici, 2000. First volume is history. Second volume is texts.

Goddard, Hugh. *A History of Christian-Muslim Relations.* Edinburgh: Edinburgh U.P., 2000. An engaging account of this history from before Islam to the present.

Southern, R. W. *Western Views of Islam in the Middle Ages.* Cambridge, Mass.: Harvard U.P., 1962; reprint, 1978.

Watt, W. Montgomery. *Muslim-Christian Encounters: Perceptions and Misperceptions.* London: Routledge, 1991.

Christian-Muslim Relations—Present Perspectives

Anees, Munawar Ahmad, et al. *Christian-Muslim Relations: Yesterday, Today, Tomorrow.* London: Grey Seal, 1991. An interesting Muslim perspective.

Azumah, John Alembillah. *The Legacy of Arab-Islam in Africa: A Quest for Inter-religious Dialogue.* Oxford: Oneworld, 2001. Raises difficult questions in the sub-Saharan African context.

Borrmans, Maurice. *Guidelines for Dialogue between Christians and Muslims.* Trans. R. Marston Speight from the French. Mahwah, N.J.: Paulist, 1990. An important work based on Roman Catholic teaching concerning dialogue with Muslims.

Brown, Stuart E. *Meeting in Faith: Twenty Years of Christian-Muslim Conversations Sponsored by the World Council of Churches.* Geneva: World Council of Churches, 1989. Helpful for a quick overview of what has been discussed.

Caspar, Robert. *Trying to Answer Questions.* Rome: Pontificio Istituto di Studi Arabi e Islamici, 1989. Answering Muslims' questions from a Roman Catholic perspective.

Chapman, Colin. *Islam and the West.* Carlisle, UK: Paternoster, 1998. Basic Christian reflection on the history of Christian Muslim relations and contemporary issues of human rights and education.

Cragg, Kenneth. *The Call of the Minaret.* 3rd ed. Oxford: Oneworld, 2000. A classic by an Anglican bishop. Sympathetic and inciteful intepretation of Islam with an extended Christian response.

Cragg, Kenneth. *Jesus and the Muslim: An Exploration.* Oxford: Oneworld, 1999. Explaining the Christian view of Jesus to a Muslim.

Cragg, Kenneth. *Muhammad and the Christian: A Question of Response.* Oxford: Oneworld, 1999. On how a Christian might regard Muhammad.

Goddard, Hugh. *Christians and Muslims: From Double Standards to Mutual Understanding.* Surrey, UK: Curzon Press, 1995. An introduction to both religions with historical and sociological comparisons.

Goddard, Hugh. *Muslim Perceptions of Christianity.* London: Grey Seal, 1996. Focus on Muslim views of Christianity in twentiety-century Egypt.

Kateregga, Badru D., and David W. Shenk. *Islam and Christianity: a Muslim and Christian in Dialogue.* Scottdale, Pa.: Herald Press, 1997. A theological introduction by a Muslim and a Christian with mutual responses.

Kirkwood, Neville A. *Pastoral Care to Muslims.* Binghamton, N.Y.: The Haworth Pastoral Press, 2001. A book for hospital chaplains who provide pastoral care to Muslims.

Nickel, Gordon. *Peaceable Witness Among Muslims.* Scottdale, Pa.: Herald Press, 1999. A pacifist theology of witness by a Mennonite.

Tingle, Donald S. *Islam and Christianity.* Madison, Wisc.: InterVarsity Press, 1985. A concise booklet of thirty-two pages comparing the two faiths.

Zebiri, Kate. *Muslims and Christians Face to Face.* Oxford: Oneworld, 1997.

Christian Communities in the Middle East

Cragg, Kenneth. *The Arab Christian: A History in the Middle East.* Louisville, Ky.: Westminster/John Knox Press, 1991. Interesting theological reflection, but weak on Christianity in the early Islamic era.

Horner, Norman A. *A Guide to Christian Churches in the Middle East.* Elkhart, Ind.: Mission Focus, 1989. Basic facts and figures on churches in the Middle East and North Africa.

Pacini, Andrea, ed. *Christian Communities in the Arab Middle East: The Challenge of the Future.* Oxford: Clarendon Press, 1998. Essays by different scholars with extensive supporting factual information.

Partick, Theodore Hall. *Traditional Egyptian Christianity: A History of the Coptic Orthodox Church.* Greensboro, N.C.: Fisher Park Press, 1996.

Van-Doorn-Harder, Nelly, and Kari Vogt, eds. *Between Desert and City: The Coptic Orthodox Church Today.* Oslo, Instituttet for Sammenlignende Kulturforskning, 1997. Essays by different scholars on non-political aspects of the church.

Wessels, Antonie. *Arab and Christian? Christians in the Middle East.* Kampen, The Netherlands: Kok Pharos Publishing House, 1995. History and interpretation of the contemporary situation.

Index

The Author

David W. Shenk was born and raised in a Christian missionary home in Tanzania. For ten years he was involved in educational work in Islamic Somalia and then lectured in comparative religion and church history at Kenyatta University, Nairobi, Kenya for six years. He served as academic dean and professor of theology at Lithuania Christian College in Lithuania from 1998-2002. Since 1980, Shenk has been based at Eastern Mennonite Missions headquarters in Salunga, Pennsylvania, where he helps to coordinate interfaith commitments. He is the author of many books, including *A Muslim and a Christian in Dialogue*, *Global Gods*, and *Surprises of the Christian Way*.